CULTURAL ALLOTROPY

CULTURAL ALLOTROPY

A Study Through Some Indian English Novels

VINAY BHARAT

PARTRIDGE
A Penguin Random House Company

ISBN: Softcover   978-1-4828-5592-0
              eBook   978-1-4828-5591-3

To order additional copies of this book, contact
Partridge India
000 800 10062 62
orders.india@partridgepublishing.com

www.partridgepublishing.com/india

CONTENTS

ACKNOWLEDGEMENT

My research on *Cultural Allotropy: A Study in Some Indo-English Novels* would not have been complete without the co-operation of some persons and institutions. I record my deep sense of thankfulness to all of them.

For dexterous guidance and putting her heart and soul in it, I will remain ever grateful to my mentor and supervisor, Dr. Lily Kawa, Associate Professor, Department of English, Ranchi Women's College, Ranchi.

For his special care and affection, I am grateful to Dr. S. M. P. N. Singh Shahi, Head, University Department of English, Ranchi University, and Ranchi. I also extend my gratitude to Dr. K. Kumar, Former Head, University Department of English, Ranchi University, Ranchi and Dr. Victor Tigga, Former Vice-Chancellor, S.K.M. University, Dumka for their paternal guidance and words of encouragement. My special thanks and reverence to Dr. R.N. Sinha, Dr. B.P. Sinha, Dr. V.K. Sinha, Dr. A.B. Sharan, Dr. B. Chatterjee, Dr. P. Sahay and all my teachers who taught me the value of hard and honest work.

My reverence is due to Dr. J. Ahmed, Former Principal, Marwari College, Ranchi, Dr. U.C. Mehta, Principal, Ranchi College, Ranchi and Dr. Ranjit Singh, Principal, Marwari College, Ranchi for their timely help and support.

My sincere thanks are due to the Librarian of Sahitya Akademy, New Delhi for his promptness in responding to requests for books and other research materials. I thank all my colleagues and friends who often enquired about and took interest in the progress of my research work. Their oft-expressed good wishes meant much to me.

Last but not the least, my gratitude is due to my parents Ms. Parvati and Prof. Rameshwar Choudhary, Bhabhi Ms. Shikha, Bhaiya Mr. Vijay Bharat, Jeeju Mr. Rajesh, Di Ms. Punita and my loving thanks go to my beloved wife Archana, my kids Pranjal, Anurati, Ishi, Yathartha and Aahnvi who continued to bear with me during the research work, as I could not give them the time which was theirs.

Vinay Bharat

Chapter - I

INTRODUCTION

In the fast shrinking modern world, the state of a static cultural identity is simply unthinkable. The frequent interaction among people of different and contradictory sets of values, thought processes and the attitude towards life result in a process of conscious and sub-conscious give–and–take and the change is visibly clear from attire to mannerism. Nothing serious is involved here. But on the other hand, there are people who have had the misfortune of being colonized; such people have to face a kind of alien cultural flood threatening, in some cases, to submerge the native tradition and culture. Most of such countries especially the non-whites have been subjected to a situation of multi-culturalism, i.e. the presence of more than one cultural trait in its people. They grow together but this togetherness is not without tension and the tension in togetherness is manifested in a response to life that is all confused and uncertain.

Centuries of political intervention and subjugation by foreign countries results in the presence of a mixed culture and this side - by - side flourishing of two cultures seems now an accepted fact – a part of man's consciousness. But the presence of two contradictory sets of values – one not fully accepted and the other not totally rejected – gives rise to a difficult situation in the face of the conflicting claims of the two. This gives rise to a mixing of cultures - a blend which in other words may be called "cultural allotropy", that is, existence of the culture of a particular region in two or more forms, having different and mixed properties at the emotional or intellectual level at a given point of time. In a recent survey done by a news channel the Delhi-ites responded differently on the issue of national anthem. For some, it was "jana-gana-mann", for others it was "vande matram". Had only this been the limit, it was digestible, but for many youngsters it was a Bollywood number, sung and composed by Shankar Mahadevan. This type of 'rainbow'-culture creates allotropy where men of different cultures and values live under the same roof. A cafeteria of a Call Centre of Noida becomes a sort of allotropic hub and appears like multi-lingual radio stations where Voice of America, BBC, Vividh Bharati can be heard together blended with American jazz, British Opera and Indian Classical music at the same time.

This very situation of cultural allotropy has inspired several creative works of art that forcefully delineate the complexity of the situation. India also had the misfortune of being colonized by the British people for about two hundred years, as a result of which a mingling of the two cultures, i.e. Indian and Western, in the Indian society is a common thing witnessed. In the complex fabric of contemporary Indian civilization, the two most easily discerned strands are the indigenous Indian tradition and the imported European conceptions. "Almost every educated Indian today is the product of the conflicts and reconciliations of the two cultures,"[1] right from Sam

Pitroda, the Father of India's Communication Revolution (whose original name is Satyanarayan Gangaram Pitroda, re-christened as 'Sam' during his American exposure) to Sarita Choudhury, the Hollywood actress, whose life is a melting pot of cultures (born in England to British and Indian parents, and educated in Ontario, Canada), we have many more such examples including Ganesh in *A House for Mr. Biswas* by V.S. Naipaul, who changes his name to Gareth.

What is generally true of the educated Indian is especially true of the Indian writer, because a writer is concerned with the springs of human action and with the motivation behind human behaviour. As literature is the mirror of the society the peculiar trait could not have escaped the sensitive minds of the creative writers. The Indian novel in English explores this fact in various ways.

This cultural conflict or synthesis, as the case may be, has for some reason or the other, always assumed a vital significance for the Indian novelist who writes in English. As early as 1909, Sarath Kumar Ghosh wrote a novel called *The Prince of Destiny* dealing with the inter–cultural theme where the hero, the prince of a native Indian state, has to choose between the love of an English girl and marriage with an Indian princess. And as late as 1960, J.M. Ganguly's *When East and West Meet* shows that the East – West motif has not yet exhausted itself.

Like all post–colonial literatures, Indian writing in English is an outcome of the interaction between the imperial British culture and the native Indian culture. Its relationship with the mainstream English literature reflects the changing dynamics of power between the imperial authority and the colonized subject – from a relationship of filiations to that of affiliation, to that of an assertion of independence, Indian writing in English, soon developed characteristics and qualities of its own which were in marked contrast with those of the metropolitan literature. It was firmly rooted in the Indian soil and culture. Like all other Indian Literatures, Indian writing in English can be said to be constituting and reflecting the Indian culture.

However, doubts and questions on this still persist. Being a product of what was once the imperial language and the native culture, Indian writing in English has become a heavily contested site for writers and critics alike. Writing in English involves a deliberate choice on the part of a writer and he must inevitably grapple and come to terms with the question – why write in English when one has the choice and freedom of writing in one's own language or mother tongue. In a multi-cultural and multi-lingual society like ours, we have a long and continuous tradition of regional literatures of varying richness, depth and complexity, which continued to be produced even during the height of the colonial power. Implicit in this question is a host of related questions and issues: the question of 'Indianness' in Indian writing in English, the adequacy of the borrowed imperial language to capture and portray the native Indian culture and sensibility, the competence and ability of its practitioners to use it creatively, the suitability of the inherited literary forms, etc.

These questions are "predicted upon a desire to achieve literary decolonization, a desire to retrieve a pure pre-colonial past. Such a desire is only logical to a society which has suffered the consequences of colonization, but given the hybrid nature of our post – colonial society, such a desire is impossible to achieve. In fact, not only writings in English, but all other regional literatures are cross – cultural products now, bearing the marks and traces of colonization. In fact, many critics are of the view that the hybrid nature of our society is a source of strength rather than a weakness."[2]

Commenting upon the hybrid nature of post – colonial writings, Taher Ben Jalloun, a writer from Morocco, says:

> *We have two cultures; it's as if we had two mothers and two fathers. Perhaps we don't have total control, like writers in the West, but we have two possible inner worlds. I think we are doubly clever: firstly, to use the narrative techniques of the West and secondly to exploit the narrative traditions, of the folklore, the stories from our respective court-list. And we've come up with a third type of literature. Like Western writing which is essentially provincial, egocentric and inward looking, we have created literature which is open to other cultures and situations.*[3]

The above comment of Jalloun points to three significant features which characterize all post – colonial literatures including Indian writing in English – appropriation, resistance, subversion and reconstruction.

The circumstances and purpose of the introduction of the English language and English education in India have been a subject of extensive research and commentary and they are too familiar to be recounted here. However, a brief comment is in order. While the British wanted to maintain political control by establishing cultural hegemony over us through the introduction of English education to a certain extent, they had succeeded in achieving their goal. As Anna Guttmann observes:

> *Macaulay's Minute which sought to facilitate British rule by creating "a class of persons … Indian in colour and blood but English in tastes, in opinions, in morals and in intellect" – had clearly succeeded where the Nehrus are concerned, at least in matters of taste and linguistic usage.*[4]

It also produced results and effects quite contrary to their expectations. Rajeshwari Sunder Rajan comments:

> *… though the overt purpose of English education – which was to create an amenable native elite population that would be impressed by, conform to, and propagate the values of the secular English book – was undoubtedly served, the English text was also, in complex and mediated ways, appropriated for political representation, for articulating demands, and for questioning to rulers.*[5]

A group of people acquired English education and began to question England's presence and position in India with intellectual weapons which English education had bestowed upon them.

This was true of Indian writers in English, too. The creative writers appropriated the western literary forms and techniques – the forms of fiction, the metrics of poetry and the conventions of theatre – and sought to dismantle the privileged position enjoyed by the 'centre'. In the years following independence, however, a number of novels have appeared where the conflict between the two cultures is not on the social but on the personal level; whose theme, in broad terms, may be called an individual's search for identity in a changing India. The definition of 'East' as well as of 'West' varies from novel to novel, but each tries in its own way to grapple with the problem that has continued to concern the Indo-Anglian novelist for more than fifty years.

To a certain extent this interest is noticeable also in the novels of the period written in the Indian languages. S.H. Vatsayan has noted in a survey of modern Hindu literature that "the search for a satisfactory attitude towards the west and an emotionally and spiritually significant image of the east"[6] marks the Hindi novels after the Second World War. But, as Meenakshi Mukherjee observes:

> *The Indian novelist in English is more seriously and consistently involved with the East -West theme than his counterparts in the Indian languages, if only because this very choice of language indicates an awareness of and exposure to a culture other than the traditional Indian, we assume that an Indian, when he writes in English, does so only because it comes most naturally to him.*[7]

Balachandra Rajan argues that "the real necessity of a writer is the necessity to render his individual vision without compromise into a public language – If that language happens to be English the creative choice must be respected and one should judge by results rather than by dismal prophecies of what the result must fail to be."[8]

The need to realize oneself creatively in English, however, presupposes a familiarity with the language which goes along with a greater degree of exposure to western culture than what the average educated Indian undergoes. The latter, in spite of all his English education, is usually more at-home in his regional language. The majority of the Indo-Anglian writers today have had at least part of their education, abroad. Because of their intimate experience of a culture other than their own, they are made aware of their Indianness as well as of the difference in the two systems of values: one rather acquired, the other inherited and often taken for granted. The inter-cultural nature of his own being becomes for such a writer a theme of profound interest. Therefore, the search for one's identity is found to be a common and recurrent theme in Indo-Anglian fiction.

Professor David Mc Cutchion, introducing his collection of essays called *Indian Writing in English* (1969), says that the main interest of Indo-Anglian writing is that it is Indian, and that inquiries must therefore be directed towards an examination of the circumstances that produce it and to find out how far it is derived from non-Indian sources. This documentary approach, he adds, is based on the view that "we read all literature not only for aesthetic or vicarious emotions but to learn about our fellowmen, and to the extent nations are idiosyncratic we learn about national behaviour too." Paul C. Verghese in this light puts forth a list of questions:

> *Should Indianness be thought of as indispensable to all writing done by Indians? Should Indianness be regarded as the most important criterion of*

*criticism? How Indian should Indian writing
be in English?*[9]

Indian writing in English, in view of its copiousness, can no longer be dismissed as "a curious and exotic chapter in English literature", as K.M. Panikkar once put it, or described derisively as a nascent literature which will not live out of its infancy.

The distinctiveness of this writing primarily stems from its Indianness. This is true of every national literature, for the roots of any form of literary expression are nourished by the attitudes and behaviour of the people who have established patterns of life and developed traditions that have emerged over the years. In this sense it is only natural and legitimate to insist that Indian literature in English has its own national distinctiveness: The kind of insistence is seen in the West - Indian and Nigerian literatures, too. There is nothing wrong in this.

Moreover, Indianness is a nebulous term and can be interpreted differently. For instance, while Prof. Mc Cutchion speaks of Indianness as "life-attitudes" and "modes of perception" and in view of "the problem the writer has to face in order to be neither an imitation of Westerner nor a picturesque Indian, Prof. V.K. Gokak defines it as "a composite awareness in the manner of race, milieu, language and religion – an awareness leading to tolerance and broad-based understanding, an integral awareness of the Indian heritage, not a fragmented approach to it, a simultaneous cultivation of science and spirituality, a passionate involvement in the implications of the Time Spirit as well as of Eternity."[10]

For C. Paul Verghese, the concept of Indianness is simpler. To him 'Indianness' is nothing but depiction of Indian culture, which as K.M. Panikkar defines it as, "the complex of ideas, conceptions, developed qualities, organized relationships and courtesies that exist generally in a society and includes a community of thought, a similarity of conduct and behaviour, a common general approach to fundamental problems, which arise from shared traditions and ideals."[11]

Further, Professor Gokak's concept is not acceptable for two reasons. Firstly, it is too idealistic to be reflected in a literary work and is bound up with the philosophies and religions of India. To him "a true Indian is one who is intensely aware of the gifts of eternity and of his epoch, of eternity and the past as well as the milieu and the moment of spirituality and service." Secondly, he tends to equate Indianness with an all – embracing international or catholic outlook by saying that "to be a true Indian is also to be on the way to becoming a true world citizen tomorrow." To accept Prof. Gokak's definition is to base the distinctiveness of Indian writing in English on the philosophies and spirituality of India, and not on the secular aspects and values of Indian Culture.

Paul C. Verghese writes back:

> *What I mean by Indianness in Indian writing in English is the sum total of the cultural patterns of India and the deep-seated ideas and ideals – political, economic, secular and spiritual – that constitutes the mind of India and is reflected in her writing. We have this kind of Indianness in our regional literatures, but we do not make much of it. This is because Indianness here is*

taken for granted. There is no clash between the culture and the languages which express it. In Indian writing in English however, the language may seem to clash with a culture for which it is not a natural medium. It is this discord between culture and language that has so far compelled the critic of Indo-Anglian writing to make the authenticity of its Indianness the basis of his critical studies.[12]

But should the critic look for Indianness in a work totally ignoring its literary quality? Perhaps he is right in assuming that the literary quality of a work is inseparable from its Indianness, all the same, he should concede that whatever experience of life a writer chooses to express should be authentic. If the experience is Indian it should be authentically Indian.

Kamala Das has written:

The language, I speak becomes mine, its distortions, its queerness .. All mine, mine alone. It is half English, half Indian, funny perhaps, but it is honest. It is as human as I am human…

Even Raja Rao writes back:

We cannot write like the English. We should not. We can write only as Indians. Our method of expression therefore has to be a dialect which will someday prove to be as distinctive and colorful as the Irish or the American. Time alone will justify it.[13]

Even the protagonist Agastya (rather, August, as he prefers to be called) of Upamanyu Chatterjee's "English August" agrees,

> *Amazing mix, the English we speak, Hazar fucked. Urdu and American. I'm sure nowhere else could languages be mixed and spoken with such ease.*[14]

For the term "Indian experience of Life" there is no one definition. It varies from novel to novel, poem to poem, and play to play. It is for the writer to decide what his experience of India means to him; it is again for the writer to persuade the reader of the authenticity of his experience. The levels of experience and their realization vary from writer to writer, and sometimes even from one work to another, by the same author.

It is this aspect of the writer's experience and expression of it that distinguishes the work of one writer from another, say the works of R.K. Narayan from those of Arun Joshi, and also between two works by the same author. R.K. Narayan's Malgudi having scientific orientation in *The Man - Eater of Malgudi* is absolutely orthodoxical in *The Bachelor of Arts*, based on 'horoscopes'. Mulk Raj Anand's India is political, economic and proletarian in almost all his novels.

No one can mistake the authentic Indianness in R.K. Narayan, Bhabani Bhattacharya and other writers of the same line. This cannot he said of the later novels of Kamala Markandaya, namely *Possession* and *The Coffer Dams*. Her India in these two novels is a far cry from the India with which those of us living in India are familiar. Perhaps

Kamala Markandaya's failure in these novels is the result of her having been an expatriate writer with little or no touch with India for a long time.

My proposed thesis deals with the problems observed in the delineation of characters in their respective novels written by such expatriate writers like Kamala Markandaya, Arun Joshi or Ruth Prawer Jhabvala.

The dilemma that the expatriate writer faces is whether or not to deal with an Indian theme or a theme directly concerned with his immediate experience. Perhaps it is better for an expatriate writer to draw on his wider experience and extended vision. This is how Arun Joshi has solved the dilemma; his novel *The Foreigner* has the Indian sutra, or non-attachment in its centre but there is no point for the critic looking for Indianness in the central character.

A novel like this makes the critic of Indian literature in English sit up for he cannot evaluate it on its Indianness. He can judge it only on its literary quality and on the authenticity of the experience which the writer, purports to communicate. Nor can he condemn it on the basis of its un-Indianness; for the writer has a right to select themes from within his experience and his environment. Besides, in a world that has shrunk in space and time, no novelist can be expected to be national in the choice of his themes. He is likely to become absorbed in the universal environment and to transcend his immediate environment. Sindi Oberoi, the protagonist of Arun Joshi's *The Foreigner* is a mouthpiece of all the globalized citizens across the world:

> *My foreignness lay within me and I couldn't leave myself behind wherever I went.*[15]

In fact, Sindi bears no flag, he owns no territory; he may simply be called an 'allotrope' — "the existence of the same person on two or more forms, having different properties at the intellectual or emotional level."[16]

Sindi, in fact, sets a superb example of cultural allotropy. Sindi is a simple human being; he carries innumerable unanswerable questions and behaves differently on different occasions. He is an ideal representative of the modern cross-road culture. He is all conflict. Sindi is right when he admits that his foreignness lay within him. But what exactly does he mean when using the abstract noun 'foreignness' and what exactly is "Indianness" then? Keeping the character of Sindi in mind, if we listen to what R.K. Narayan has to say, the clouds of doubt may disappear and we might be self – answered. To quote R.K. Narayan:

> *We (Indians) believe that marriages are made in heaven and a bride and groom meet, not by accident or design but by decree of fate, the fitness for a match not to be gauged by letting them go through a period of courtship but by a study of their horoscopes: boy and girl meet and love develops after marriage rather than before our social circumstances not providing adequate facilities for the triangle. We, however, seek excitement in our system of living known as the 'joint family in which several members of a family live under the same roof.*[17]

If R.K. Narayan's statement be our parameter to adjudge our Indianness, we find nothing Indian in Sindi, except that he carries an Indian blood from his father's side. He exhibits no particular shade he can be identified with. First, he falls in love with Anna, a minor artist separated from her husband and then with Kathy, who finally leaves him. Then he moves to Boston only to establish intimacy with June Blyth, an attractive young girl. But thanks at last to his Indian 'Id' that makes him visit India where he tries to dig out his instinctive roots out of the debris of his own rootlessness. And that leaves him more tensed, more puzzled, more barren.

This is not the problem of Sindi alone. But Sindi is a superb example of this cultural allotropy personified. Basically, the present day world is on the cross – roads. Although the roof is the same, one is an insider; another is an outsider. If Indian Culture be a coin, its one side will bear the carving of Anita Desai's comment, "I was born in India and I am not an outsider."[18], while its other side will be marked by Ruth Prawer Jhabvala's statement:

> *I have lived in India for most of my adult life.*
> *My husband is Indian and so are my children. I*
> *am not, and less so every year.*[19]

Coming once again to the language part, English has 'not only sent down its roots to 'market place' and the 'village green' but it has seeped down into our existential roots, too. A scene from *English, August* will amplify the point:

> *A hooligan offered Kumar a paan, which he*
> *stuffed into his mouth. 'Haha, you look the*
> *English type'. 'the English type?'*

> *'Any Indian who speaks English more fluently*
> *than any Indian language he speaks I call the*
> *English type, good, no?'*

> *yes, Sir.*[20]

The question that was raised in all seriousness by Prof. Raj Kumar in his presidential address at the All - India English Teachers' Conference held at Bhubaneswar in Dec. 1970, is quite apt:

> *Is it possible for us to think of a new language*
> *for a new India which I may provisionally call*
> *'Indish' – a language having the alphabet, the*
> *framework and basic structure of English, in the*
> *Roman script, but an organic language growing*
> *freely and assimilating new words, new ideas,*
> *new constructions, new idioms, even, if necessary*
> *new letters of the alphabet, from each one of the*
> *regional languages of India?*[21]

The plea which he made for the evolution of 'Indish' as a necessary solution to the knotty language problem of India was certainly a spirited one, and sounded novel and revolutionary to many of the delegates. He recommended the adoption of 'Indish' as the 'lingua franca' for the country – "a common language as the medium of communication and government work in the whole country" – and even foresaw the coming into existence of 'Indish literature' – "a rich and exotic dish of many flavors" from all over India gaining "recognition at the national and international levels." 'Indish' he felt, would meet with "no resistance or ill – will" from any part of India because of its association with regional languages. In short, it would be English that is becoming "un-English every day."

The use of English by Indian writers is not to be confused with Prof. Raj Kumar's concept of 'Indish'. Mulk Raj Anand, in a paper read in a seminar on Austrian and Indian literatures held in New Delhi in January, 1970 drew a distinction between "the higgledy – piggledy spoken English in our country" and "the imaginative use of the same language" by creative writers in what he chose to call "Indian – English." He said:

> *I would like to define two kinds of English by entitling the imaginative transformation of Indian – English as 'Pigeon – Indian and the anyhow speech as 'pidgin English', without associating myself with the latter definition with the British contempt implied in the word 'pidgin'. I only wish to indicate that while 'Pigeon – English' soars, 'Pidgin – English' remains in gutter...*

The point Mulk Raj Anand makes is that "pigeon – Indian" or "Indian English" is derived from 'Pidgin English' which consists of expressions like 'Thank you ji', 'Hello ji', 'By good yaar' and sentences like 'Have you finished your Khana?' and of the large number of Indian words increasingly used by both Indians and foreigners in English. What Indian writers in English like R.K. Narayan, Bhabani Bhattacharya, Upamanyu Chatterjee have sometimes done, successfully or unsuccessfully is to exploit this "hang – over of the mother-Tongue" as well as the idioms and proverbs peculiar to Indian languages for their artistic purpose, that is, for the expression of fictional reality.

There is nothing new in this use of English by creative writers. Writers like Chinua Achebe in Nigeria have made it even as V.S. Naipaul has successfully used in his novels, the peculiarities of the spoken English of the people of the West Indies. Again, it is this kind of creative use of English that we find in writers like James Joyce and William Faulkner. Prof. S. Nagarajan also gives his opinion in this regard:

> *Indian English is a mode of style which is created by the author himself. It is not ungrammatical, unidiomatic English or Cantonment English or the English of the railway shunting yard. You do not get Indian English in all writing by Indians or in all writing about India. The justification of Indian must be that to the native virtue of the English language it adds an element of extra beauty and colour, strangeness and wonder, and truth. Its test of success is that it recreates Indian life in all its shame and glory, its beauty and rottenness.[22]*

The most important problem concerns the suitability and adaptability of English as a medium for the Indian novelist. There are many Indians who believe that the writer in India ought not to write in English because, they say, it is a foreign language and to write in English is a kind of disservice to the nation and is quite incompatible with our national pride. A few others take an apparently scientific stand and argue that only through an Indian language can an Indian consciousness be expressed and that the attempt of the Indian novelist in English to depict the life of those whose emotional and intellectual life is fashioned by a different language, is characterized by a total absence of the mutual nourishment between the writer and his society. They also point out that since he writes for a Western audience he will inevitably fail to present a true image of India as much as in his own interest he will try to create an image that is most saleable.

The question of language is one involving the fundamental right of the creative artist to express himself in whatever language he likes. As Bhabani Bhattacharya says:

> *The Indian writer must be free to use any language he likes unharassed by criticism, either tacitly implied or plainly stated, and by any kind of compulsion, direct or indirect, which may come out of the strengthening mood of linguistic chauvinism… The concept of freedom will have to include the medium of expression to which the writer, out of his inner urge, commits himself… It is far more difficult to write creatively in a foreign language than in one's own. But that must be regarded as the writer's own business.*[23]

Commenting on the dilemma faced by the Indian creative writer in the choice of a medium, John Wain says in his *Essays on Literature And Ideas* (London, 1963, p. 254) that if he were in the position of an Indian writer hesitating between English and Marathi he would certainly choose to write in Marathi and let the big sales and wide publicity take care of themselves.

The concept of an Indian English is generally dismissed on the ground that it can only be 'bad' English or 'baboo' English. This is, as Ellis Underwood puts it, "because of the notion that the characteristics of 'Indian English' are 'a fondness for "tall" writing, a delight in "six foot" words and grand expressions, magniloquence of style ... coupled with colloquialisms, the use of 'fine imagery often derived from ancient classical sources', the practice of 'interlarding or ... embellishing ... periods with misplaced or misguided idioms or phrases, forced allusions, tags quotations and such bits of Latin or French as those picked up second – hand' and mistaking 'garishness for splendor, tinsel for ornament."[24]

C. Paul Verghese writes,

> *'Indian English' establishes an Indian idiom of English as opposed to the English idiom of British English, the American idiom of American English and the Australian idiom of Australian English. In other words, the Indian social, cultural and linguistic set up has affected the features of the English language as used by the Indian creative writers in English, especially the novelists, and 'Indian English' is only a variety of English whose characteristics stem from the life and culture of the people of India. And the Indianness of it consists in its cultural overtones and undertones and not in a legalization of the ignorant misuse of English.*[25]

Indian English is not 'baboo' English; nor is it the type of English satirized by Nissim Ezeikel in his poem *Very*

Indian Poem in English published in the September 1967 issue of *Literature East and West* (New York):

> *You want one glass lassi?*
> *Very good for digestion/*
> *With little salt lovely drink,/*
> *Better than wine:/*
> *Not that I am ever tasting wine.*
> *I am the total tee-totallar,*
> *Completely total,/ But I say/*
> *Wine is for the drunkards only.*

Also it cannot be said that indiscriminate use of Indian words in English by an Indian writer makes his English Indian.

The creation of an Indian consciousness is another problem which the Indian writer in English faces today. "The Indian writers in English are also not infrequently charged with projecting a distorted image of India abroad with their eye on the sole prospects of their work. It may be that some of them are salesman but then this is so among all writers in all languages"[26].

Surely the Indian novelist in English makes an attempt to deal with the cultural problems of a modern India, even when the choice of setting in a way restricts his freedom to give his novel an Indian character. This awareness of India as a nation is at the back of his mind, especially because he is writing for an audience both inside and outside India. For example, Kamala Markandaya's *Possession*, which is a weird mixture of rural life, a Swamy, and declining royalty – all veneered with the theme of East – West cultural contact. *The Coffer Dams* which is her prominent novel is also not free from the bizarre characteristic of her *Possession;* the novel is a mixture of tribal life, impact of machinery and industrialization and East – West cultural contact presented in an unconvincing manner and style. Arun Joshi's treatment of the theme of loneliness and the problem of rootlessness in his *The Foreigner* finally leads him to advocate the ideal of non-attachment as a solution to the problem of loneliness and rootlessness. The novel is a satisfying one though it lacks the psychological depth. In this proposed thesis it has been discussed in detail in the succeeding chapters.

The term 'Indianness' always poses endless questions, and while attempting to answer these questions, certain terms occur time and again. One of those is 'values'. In this distinction between eastern and western values, we tread dangerous grounds. Nevertheless, in spite of the constant overlapping and interchangeability of values, some kind of basic difference does exist between the two civilizations.

The American sociologist Clyde Kluchohn has indicated one way of defining the vague term 'values' when he says:

> *It should be possible to construct in general terms the views of a given group regarding the structure of the universe, and the relations of man to man. These views will represent the group's own definition of the ultimate meaning of human life.*[27]

Sociologists, anthropologists and philosophers have tried many times to define the precise nature of oriental and occidental value systems. Among these definitions the most comprehensive and least controversial seems to be the one suggested by Cora Du Bois[28]. She sums up the entire issue in three questions:

(1) What is man's relation to nature?
(2) What is man's conception of time?
(3) What is man's relation to man?

With regard to the first question, namely, man and nature, we find man can accept the forces of nature as invincible (like the local folks in *The Coffer Dams*) or he can strive to master nature through the application of science on the form of technology (as Mackendrick or Clinton of *The Coffer Dams*).

As for the concept of time – the second question – man can either look backward to a lost golden age (like Agastya of '*English, August* or the protagonist of *Heat and Dust*) or forward to an even more perceptible world; that is, have belief in progress (like Nataraj of *The Man-eater of Malgudi*). As regards the third question, society can either be envisaged as a strict hierarchical order where each man performs duties allotted to him, or man can look upon himself primarily as an isolated individual (like Sindi Oberoi of *The Foreigner*), charged with cherishing and developing his unique potentialities.

At the same time, Richard Lonnoy, believes that the impulse to partake of both Eastern and Western values have induced a type of cultural pathology:

> *Such dualism is not dialectical symbolism; it is more like the double alienation referred to in* connection with schizoid tendencies.[29]

Ayyub, the editor of *Quest*, has expressed a similar concern for the plight of the Indian intellectual:

> *He realizes that he cannot resist long the charm and power of the West; and yet this is felt as an act of disloyalty, almost a form of spiritual matricide.*[30]

Similarly, S.N. Ganguli, an Indian intellectual of some repute himself has remarked that when the West intruded on India: "Modern India become an alienated India; alienated from the India that was real."[31]

But resistance and subversion is only half the story, the other half is reconstruction. The challenge which Indian writers in English have faced was one of creating a distant voice of their own, of making the language bear the burden of their experience. Raja Rao has put it very aptly in *The Preface* to *Kanthapura*:

> *One has to convey in a language that is not one's own. One has to convey the various shades and commissions of a certain thought movement that look maltreated in an alien language… After language, the next problem is that of style. The tempo of Indian life must be infused into our English expression, even as the tempo of American or Irish life has gone into the making of theirs.*[32]

The history of Indian writing in English is the story of how the writers have overcome these challenges and have created a unique voice and style which have established Indian writing in English as a discrete national formation.

An in-depth analysis of the British political machinations at this time makes D.P. Mukherjee observe that it is for the first time that 'an alien civilization impinged upon every detail of Indian life, changed its pattern and created new values, this Indian wealth ceased to become treasures, money became capital, goods became commodities, land became a source of monopoly – rent and the self sufficiency of rural economy was transformed into the interdependence of urban and world economy. Not only this, the entire facade of introducing the English system of education in India with a view to bringing about enlightenment was an attempt at making cultural inroads into the Indian identity turning it alien to its roots and thus making it loyal to the British designs of perpetuating its rule in India. In fact, the main aim of colonialism is to change consciousness by the superimposition of an alien order on the native order, so that the individual is divided in his loyalties towards himself and his community, thus developing a 'marginal' personality. The intentions contained in the minutes of Lord Macaulay on the introduction of English education in India did not mince words on this issue. Though the move was welcomed by some of the intellectuals as ushering in 'modernity' it led to alienation of the Indian from his roots. The attempts made by some of the nationalists to remind the people of their ancient heritage, were labeled as 'revivalism'.

The roots of colonialism, in fact, lie in the maximum disorientation of the ruled which is achieved either by keeping them ignorant of the real exploitative designs of the colonialists or by misleading them to a belief in the colonialists as saviours. This leads to the creation of a deliberate cultural –cum- epistemological colonialism destroying and negating the basic integrity of a civilization, crippling the colonial victim. Gandhiji, too, diagnosed that dehumanization was the very basis of the western civilization, epistemology and all the allied political structure and strategy applied to the governance of the colonized. Stokely Carmichael writes,

> *We want to talk about cultural integrity versus cultural imposition, because that stems from definitions... I thought the best thing the white man could do for me was to leave me alone, but Rudyard Kipling told them to come and save me because I was half savage, half child. It was very white of him. What has happened is that the West has used force to impose its culture on the third world wherever it has been. If a few settlers left England to go to Zimbabwe, there was no reason for them to rename that country after themselves, Rhodesia, and then force everybody to speak their language, English.*[33]

He further oozes out the venom,

> *The West with its guns and its power and its might came into Africa, Asia, Latin America and the USA and raped it. And while they raped it they used beautiful terms. They told the Indians 'we're civilizing you, and we're taming the West... So what the West was able to do is impose its culture and it told everyone 'we are better, we are civilized', so that all other non-western people have been stripped of their own culture.*[34]

English, in India, as a result, has not only sent down its root to 'market place' and the 'village green' but it has seeped into our existential roots, too. Have we been "stripped of our own culture", I shall try to get the answer of this question in my later chapters. But, one thing is clear that the question of "cultural allotropy" in a culturally rich country like India arose only after the colonial rule.

References:

1. Meenakshi Mukherjee, *'East – West Encounter'. The Twice Born Fiction.* Delhi: Pen craft International, 2001. p. 69.
2. Bill Ashcroft Gareth Griffiths and Helen Tiffin. *The Empire Writes Back: Theory and Practice In Post Colonial Literatures.* London: Rutledge, 1989 p. 24.
3. Tahen ben Jalloun in an Interview with Vaiju Naravane in *"The Sunday Times of India:* Delhi Edition, Jan. 28, 1996.
4. Anna Guttmann. *The Nation of India in Contemporary Indian Literature.* New York: Palgrave, Macmillan. 2007. p. 16.
5. Rajeshwari Sunder Rajan. *The Lie of the Land: English Literary Studies in India"*, Delhi: Oxford University Press, 1992, p. 12.
6. S.H. Vatsayan. *Contemporary Indian Literature*, N. Delhi: Vikash Publication, 1959, p - 93
7. Meenakshi Mukherjee. *The Twice Born Fiction*, op. cit., p. 70.
8. Balachandra Rajan. *'Identity and Nationality'. Commonwealth Literature*, London: John Press, 1965, p. 108.
9. C. Paul Verghese. *'Indian Writing in English'. Essay in Indian Writing in English,* N. Delhi: NV publications, 1975, p.1.
10. As quoted in C. Paul Verghese. *Essay On Indian Writing in English, ibid.,* p. 2.
11. *ibid.,* p. 2.
12. *ibid.,* p.3.
13. c.f. Raja Rao. *'Foreword'* to *Kanthapura,* Madras: Oxford University Press, 1938.
14. Upamanyu Chatterjee. *English August: An Indian Story.* London: Penguin Books in association with Faber & Faber, 1988. p.1
15. Arun Joshi. *The Foreigner.* Bombay: Asia Publishing House, 1968. p. 58.
16. Dr. Lily Kawa and Vinay Bharat. *'Cultural Allotropy in Some Indo-English Novels'*, http.//www.zgyn.com/ literature

17. R.K. Narayan. '*English In India: The Process of Transmutation*,' *The Times of India*, Bombay: Dec. 2nd, 1964.

18. Anita Desai. *The Indian Writers' Problems,* London: Language Forum, 1970, p.38

19. Ruth P. Jhabvala. *Autobiographical Essay: Living in India.* London: London Magazine, Sept., 1970, p. 41.

20. Upamanyu Chatterjee. *English: August,* op. cit., p. 23.

21. As quoted in C. Paul Verghese's *Essay on Indian Writing in English*, op. cit., p.8.

22. Prof. S. Nagarajan. '*A Study of English Literature in India".* *Commonwealth Literature*, London, 1965

23. Iqbal Bekhtiyar.ed. *The Novel In Modern India,* Bombay, 1964. p. 43.

24. Ellis Underwood. *Indian English and Indian Character,* Calcutta: OUP, 1885. pp. 10-33.

25. Paul C. Verghese. *Problems of the Indian Creative Writer In English.* Bombay: Somaaiya Publications, 1971. p. 109.

26. *ibid.,* p. 109.

27. Clyde Kluchohn. '*Values and Value Orientation in the Theory of fiction'. Towards a General Theory of Action.* eds. L. Parsons and E. Shils. Cambridge: Mass., 1951. p. 410.

28. Cora Du Bois. '*The cultural Interplay between East and West'. The East and West Must Meet: A Symposium.* East Lansing: Michigan, 1959. p.7.

29. Richard Lannoy. *The Speaking Tree: A Study of Indian Culture and Society,* London: Oxford University Press, 1971. p. 414.

30. *ibid.,* p. 417.

31. S.N. Ganguli. *Tradition, modernity and Development: A study in Contemporary Indian Society.* N. Delhi: Macmillan, 1977. p. 15.

32. c.f. Raja Rao. '*Foreword*' to *Kanthapura*.op.cit.

33. Stokley Carmichael. *The Dialectics of Liberation*, ed., David Cooper. Great Britain: Penguin Books, 1968. p.156.

34. *ibid.,* p.157.

Chapter - II

HISTORICAL BACKGROUND

The rise of the novel in India was not a purely literary phenomenon, it was a social phenomenon as well. It was associated with the social, political and economic conditions which were comparable with those which favoured its rise in England. "In comparison with the regional literatures of India such as Bengali, Punjabi and Telegu which have existed for many centuries, or with Tamil which is even older, Indian English literature is very young. Nevertheless, it already has its own history".[1]

India came into contact with the West in the pre-Christian era as a result of the invasion of Alexander, the Great. For more than two thousand years India has been in trade with many Western countries. The journey which began from Vasco de Gama's voyage to India in 1498 continued till the nineteenth and the twentieth century. Portugal being the first, became interested in trade and commerce with India. This was also not without political implications. In fact, the process of European colonization began as early as November, 1510 when Alfonso de Albuquerque captured Goa. In the middle of the 17th century, they started losing the Moghul Emperor's favours. Shahjahan rained death and disaster on them when the Portuguese held the two slave girls of Mumtaz Mahal in 1632. To aurangzeb, they became an eyeshore for their piracy and robbery, avarice and rapacity, religious interference and clandestine practices.

Marhatta navy was cutting down their trade. Portuguese commercial supremacy was under fire when a triangular contest between the Portuguese and the Dutch, the Pouruguese and the English, and between the Dutch and the English soon engulfed the Indian poiltical scene. The French came last and were the last to be wiped out by the English. By the beginning of the second half of the 18th century, the English shone brilliantly against the flickering glow of the dying Moghul Empire. Meanwhile, they began to delve in the field of education also as to prepare clerks and translators in their administrative offices.

Although the first English School was established in 1718 for the benefit of the children of the officers of the Company, it took more than one hundread years for English education to become an official policy. Meanwhile, missionaries had established quite a few educational institutions imparting English education. "A few institutions, like the Hindu College, were founded by people who were interested in public welfare. The Anglicists, under the leadership of Raja Rammohan Roy, could at last presuade the government to introduce Western science and philosophy through English education (1835). The introduction of the Western system of education was a major landmark in the history of modern India, as it paved the way for a new awareness in the English educated Indians."[2]

While Indians were beeing "anglicised", interestingly, a section of the British population was being "Indianised". Indilogists like Sir William Jones and Sir Thomas Munro came to be called "Brahmanised Britons" because of their intellectual identificaiton with India. They admired Indian culture and deprecated the idea of introducing Western civilisation or Christianity into India.[3]

M.K. Naik informs that many British people were "going native", and that, "some of them saw nothing wrong in taking Indian mistresses and, a few, even wives."[4] Some of them embraced Oriental religions and lived like Indians. Mirza Moorad Alee Beg Gaekware, the author of *Lalun the Beragun*, was an Englishman by birth, "a scion of old Hampshire family of Milford" but "became a Mussalman."[5]

It is the Englishman again who performed the yeoman's service by introducing and interpreting Indian culture and religion to the West through translations treatises and commentaries. Sir William Jones founded the Royal Asiatic Society of Bengal in 1784. H.T. Colebrooke wrote *Digest of Hindu Law on Contracts and Succession* (1797 – 98), and James Prinsep discovered the clue to the Asokan inscriptions.[6]

While on the political front, the impact of the West made Indians more and more conscious of their rights and privileges at the levels of culture and religion; the resistance at the initial stage gave way to a synthesis. In the nineteenth century, there prevailed a general inclination towards assimilation and synthesis rather than opposition. There was an atmosphere of suspicion and distrust in some quarters, no doubt, but in spite of that, East-West encounter resulted in a benign synthesis.

The theme of East-West encounter is a popular theme taken up by the novelists in their works. At some other times, there are passing remarks or situations touching the theme. Lal Behari Dey's novel *Govinda Samanta: Or Bengal Peasant Life* (1874) reflects the author's attitude of reform in the context of a traditional rural society. His novel also deals with the problems of English education. According to Viswanath S. Naravane, "..the coming together of East and West is one of the most significant developments of the modern age."[7]

Leaders like Raja Rammohan Ray, Debendra Nath Tagore, Keshub Chandra Sen, Iswar Chandra Vidyasagar, Swami Dayanand Saraswati, Swami Vivekananda and Syed Ahmed Khan believed in the assimilation of the essence of both the cultures and religions as the most desirable goal of modern India. Naravane has quoted Ronaldshay to drive home his point:

> *Keshub Chandra Sen, more than, perhaps any other man, showed that the gulf between Europe and Asia might be bridged without the sacrifice of anything fundamental in the race genius or race – culture of either. He showed how East and West might be complementary rather than antagonistic to one another.*[8]

The encounter between East and West, according to Gopal Krishna Gokhale led the Indians to look at things in a different perspective and "a re-examination of the whole of their ancient civilization."[9] This also brought them into "violent collision with their own society." In his famous lecture, "East and West in India", presented at the Universal Races Congress in July, 1911 Gokhle further pointed out that the "teaching" of the West served Indians "both as a corrective and a stimulant to their old civilization."[10]

Krupabai Satthianandan has treated this theme of cultural collision and synthesis in both her novels, although

Saguna: A Story of Native Christian Life (1880 – 90), her autobiographical novel, shows more involvement with the issue. Krupabai Satthianadan belonged to a family of Brahmins in Gujurat converted to Christianity. The story of the conversion has been narrated by her in *The Story of a Conversion* (1891), poignant with the basic questions involving faith and belief. She had received good education and had exposure to the high class native Christians as well as Europeans. In *Kamala: A Story of Hindu Life* (1892 – 94), she presents the conflict between the true essence of Hinduism and the superstitions and conservative way of life led by the Hindus in general.

Saguna is more deeply pre-occupied with the interaction between the two cultures. Harichandra, the prototype of the author's father is the embodiment of a cross – cultural psychological situation. To young people like Harichandra, English education meant liberal and modern ideas, but to many others, it merely meant the blind imitation of the Western habits and manners. As a young, educated Brahmin, Harichandra had a very open mind ready to be influenced, and also to think and ask questions.[11]

After long thinking and self - rationalizing with his own self and with his scriptures, Harichandra embraces Christianity. His conversion shocked the community, but he found that "some of those with whom he argued could not but acknowledge that Christianity had in it, in a more highly developed form, truths which were only dimly outlined in the Hindu 'shastras'. But their objection to the religion of Christ was that it was a foreign religion, the religion of the conquerors, and that it was therefore very unpatriotic for an orthodox Hindu to exchange his own faith for that of the foreigners".[12]

So, all we can say is that the rise of the novel in India was not purely a literary phenomenon. It was a social phenomenon as much, rather the fulfilment of a social need. As Ralph Fox points out:

> *The novel is the most important gift of the burgeois, or the capitalist civilization to the world's imaginative culture. The novel is its great adventure, its discovery of man...*[13]

The growth and the development of the novel ran parallel to the industrial development and the growth of the modern burgeois society in Europe. In India too, the novel could develop and become popular with the advent of the British rule which set in the process of industrialisation and the rise of middle class in the nineteenth century. Likewise, the social climate in the nineteenth century Bengal seems to have been not very much different from what it was in eighteenth century England. The emergence of the middle classes took place first in Bengal because the historical situation in Bengal during early British rule was most favourable to the emergence of what economists call 'money economy' to which was oriented the rise and growth of a modern urban middle class. Accounting for the popularity of fiction in the nineteenth century Harish Raizada says:

> *As the appeal for improving the condition of Indian people and the relationship between India and England was to be made to the English rulers, many of the Indian writers chose to write in English, and as novel was a literary genre most suited to the proper representation of life and its*

> *problems, they took to fiction for expressing their views.*[14]

Many upper class Bengali families constituting the urban aristocracy in the late eighteenth and nineteenth centuries were fast stepping down the ladder to the middle rungs by the middle of the nineteenth century:

> *The composition of the urban Bengali middle class was changing and with it its outlook and behaviour as well ... Money and intellect, the two motive powers of modern times, stylistically and objectively corrected, were now united together in moulding the destiny of the urban Bengali middle class...*[15]

Bangdoot, the Bengali weekly, wrote in 1829 welcoming "the rise of this new class in a confident and optimistic tone while *Sambad Prabhakar*, the most popular Bengali daily of the time, wrote in 1853 strongly criticizing the economic parasitism of the Bengali middle class and again in the nineties lamenting the sad degeneration of the middle class Bengalis into a "tribe" of cringing employees and servants, without any hope of regeneration in the near future".[16]

It should also be remembered in this context that the advantages of English education were reaped mostly by the middle class Hindus, the Hindu aristocracy and the muslim community generally holding aloof from it.

Thus the social climate of Bengal during the first half of the nineteenth century was powerfully conditoned by the rise of the middle classes, the spread of English education and the consequent impact of western ideas and culture, the growth of the press, a resuscitation of the Hindu religion and change of religious and moral values brought about by the great reforms of William Bentinck and the teachings of Raja Rammohan Roy and the emergence of a rationalistic view of life.

Dr. Karanth, who in an article entitled, "How Deep is Western Influence on Indian Writers of Fiction", published as early as 1967 had analysed the relative impacts made on him as a novelist by native literatures and many of the classics of European and English fiction, took more or less a similar stand on the question, in the paper he presented at the seminar, on 'The Rise of the Indian Novel". He was of the view that our early novels were inspired by the early English novels and not by Indian epics, *puranas, jataka* stories or fables.

According to Karanth, all our ancient literary works such as epics, puranas, tales and fables could neither, by their very nature, provide the seeds for this particular literary form nor exercise any healthy influence on its development because of their highly moralistic, didactic and idealistic pre-occupation which militated against a more realistic and humanistic intererst in the spatio-temporal realities of existence such as was necessary for a novelist.

As against these views of Karnath, K. Krishnamoorthy's paper on *The Makings of the Indian Novel* sought to maintain that "the novel was not entirely new to Indian literature which contained many of the ingredients of the modern novel".[17]

A good example may be Romesh Chandra Dutt's works which have vibrations that have stood unwithered till date. Even time could not tarnish it. R.C.Dutt transcreated the Ramayana and the Mahabharatha into English, wrote six novels in Bengali. He himself rendered into English his two novels- *Sansar* and *Madhavi Kankan-* under the captions *The Lake of Palms* (1902) and *The Slave Girl of Agra* (1909) respectively. *The Lake of Palms* is based on the theme of social reformation and advocates the cause of widow remarriage. His two English transactions are conspicious for social realism, historical element, vividly portrayed characters and a graceful and polished style.

Joginder Singh, who is well-renowned for writing Guru Nanak's biography, Sikh Ceremonies, was a celebrated novelist whose fame as a novelist rests on *Nur Jahan* (1909), *Nasrin* (1915), *Kamla* (1925) and *Kamini* (1931). *Nur Jahan* should not go unnoticed as it appeared as a serial in *The East and The West*, portraying the famous romance between the Moghul prince, Salim and Mihar-ul-Nisa, the beautiful daughter of Ghias Beg.

Bal Krishna's *Love of Kusuma* (1910), a novel on the social life in the Punjab, mixes realism and romance in the delineation of Mohan and Kusum.

S.K. Ghose is considered as one of the best and most talented Indian English novelists of this period. Ghose's *1001 Indian Nights* (1905) and *The Prince of Destiny* (1909) are two celebrated novels of remarkable literary interest. The Publishers of *The Prince and Destiny* in the Preface to the first edition say:

> His romance is a presentation of India by an Indian. It draws a picture of Indian life from the inside, with its social customs and mortal ideas, its eternal patience, its religious fervour, its passionate love.[18]

The Prince of Destiny is remarkable for the vividly drawn characters. The hero, Barath, presents a union of the highest ideals of the East and the West. He is a believer in non-violence, love and forgiveness and wants to win over the Englishmen by the power of love and not by the power of the sword.

Bankim Chandra's *Rajmohan's Wife* and Lal Bihari Dey's *Govinda Samanta* are the first real Indian novels. Bankim was a superb story teller and carried the readers off their feet by the sheer flow of narrative. He had an imaginative vigour which gave to his characters life and vitality. They showed an astonishing vigour of the Bengali language combined with beauty and simplicity and also revealed a new world of romance and idealism. Some of his novels were translated into English, one into German, and this raised the prestige of Bengali literature in the eyes of the eudcated classes.

The real question before the student of Indo-Anglian fiction is not how imitiative that fiction has been of the western form but how original and innovative it has been. Referring to Raja Rao as the first great Indian writer of English prose and Michael Madhusudan Dutt as the author of *The Captive Indian* M.E. Derret observes:

> Others who imitated English forms and expressions admirably could not convey through them the Indian modes of thought and feeling, so that their works lacked the necessary depth and sincerity and were mere imitations.[19]

It cannot be said of writers like Toru Dutt, Lal Behari Dey, S.K. Ghosh, Swarnakumari Ghosal, Madhaviah and

Joginder Singh that they wrote only to show that they had a command over English. There were among them too many to whom English was the chosen language of intellectual communication. Most of these writers viz., Rajam Iyer and Madhaviah felt equally at home both in their own language, i.e. Tamil and in English, together with an inner compulsion not out of a desire to demonstrate their ability to write in English, or to impress the Western readers.

The history of novels based on the theme of East - West Cultural meet and encounter has been scripted well in E.F. Oaten's *A Sketch of Anglo - Indian Literature* (1908), the first important paper on the subject, uses the term 'Anglo-Indian' to cover all writing in English about India, and makes no distinction whatever, between writing in English by Indians and writng on India by Englishmen. Even as late as 1934 Bhupal Singh uses the term to cover both classes of writing. Since the publication of Dr. K.R. Srinivasa Iyengar's *Indo-Anglican Literature* (1943) and *The Indian Contribution to English Literature* (1945), Indian writing in English by Indians has been recognized as a distinct entity and the term *Indo-Anglian* has begun to be used to describe Indian creative writing in English. The term *Anglo-Indian* has been retained to describe writings by Englishmen in which either the subject is India or there is material borrowed from Indian life.

Some writers like Alphonso- Karkala perfer the term *Indo-English* to *Indo-Anglian* even while referring to writings by Indians in English. But there is another class of writing in which the writers are Indian and the subject is Indo-British relationship or what may be called the colonial encounter. Some of the early writers of English fiction in India have given us novels in which the theme is Anglo-India, the India which was the scene of social and cultural confrontations between the Englishmen and the natives. These writings, though small in number, have a significant place in the histroy of the Indian novel in English.

Among the novels of this class there are only two which come under the scope of the present study as it has already been discussed above. They are S.M. Mitra's *Hindupore* (1909) and Sarat Kumar Ghose's *The Prince of Destiny* (1909). Novels with intrinsic merits of their own, they are concerned with Indo-British social and cultural relationships broadening into a study of East-West encounters.

Needless to mention, *The Prince of Destiny* was, in fact, the first Indian novel in English to have the East-West motif as its theme and during the fifty years following its appearance, it has had a number of successors.

Viney Kirpal in an article entitled *An Overview of Indian Fiction: 1920 – 1990's* writes that Indian English fiction can broadly be categorised into two periods -

(1) The Indian English novel between the 1920's - 1990's and
(2) The Indian English novel since the 1980's.[20]

Though the novel in Indian Literature had been in existence for nearly a hundred years, the development of the Indian English novel could be telescoped into a span of less than forty years (1920s -1960s) with the various phases of the different regional language novels overlapping. These phases as broadly identified by Mukherjee are:

| Ph. I | (1920s) | The Historical novel |
| Ph. II | (1930s &, 1940s) | The novel of social reform and political change. |

Ph. III   (1950s & 1960s)   The novel of self-identity
                            including the
                            psychological.[21]

The seminal Indian English novel which set out
to subvert the colonizer's view of India was Raja Rao's
Kanthapura (1938). With its ingenuous mixing of myth
and history, it is the outstanding Indian English novel of
nation - building.

The national freedom movement, with Gandhiji as the
hero of the times, is also the subject of a few later historical
Indian English novels viz. R.K. Narayan's *Waiting for the
Mahatma*, Nayantara Sahgal's *A Time to be Happy* (1952).
We may also mention A.S.P. Ayyar's *Baladitya*, Dewan
Sharar's *Eastern Tales*, Dhirendra Nath Paul's *The Mysteries
of the Moghal Court* and Joseph Furtado's *Golden Goa*,
which are some unforgettable works of historical fiction
written during this period. The Indian historical novel,
therefore, continued to be produced in the 1950s although
its peak period was the 1920s through the 1930s. In fact,
during 1920s and 1930s, the Indian English writer basked
in the broad and radiant sunshine of Gandhian ideology.
No discussion of Indian English novel would be complete
without the assessment of the everlasting influence of the
Mahatma. Meenakshi Mukherjee writes:

> The most potent force behind the whole
> movement, the Mahatma is a recurring presence
> in these novels, and he is used in different ways
> to suit the design of each writer. He has been
> treated variously as an idea, a myth, a symbol,
> a tangible reality, and a benevolent human

being. In a few novels he appears in person, in
most others his is an invisible presence.[22]

In Raja Rao's *Kanthapura* and *The Cow of the Barricades*
the Mahatma never appears in person but his presence is felt
everywhere. In R. K. Narayan's *Waiting for the Mahatma*, the
Mahatma appears to be a warm human being. In Anand's
Untouchable Mahatma Gandhi appears as a crusader of
the evil of untouchability. The Indian English novel of
this period deals directly with the national experience
as the central theme. The various momentous events of
this turbulent period like - Mahatma Gandhi's passive
resistance movement against the Black Rowlatt Act, the
inhuman massacre in Jallianwallah Bagh in Amritsar, The
Khilafat Movement, the boycott of Simon Commisssion,
the prohibition and the boycott of foreign goods, the Civil
Disobedience Movement of 1930, the famous dandi March,
the Government of India Act 1935, the emancipation of
women, the Quit India Movement of 1942 and many other
facets of the Gandhian movement are vivdly described in
the novels written during this period.

The East-West encounter or the cultural conflict is
another important theme in the novel of this period. In
the novels written during this era the East-West encounter
operates as the conflict between the pre-Industrial modes of
life and mechanisation in Venkatraman's *Murugan the Tiller*
and Chintamani's *Vedantam, the Clash of Traditions*. What
distinguishes the Indian novel in English during this era is
the rise of the regional novel. The novelists who come from
various regions and states brought regionalism and local
colour in their novels. A. Madhaviah, K.S. Venkatramani,
Shankar Ram, Raja Rao and R.K. Narayan pioneered the

regional novel about South. D.F. Karaka and Amir Ali wrote about Maharashtra, especially Mumbai.

The Indianisation of English is the most outstanding achievement of Indian English novelists of this period. What distinguishes their English is the regional and local colouring they have imparted to English in order to make it an authentic and powerful medium for the expression of regional sensibilities and peculiarities. The English of a writer from the North differs from that of the South. In the Post-Independence era, the novel in English came to maturity and attained full flowering.

Here comes into picture the famous trio of the Indian English novel - R.K. Narayan, Mulk Raj Anand and Raja Rao. They began writing during the Gandhian era only and won great acclaim but their mature works belong to the dawn of Freedom. They were, in fact, the harbingers of the true Indo-English novel. Bhabani Bhattacharya was also a contemporary of these novelists, but he started writing fiction just after the Indian Independence.

The writings of these novelists steered the Indian English novel in the right direction. They defined the area in which the Indian novel was to operate, and brought the Indo-Anglian novel within hailing distance of the latest novels of the West. K.R. Rao writes:

> They laid the foundation for the genuine Indo-Anglian novel, each imparting to the Indian experience a dimension of individuality based on their approach to content and form.[23]

Mulk Raj Anand (1905-2004) has been the most prolific of the trio. His contribution to Indian English fiction of social relism is exceptionally great. His *Untoucable* (1935), which was left untouched by British publishers before being recommended by E. M. Forster to Lawerence and Wishart to accept it, depicts the story of the low caste boy, Bakha. It is primarily a tragic drama of an individual caught in the net of the age-old caste system. In *Coolie* (1936), he presents a poverty-stricken protagonist, Munno. Both novels are "a plea for the downtrodden, the poor and the outcast, who face economic hardship and emotional humiliation in a rigid social structure."[24] His *Two Leaves and a Bud* (1937) depicts the story of a middle-aged peasant, Ganger, from a village in Punjab.

Among Anand's other novels are *The Village* (1939), *Across the Black Waters* (1941), *The Sword and the Sickle* (1942), *The Big Heart* (1945), *Seven Summers* (1951), *The Private Life of an Indian Prince* (1953), *The Road* (1963), *Mourning Face* (1970), *Confession of a Lover* (1976), and *Nine Moods of Bharata: Novels of a Pilgrimage* (1998).

Anand's novels portray vividly the wretched condition of Indian rural society. He is one who "believes that literature must serve society, solve their problems and guide them."[25] He is considered the Indian version of Charles Dickens as far as the treatment of social theme is concerened.

R.K. Narayan is a product of the South Indian Hindu middle class family. He remained aloof from the contemporary socio-political issues and explored the South Indian middle class milieu in his fiction. He is a writer with full commitment to Hindu ideas. He created an imaginary small town named Malgudi and depicted middle class life in that town in almost all his works. Before Independence Narayan produced *Swami and Friends* (1935), *The Bachelor of Arts* (1937), *The Dark Room* (1938) and *The English*

Teacher (1946). His fictional art seems to reach maturity in his novels which appeared after Independence: *The Financial Expert* (1952), *The Guide* (1958), and *The Man-Eater of Malgudi* (1962). *The Guide* represents perhaps, the most sophisticated example of narrative technique in the Indo- English novel.

Narayan succeeded in universalising his Malgudi, through a local town, as Hardy universalised his 'Wessex'. The inhabitants of Malgudi – although they may have their local identity – are essentially human beings having kinship with all humanity. In his novels we meet college boys, teachers, guides, tourists, municipal members, and taxi drivers of Malgudi, but through the provincial themes he forges a universal vision. He "peoples his novels with caricatures rather than characters."[26]

Raja Rao (1908- 2006), whose "advent on the literary scene has been described as the appearance of a new star shining bright"[27] is the youngest of the trio. His *Kanthapura* (1938) is perhaps the finest representation of the Gandhian whirlwind in Indian English fiction. It is the story of a village with the same name. It presents the Gandhian ideology of non-violence and abolition of untouchability. Like its spirit, the form and style of *Kanthapura* also follow the Indian tradition.

The Serpent and the Rope (1960), winner of the Sahitya Academy Award in 1963, is considered a landmark in Indian-English fiction and traced as "few Indian English novels" which "have expressed the Indian sensibility with as much authenticity and power as *The Serpent and the Rope*."[28] *The Cat and Shakespeare* (1965), a metaphysical comedy, is an example of philosophical fiction.

> *Fantasy and reality, mysticism and mammonism,*
> *the past with its age- old philosophy and the*
> *present of the global war – are all mixed together*
> *in this brief, teasing fable.*[29]

His other prominent works are *Comrade Kirillov* (1976) and *The Chessmaster and His Moves* (1988). Raja Rao's place in the realm of Indian English fiction is safe as the most Indian of novelists writing in English, as a stylist, a symbolist, a myth- maker, the finest painter of the East-West encounter and a philosophical novelist.

Meenakshi Mukherjee in one of her essays entitled *The Anxiety of Indianness In Our Novels in English*[30] observes that the three pioneering writers who began their careers almost simultaneously in the 1930s may have been poles apart in their ideology, background and narrative modes, but they shared an unspoken faith which could then be rendered through particularized situations. In *The Serpent and the Rope*, Raja Rao constructs an advaitic brahminic India; Anand's novels, on the other hand, expose the claims of the high culture by taking up the cause of the paradigmatic Indian poor. R.K. Narayan's "Malgudi" has a metanymic relationship with India as a whole.

Bhabani Bhattacharya (1908) is a contemporary of Mulk Raj Anand, R.K. Narayan and Raja Rao, though he began his career as a novelist relatively late with *So Many Hungers* (1947). His novels show social commitment as deep as Anand's but critics have not rated him as highly, perhaps because his novels are much more entertaining *So Many Hungers* deals with the Bengal famine of 1942; Bhattacharya effectively presents the misery caused by the famine as well as wartime black marketeering. *Music for Mohini* (1952) is a lighter novel, dealing with city bred evil going to a village home after the arranged marriage. *He Who Rides A Tiger* (1954) is his best work.

Manohar Malgonkar, one of the popular Indo-English novelists of the modern era, started his career after Independence with the publication of *Distant Drum* (1960). He is an artist of the first order. He excels in literary sensibility and critical maturity; he "subtly makes a landmark as a historical novelist."[31] *Distant Drum* is a documentary of army life in its various aspects and a celebration of the army code as developed by the Britishers in the army. *Combat of Shadows* (1962) derives its title and epigraph from the *Bhagwad Gita*. *The Princess* (1963), undoubtedly Malgaonkar's best novel, is also a successful political novel. It reveals the bright side of the princely world. The theme of *A Bend in The Ganges* (1964) is Partition while *The Devil's Wind* (1972) deals with the great Revolt of 1857.

Meanwhile, Khushwant Singh came into limelight as a crude realist with the publication of his *Train to Pakistan* (1956). In this novel he deals with the impact of Partition in a small village on the India - Pakistan border. His second novel *I Shall not Hear the Nightingale* (1959) shows an ironic picture of a Sikh joint family symbolizing different Indian reactions to the freedom movement of the 1940s. His later novels include *Delhi* (1992), covering more than eight hundred years in the life of a city, which has been the heart of India in more than one sense, and *The Company of Women* (1999). His crude realism finds a place in each of his novels.

Another novelist of this period is J. Menon Marath whose realism is deeply rooted in his native land Kerela, as Khushwant Singh's is the Punjab. He wrote *Wound of Spring* (1960), *The Sale of the Island* (1968) and *Janu* (1998).

Balchandra Rajan presents a blend of realism and fantasy, the two conspicuous strains in the Indian English fiction of the 1950s and 1960s. Unlike his contemporaries, Rajan's realism is less social than psychological in his first novel *Too Long in the West* (1961). It is a comic extravaganza.

Chaman Nahal is another novelist who, began his career late, though he published a book of literary criticism. His works suffer from an over-involved style where the English professor's presence can be felt always. *Azadi* (1975) is written in a very different style. It is a straight forward account of a rich Hindu family uprooted because of the partition of the Punjab, and their painful journey to India. *The English Queens* (1979) is a pure comedy with a touch of the fantastic. It is a good satire on the English - speaking elite in India, out of touch with reality and its own culture.

After the 1960s Indian English fiction, like its Western counterpart, shifted its focus from the public to the private sphere. The mass destruction caused by nuclear weapons in World War - II brought unrest and anxiety all over the world. The situation gave rise to psychological disorders and loss of moral values, and profoundly disturbed man's mental peace and harmony.

Indian novelists, too, could not remain aloof from these currents and henceforth they were not exclusively concerened with the exploration and interpretation of a social milieu, but dealt with new subjects of human existence and man's quest for self in all its complicated situations. This shift of focus in Indian English fiction becomes clearer particularly with Anita Desai and Arun Joshi who explore the agonised existence of modern man in their writing which "changed the face of Indian English novel".[32.]

Anita Desai, one of the literary luminaries of contemporary Indain fiction writing in English, is "the most prominent among the Indian English novelists who have tried to portray the tragedy of human souls trapped in the circumstances of life. She is more interested in the interior landscape of the mind than in political and social realities".[33] In her novels Indian English fiction has acquired a depth which it seldom had before. The combined influence of the great philosophers of the West and the fast- changing elements in the social structure of India has had a great impact on Desai. She makes each work an exploration of the inner self. Her works bring themselves closer to the form of existentialism. The main issue of concern in her novels is the loneliness of individual life. Through her novels, *Cry the Peacock* (1963), *Voices in The City* (1965) and *Bye – Bye Blackbird* (1971), she has added a new dimension to the saga of Indian women novelists in English fiction.

Anita Desai effectively deals with the East – West Encounter theme in *Bye – Bye Blackbird* when she writes about the homesick Indian immigrant in England. Her Akademi Award winning novel, *Where Shall We Go This Summer* (1975) is a sensitive examination of upper middle class life. Sita, a house wife in Bombay (now Mumbai), is sick and tired of her conventional routine. Past middle age mother of four and pregnant for the fifth time she does not want the child to be born into the stifling environment in which she lives. It "depicts the inner - outer world of its protagonist Sita and her fatigue for life."[34] Her other works, *Fire on the Mountain* (1977), *In Custody* (1984) and *Fasting, Feasting* (1999) also deal with similar existential questions tormenting the individuals. She is a dominating figure in the twentieth century Indo-Anglian fiction.

By the end of the nineteen sixtees and the early seventies some fresh faces appeared on the Indian English fictional scene, the most prominent of them were Chaman Nahal and Arun Joshi.

Arun Joshi (1939-1993), like Anita Desai, has recorded the modern man's traumas and agonies in his novels with rare competence and gravity. As Shyamala A. Narayan puts it:

> *Arun Joshi presents an India riddled with corruption. Even God can be propetised, by gifts in black money to his temples, where the priests themselves are corrupt as the narrator. Hypocrisy is so all pervasive that the narrator himself is not free from it.*[35]

His five novels, *The Foreigner* (1968), *The Strange Case of Billy Biswas* (1971), *The Apprentice* (1974), *The Last Labyrinth* (1981), *The City and the River* (1990) and a collection of short stories have won him high critical acclaim and a recognition as an author of rare sensitivity and exceptional talent.

As a study in cross cultures, *The Foreigner* has been compared to *The Bostonians, The American* and *The Ambassadors*. The working of the personal and human problem against the background of cultures follows the same delicate pattern as of Henry James. According to *The Journal of Indian Writing in English,* it "marks as definite improvement over all other novels in English on the East-West muddle."[36]

Among Joshi's contemporaries, Chaman Nahal is an important novelist. His most outstanding work before the eighties was *Azadi* (1975), one of the most prominent novels on the theme of Partition. His other novels before the eighties are *My True Faces* (1973), *Into Another Dawn* (1977), and *The English Queens* (1979). Among his novels after 1980 are: *The Crown and The Loincloth* (1981), *The Salt of Life* (1990), and *The Triumph of the Tricolour* (1993).

Feminism as the assertion for a discrimination – free existence for women is the second dominant theme that has been the subject of the Indain English novel since the 1930s. An important feature of this period was the growth of Indian women novelists writing in English. Their appearance added a new dimension to Indian English novel. It is only after India gained freedom that they have begun enriching Indian English fiction. The domionant figures are Ruth Prawer Jhabvala, Kamala Markandaya, Nayantara Sahgal and Anita Desai.

Kamala Markandaya, one of the most dazzling and renowned Indo-English novelists, exihibits a broad and rich variety of setting, characters, and themes. Her debut novel *Nectar in a Sieve* (1954), a tragedy coaxed by economics, is a narrative of doleful trials and tribulations of a peasant couple, Nathan and Rukmani, of a South Indian village. Her second novel, *Some Inner Fury* (1957), is primarily a political novel while her *Silence Of Desire* (1961) depicts the conflict between Indian spiritual faith and modernism born of India's contact with the West. Two of her novels, *A Handful of Rice* (1966) and *Two Virgins* (1973), however covertly, show how the modernism brought in by the West inspires the protagonists to revolt against their traditional enviornment and seek their fulfilment by shaping their careers independently.

In *The Coffer Dams* (1969) Markandaya deals with the theme of the East – West encounter from a different angle by presenting the conflict between technological power and the forces of nature symbolised by a turbulent South Indian river. Some of her other prominent works are – *The Nowhere Man, The Golden Honeycomb* (1977), *Pleasure City* (1982). In all her novels Markandaya has treated the theme of East-West confrontation more comprehensibly than any other Indian English Novelist.

Ruth Prawer Jhabvala creates difficulties for her Indian readers and critics. In one of her articles published in London Magazine, Sep. 1970, she has definitely declared, "My husband is Indian, and so are my children I am not, and less so every year". K.R. Srinivasa Iyenger rightly observes:

> *One might, however, include her novels among her children, and in that sense her fiction 'is' Indian. She has been dividing her time between creative fiction and film - scripting between (as she has confessed) the "silence, exile and cunning" (James Joyce's formula) that the formula demands and the "glare of sublimity under which films have to be produced.*[37]

She takes an amused look at arranged marriages in India with her Jane Austenian tongue – in – cheek style and presents an ironic survey of the East-West confrontation. Her early novels *To Whom She Will* (1955), and *The Nature of Passion* (1956) are exquisite comedies of urban middle - class life in the nineteen fiftees and sixties. Her other novels include *The Householder* (1960), *Get Ready for Battle* (1962), *A New Dominion* (1973). About her *Heat and Dust* (1975), *The Guardian* writes, 'Her russle with India is one of the richest treats of contemporary literature'.[38] In all her novels, be it *In Search of Love and Beauty* (1983), *The Continents* (1987), *Poet and Dancer* (1993) or *Shards of Memory* (1995), she observes keenly the strangeness of human behaviour and presents it with gentle irony and good-humoured satire.

Nayantara Sahgal, whose forte is politics, is a leading practitioner of the political novel in India. In addition to the obvious political theme Sahgal shows her preoccupation with the modern Indian woman's search for sexual freedom and self-realization. Her novels include *A Time to be Happy* (1958), *This Time of Morning* (1968), *Storm in Chandigarh* (1969), *The Day in Shadow* (1971), *A Situation in New Delhi* (1977), *Rich Like Us* (1985), *Plans for Departure* (1985) and *Mistaken Identity* (1988). In all her novels the political turmoil of the outside world and the private torment of individuals are woven together.

After 1980 began the perid of the so-called "new" fiction. In this period a force of new novelists emerged. It includes Salman Rushdie, Vikram Seth, Upamanyu Chatterjee, Shashi Deshpande, Shashi Tharoor, Shobha De, Amitav Ghose, Amit Chodhary, and Arundhati Roy.

Sashi Deshpande is the novelist with the most sustained achievement. Having published eight novels - she seems to grapple with the identity crisis of the contemporary women in her works. Her prominent novels include *The Dark Holds No Terrors* (1980), *If I Die Today* (1982), *A Matter of Time* (1996) and *Small Remedies* (2000).

Salman Rushdie's *Midnight's Children* (1981) heralded a new era in the history of Indian English fiction. His other important novels include *Shame* (1983) and *Satanic Verses* (1988). Vikram Seth is another promising writer born in Calcutta, studied in the USA, always preferred the British English to American. Seth's works are – *The Golden Gate* (a novel in verse in the year 1986), *A Suitable Boy* (1993) and *An Equal Music* (1999). His fame rests on *The Golden Gate* which depicts the theme of alienation and isolation of young urban professionals in the USA. There is a description of romantic and sexual (homosexual) relationships. His *A Suitable Boy*, 'though not a Raj Novel is truly Indian in content and theme.' [39]

Till date, Amit Choudhary has published four novels, namely *A Strange and Sublime Address* (1999), *Afternoon Raag* (1993), *Freedom Song* (1998) and *A New World* (2000).

Upamanyu Chatterjee is "a social realist for whose creative endeavour the over-reaching theme of identity and its plight in a hostile world forms what may be called the bed-rock. He has written three novels - *English August: An Indian Story* (1988), *The Last Burden* (1993) and *The Mammaries of the Welfare State* (2000). The common thread that binds all the novels is the anti - heroic image of the protagonists and other characters."[40]

Shobha De is a popular novelist. She began her career as a journalist and edited *Stardust, Society* and *Celebrity*. She is the author of twelve books. The most prominent works are – *Socialite Evenings* (1989), *Starry Nights*(1991), *Sisters* (1992), *Strange Obsession* (1992), *Sultry Days* (1994), *Snapshots* (1995) and *Second Thoughts* (1996). But "De's novels, though selling like hot cakes in India and abroad, would seem to belong less to serious literature than to pulp writing."[41]

Arundhati Roy leapt to fame with the publication of her novel *The God of Small Things*. She won the booker prize in 1997 for this debut novel and created a history. The narrative technique Arundhati Roy uses is stream of consciousness in unconventional manner.

Namita Gokhle's *Paro: Dreams of Passion* is a remarkable novel. The novel reflects the higher strata of society, the affluent business class people, politicians and bureaucrats. Namita Gokhle presents Paro's sexual exploits not merely as form of hedonism but as the expressions of a free woman.

Brinda Mukherjee has come out with two novels *The Fourth Profile* and *A Fizzle Yield*. They reveal her remarkable knowledge of the lifestyles, manners and activities of the diplomats. Kiran Desai is the daughter of the celebrated novelist Anita Desai. She has written novels like *Hullabaloo in the Guava Orchard* and *The Inheritance of Loss*. She uses the ironic mode. Bulbul Sharma's *Banana Flower Dreams* depicts the world of patriarchal suppression, child marriages, bride – burning sexual abuse etc. in a dream sequence of a hundred year old Monimala on her death bed. Jhumpa Lahiri's two novels *Interpreter of Maladies* and *Namesake* have established her as an upcoming succesful fiction-writer. *Life Isn't All Ha Ha Hee Hee* by Mira Syal is the arrival of feminism in London's East end amidst shiny salwar-kameezes, hot samosas and awakening aspirations. Indian english fiction is on the move. We have a sizable crop of writers of fiction who have been attracting readership in India and abroad.

All we can say is that the Indian English novel has passed through a tough time. There was a time when Mulk Raj Anand's *Untouchable* was left untouched by British publishers before being recommended by E.M. Forster to Lawrence and Wishart to accept it. The same happened with R.K. Narayan whose *Swami and Friends* had to wait for Graham Greene's recommendation. But today the case is different. Indian English novelists have elevated themselves by overtaking novelists whose mother-tongue is English in the race to win major literary awards."The history of the Indian English novel can thus be dubbed as the story of a metamorphosing India."[42]

Not only are the works of Indian authors writing in English surging on the best-seller list, they are also incurring and earning an immense amount of critical acclamation. "Indeed, if one begins to explore the highly curious and arresting history of Indian English literature and also experience its various facets, as expressed in Indian English literature, plays and movies and other media, he is sure to be lost amidst such profundity, in the abstract sense."[43]

Indeed, it has also been a rather lucky happening and news that the harshness of critics has also accepted Indian literature in English as one of the guiding factor of present identification, which had begun several decades ago and is still in a continuous process of metamorphosis. There appears to be an acceptance of Indian English literature as, Indian writing represents a new form of the Indian cultural ethos. This literary body has become thoroughly absorbed and is presently a dynamic element of the quintessential Indian way of life.

Indian English literature is an honest enterprise to demonstrate the ever rare gems of Indian writing in English. "From being a singular and exceptional, rather gradual native flare-up of geniuses Indian English has turned out to be a new form of Indian culture and voice in which Indians converse regularly."[44] While Indian authors-poets, novelists, essayists, dramatists have been making momentous and considerable contributions to world literature since the pre-independence era, the past few years have witnessed a gigantic prospering and thriving of Indian English writing in the global market.

References:

1. K.K. Sharma. ed. Translated Virendra Pal Sharma. Ghaziabad: Vimal Prakashan, 1982. p. 38.
2. R.C. Mazumdar. H.C. Roy Choudhury and KK Dutta, *An Advanced History of India,* New Delhi: Penguin,1986. p. 633.
3. Subhendu Kumar Mund. *The Indian Novel in English, Its Birth and Development.*N. Delhi: Prachi Prakashan, 1997. p.73.
4. K.R. Srinivasa Iyengar. *Indian Writing In English.* New Delhi: Sterling publishers Ovt. Ltd., 1984. pp. 24- 25.
5. M.K. Naik. *A History of Indian English Literature.* N. Delhi: Sahitya Akademy, 1982. p. 28.
6. P.P. Mehta. *Indo-Anglian Fiction: An Assessment.* Bareilly: Prakash Book Depot, 2nd Revised Editon, 1979. p. 373.
7. M.K. Naik. *A History of Indian English Literature*, op.cit., p. 8.
8. S. Viswanath Naravane. *Modern Indian Thought.* N. Delhi: Orient Longman, 1978. p. 38.
9. *ibid.,* p. 38.
10. Quoted in Raja Rao and Iqbal Singh. *Changing India.* London: George Allen & Unwin Ltd., 1939. p.122.
11. *ibid.,* p. 123.
12. Subhendu Kumar Mund. *The Indian Novel in English*, op. cit., p. 80.
13. Krupabhai Satthianandan. *Saguna: A Story of Native Christian Life.* Madras: Christian College Magazine, c.1948. p.17.
14. Ralph Fox. *The Novel and the People.* Moscow: Foriegn Languages Publishing House, 1956. p.82.
15. Harish Raizada. *The Lotus And The Rose: Indian Fiction in English.* New Delhi: Young Asia, 1970. p.22.
16. Benoy Ghosh. *The Economic Character of the Urban Middle Class in the Nineteenth Century Bengal. Readings In*

Indian Economic History, ed. B.N. Ganguli. N. Delhi: Asia Publishing House, 1964., pp.137 - 143.

17. K.S. Ramamurti. *Rise of the Indian Novel in English*. Bangalore: Sterling Publishers Pvt. Ltd., 1987. p. 33.

18. *ibid.*, pp. 36 -37.

19. Quoted from P.P. Mehta: *Indo Anglian Fiction: An Assessment.* Barielly: Prakash Book Depot, 1968. p.50.

20. M.E. Derrat. *The Modern Indian Novel in English*. Bombay: Sterling Publication, 1989. p. 20.

21. K.S. Ramamuri. *Rise of the Indian Novel in English*, op. cit., p. 196.

22. Viney Kirpal. *Mapping Cultured spaces: Post Colonial Indian Literature in English*. ed., Nilufer E. Barucha and Verinda Nabar.N. Delhi: Vision Books, 1989. p. 61.

23. Meenakshi Mukherjee. *The Twice Born Fiction*. New Delhi: Heinemann, 1971. p.14.

24. K.R. Rao. *The Fiction of Raja Rao*. Aurangabad: Parimal Prakashan, 1980. p.144.

25. Ram Sevak Singh and Charu Sheel Singh. *Spectrum History of Indian Literature In English*. New Delhi: Atlantic Publishers and Distributors, 1997. p.127.

26. Smruti Ranjan Behera. *The Literary Style of Mulk Raj Anand. Indian Writing In English*, Vol.III. ed., M.K. Bhatnagar. N.Delhi: Atlantic Publishers and Distributors, 1999. p.11.

27. Murali Das Melwani. *Themes in Indo-Anglian Literature*. Bareilly: Prakash Book Depot, 1977. p.31.

28. S.M.R. Azmi. *Ambiguity in Raja Rao's Second Novel 'The Serpent And the Rope'. Indian Novel In English: Critical Perspectives.*ed., Amar Nath Prasad. New Delhi: Sarup & Sons, 2000. p.34.

29. M.K. Naik. *A History of Indian English Literature.* New Delhi: Sahitya Akademy. p.169.

30. *ibid.*, p.170.

31. Meenakshi Mukherjee. *The Anxiety of Indianness Our Novels in English*. (First published in *Economic and Political Weekly*, 27ᵗʰ Nov., 1993.

32. Arjun Kumar. *Manohar Mangonkar's Novels: A True Dynamo of Historical Sense and Sensibility in Indian English Literature*, Vol. II. ed., Basawraj Naikar. New Delhi: Atlantic Publishers and Distributors, 2002. p. 105.

33. Mukesh Ranjan Verma. *Indian English Novel since 1985 in Reflections on Indian English Literature*. eds., M.R. Verma and K.A. Agarwal. N. Delhi: Atlantic Publishers and Distributors, 2002 p.1.

34. Sharada N. Iyer. "*The Blackbird's Rough Passage" Indian English Litearture*. Vol.II. New Delhi: Atlantic Publishers and Distributors, 2002. p.176.

35. Amar Nath Prasad. *Indian Novel In English: Critical Perspective*. N. Delhi: Sarup and Sons, 2000. p.112.

36. R.K. Rajan.ed. *The Growth of the Novel in India, 1950 – 80*. N. Delhi: Abhinav Publication, p. 46.

37. Quoted in The Blurb of Arun Joshi's *The Foreigner* N. Delhi: Orient Paperbacks, 1993.

38. www. Indianetzone.com/41/history-Indian English – noter htm.p. 2.

39. The blurb of Ruth P. Jhabvala's *Heat and Dust*. Great Britain: John Murray, 1975.

40. Dr. S.C. Mundra. *A Handbook of Literature in English for Competitive Examinations*. Bareilly: Prakash Book Depot, 2003. p.517.

41. Dr. R.P.Singh. *The Concept of Anti-Hero in the Novels of Upamanyu Chatterjee*. Bareilly: Prakash Book Depot,2010 p.1.

42. Dr. Arvind M. Nawale. *Indian English Fiction: An Appraisal*. www.languageinindia.com, March, 2009.

43. *ibid.,* p. 4.

44. www.indianetzone.com/2/english-Literature.htm. p. 1

Chapter - III

THE MAN-EATER OF MALGUDI

The materials of Narayan's novels broaden out from the family to the community and the nation and one notices that modernity is slowly but steadily seeping deeper and deeper. The East-West theme is thus unavoidable. But as O.P. Mathur states:

> In R.K. Narayan, this has not been presented in terms of a vast social, economic or political conflict, nor in terms of a philosophical confrontation. Its dimensions are ethical, so deep and unobtrusive that one might easily miss it altogether.[1]

Narayan is an artist of rare excellence. He carefully avoids propaganda, commitment and purpose to which Mulk Raj Anand is devoted. He is objective. Once he remarked:

> I am so detached from what I write that I don't feel anything personal in it.[2]

Narayan is the solitary example among the modern Indian English Novelists who is detached and uninvolved and "a man of letters pure and simple". Narayan's remarkable "negative capability" and self- detachment are found in all his novels.

Narayan's fictional world of Malgudi (as in the title of the novel *The Man-Eater of Malgudi*) is more than a mere setting. It is a veritable world in microcosm, rich and complex in variety but, at the same time endued with an underlying sense of stability and continuity. The novelist never deals with the physical geography of Malgudi as a set piece but the geographical details are revealed "beneath and between the events, one comes to have a strong feeling about the identity of a place. The detail suggests surely and economically, the special flavour of Malgudi, a blend of the oriental and pre - 1914 British, like an Edwardian mixture of sweet mangoes and malt vinegar."[3]

Malgudi, though purely a localized setting, has been lavishly praised for Narayan's universality of vision. In the words of Ashish Nandy:

> *What is true of Malgudi is true in the whole world.*[4]

Whereas William Walsh writes:

> *Malgudi is an image of India and a metaphor of everywhere else.*[5]

Almost the same opinions have come from all sorts of critics. D.S. Philip has not exaggerated when he states:

> *Through the depiction of the values of the Indian heritage he* (R.K. Narayan) *offers an* alternative universality *to standards and values that emanate in the West.*[6]

The middle class family life has been a common theme in all R.K. Narayan's novels and short stories. This is his milieu as a writer, and he has been steadfastly true to it all through. Narayan's milieu is typically Indian. He has reinvented the true image of India in his Malgudi novels and short stories — the image was blurred by Kipling, John Masters and others among the Western writers and by Nirad C. Choudhuri among the Indian writers. V.S. Naipaul rightly remarks:

> *He operates from deep within his society. The India of Narayan's novels is not the India the visitor sees.*[7]

R. K. Narayan does see India from the inside. Malgudi presents a vision of India in miniature.

R.K. Narayan unfolds new vistas of life in Malgudi from *Swami and Friends* to *A Tiger for Malgudi*. Malgudi itself is a good example of cultural attotrope. Malgudi in his early novels is neither village nor city, but a town of modest size. It is sleepy, small and silent. With each new novel we advance in time and Malgudi grows in importance and gains in definition. The major landmarks remain unchanged.

> *With its unlit streets and shabby buildings, Malgudi changes from an agricultural town to a semi-industrialized city after passing through various*

phases. The town expands with the opening up of colleges, bank, hotels, cinema houses and the coming up of a railway line. It has Nallapa Grove, Kabir Road, Albert mission School names quite familiar to the readers. If its market road is noisy and dirty, it can be proud of its fashionable area — Lawly Extension — where live government officials, professors, doctors and lawyers. Like the growth of an adolescent to a young, educated and modern man, Malgudi — 'the microcosm of traditional Indian society changes from 1930's to the modern times but without losing basic characters.[8]

Resisting fast change, it crawls at its own speed – envying none, outpacing none. One can feel its pulse, its throb in the pages of Narayan:

The Wind from the West blows freely and naturally through Malgudi, irreversibly altering its cultural climate and constantly winging seeds which go on sprouting and changing the face of the society, as it has blown through its creator not only giving him a clear perception of the serious and the comic that lie at the hearts of both the traditional and modern but also producing within him the bloom of an ironical, silvery laughter, "the scene of humour" creating a "glow of peculiar civilized pleasure" which is one of the distinguishing characteristics of Western culture.[9]

Narayan gives us the feel of life itself which is neither all white nor all black but the grey, twilight world of contemporary life quivering hesitantly between tradition and modernity, East and West inextricably mixed up in the minds of individuals.

> *Narayan's own attitude, towards the West is representative of the Indian attitude unsure and ambivalent like the alternate denigration and idolization that the poor Sir Fredrick Lawley received at the hands of Malgudians.*[10]

The Man - Eater of Malgudi is the story of Nataraj, the owner of a small printing press in the fictional town of Malgudi, and his encounter with an eccentric stranger Vasu, who is, by profession, a taxidermist. The placid and sacred world of Nataraj, is disturbed by Vasu's sudden intrusion, and turns Nataraj's quiet life topsy - turvy.

The opening chapter of the novel gives a detailed account of Nataraj's family and its background which reveals a mini India. The socio-cultural ambience – the economic compulsions, family and personal bonds, socio-political environment, religious, and cultural traditions, the impact of modernity on the past and the influence of the West on the East – in which, his characters move, is strikingly real. To quote E.M. Verma:

> *Narayan's people resemble the people we come across in life, and the world of which they form a part in replica of the actual world, transformed by his creative imagination.*[11]

Narayan's novels are essentially stories of Indian life. Most of them trace the growth of an individual who is

firmly rooted in the Indian social order. The protagonists –
Swaminathan, Chandran, Krishnan, Ramani, Raju, Mr.
Sampath, Margaya, Jagan, Sriram, Raman and Nataraj —
are usually the members of a Hindu joint family.

They have strong familial bonds and are deeply attached
to their prospective parents, children and grandchildren,
uncles, aunts, brothers and sisters. Even now, in spite of the
impact of modernism, the basic unit of Indian society is the
family and it is a joint family. The individual has to grow in
this environment and his character is shaped, at times it is
warped, by the overwhelming influence of the members of
the family. He has to defer to the decisions of his elders in the
family even in such important matters as choosing his career
and choosing his wife. The whole family itself observes the
age – old customs, traditions and beliefs according to the
Hindu religion. Whereas, "the Hindu man drinks religiously,
sleeps religiously, marries religiously and robs religiously"[12]
writes Professor C.D. Narasimhaiah with a sarcastic sharpness.

Malgudi is a fast - growing and progressive town. After
independence it has witnessed significant changes. The old
roads, parks and colonies are renamed after national leaders
like Gandhi, Jawaharlal Lal Nehru and Subhas Chandra
Bose. Quite parallel to it there are posh colonies and streets
named after English people — Anderson Lane, Abu lane
and Hospital Road etc. New printing Presses carrying the
weight of English names viz, 'Empire Press', 'The Sun Press',
'Golden printing', and 'Star Press' are set up with modern
machinery. Mempi Hills is not an off- streamed place, rather
it is well connected with Malgudi Station by means of buses
and taxis. Mempi Bus Transport Corporation is also there.
Thus Malgudi grows and is ready to grow and develop in
course of time.

In the midst of these changes more often under Western influences, there are some things left unchanged which only sets an example of a cultural allotropy. Its old landmarks remain and give it a look of the town with a past. On its north flows the river Sarju, the pride of Malgudi. But Sarju seems to shift its undercurrents at times.

River Saryu is some ten minutes' walk from Ellaman Street. A little down on the north east of the town, lies Nallapa's Mango groves. The river here is shallow and can be easily crossed. On the south- west of the town are situated the best localities like Lawly Extension and New Extension. Beyond the anglicized Lawly Extension passes the Trichy Trunk Road shaded with trees. Then there is the 'typical Indian' Market Road which intersects the anglicized Race Course Road. Then there are Kabir Streets, and Kabir Lane, Sarju Street which hug sagaciously with anglicized Anderson Lane, Abu Lake and Hospital road etc. It seems that Malgudi's establishments carry the flavour of both the Indian Mango juice and the westernized 'cola'.

In R.K. Narayan's novels as professor A.N. Kaul has rightly remarked, we are aware of a small though significant part of the national condition, a fundamental aspect of which is the Western influence which seems to penetrate the lives of the common men at numerous points. R.K. Narayan himself says:

> *Society presses upon us all the time. The progress of the last half century may be described as the progress of the Frog out of the well. All means of communication, all methods of speedy travel, all newspapers, broadcasts and every kind of invention is calculated to keep the barrage of*

> *attack on the Frog in the well. He will not be*
> *left alone.*[13]

As a matter of fact, the West has made deep inroads into the common man's life in Malgudi in respect of not only the geographical aspects of the town but also of the steady erosion of traditional ways of life and the rise of new values necessarily accompanying the contemporary cultural upheaval which no writer with Narayan's background of English education, with his wide sympathies apart from his comments on Christianity in *My Days* and his comprehensive and clear – eyed vision can ignore. Narayan quotes Aldous Huxley with approval:

> *What's pity? When two nations get together they*
> *get the worst of each other – Rope trick and such*
> *things from your country and mere technology*
> *from the West.*[14]

Narayan sees South India as a "fundamentally conservative society changing under the impact of the West, industrialism, modern ideas".[15]

The Man-Eater of Malgudi is at once a re-incarnation of the old Hindu myth of Bhasmasura in the modern form (a myth presented with both serious parallelism and ironic contrast in the manner of William Faulkner) and a presentation of two diametrically opposed attitudes to life. The Bhasmasura parallel is clearly indicated in the novel in more than one place, by Shastri, who tells Nataraj the narrator, less than half way through the story that Vasu "shows all the definition of a 'rakshasa' ...demoniac creature who possessed enormous, strength, strange powers, and genuine, but recognized no sorts of restraints of man or God."[16]

Vasu has been compared incessantly with Ravana, Mahisa, Bhasmasura, Daksha and many other 'rakshasas' as mentioned in the Hindu mythology. He has been presented as the anti-thesis of all Indian characteristics. Sastri is a mouth-piece of the author and an optimistic narrator representing the eternal ethics and moral of the Indian society- victory of good upon the evil forces, unlike John Milton's Satan:

> *There was Ravana, the protagonist in Ramayana, who had ten heads and twenty arms ... the earth shook under his tyranny. Still he, came to a sad end ... or take Mahisha ... who had secured an especial flavour that every drop of blood shed from his body should give rise to another demon in his own image and strength, and who nevertheless was destroyed ... then there was Bhasmasura, who acquired a special boon that everything he touched should be scorched, while nothing could even destroy him. He made humanity suffer. God Vishnu was incarnated as a dancer of great beauty named Mohini, with whom the asura became infatuated ... the demon was reduced to ashes that very second, that blighting touch becoming active on his own head. Everyman can think that he is great and will live forever, but no one can guess from which quarter his doom will come.*[17]

Narayan's novels begin when Malgudi is threatened by some newcomer, which may be the Mahatma or the movies, a taxidermist or a dancing girl. In *The Man- Eater of Malgudi*, it is the taxidermist Narayan, who flirts with the danger, but the novel ends only when the threat has been removed, when it has been blunted by the repressive tolerance of traditional India, or when it has been exposed as a rakshasa, an evil demon that, because it is evil, necessarily, destroys itself. Richard Cronin rightly states:

> *The admiration that Naipaul felt for such a writer was never likely to be other than fragile, puzzled, for Naipaul's achievement is as clearly built upon his sense of himself as deracinated, his painful and proved insistence on living in a free state, as Narayan's is founded on his participation in the values, the prejudices, the culture of the society that he depicts.*[18]

The raw material of the novelist comes from the actual world in which he lives and breathes, the people he meets in real life — his family and relations, his friends and acquaintances, official functionaries, saints and sinners, and personas of all shades and types who constitute the web of society and its institutions — social, cultural, political and religious, customs and manners, traditions and conventions, beliefs and superstitions — leave an indelible mark on his heart and soul.

The Man-Eater of Malgudi returns to a more familiar Malgudi territory. Like Srinivas in *Mr. Sampath*, Nataraj, the protagonist, is a printer with a shop in the Market – Road and his home is in the long-established Kabir Street. His printing press without 'the original Heidelberg machine' has got a complete Indian set-up.

.... Hung up a framed picture of Goddess Laxmi
poised on her lotus holding aloft the bounties of
earth in her four hands, and through her grace I
did not do too badly.[19]

The above statement reveals not only the set up of his press but his own mental set-up and beliefs. He is an Indian to the core, though he proves to be a perfect example of cultural allotrope. He is a meeting point of the East and the West, though in a very subtle way. He seems to get inclined towards Western-influenced schoolings as first he himself and then his son, "little Babu, went to Albert Mission school, and he felt quite adequately supplied with toys, books sweets and many other odds and ends he fancied."[20]

Not only this unique contrast in him. But his press has also got the cultural fusion. What to say about the hanged frame of goddess Laxmi in front of the prime seat of Queen Anne-chair, a style, directly copied from Europe. Nataraj says:

I had furnished my parlour with a high-backed
chair made of teak wood in the style of Queen
Anne.[21]

The printing press, in fact, forms the cultural trope of the Novel. Not only is a large part of the novel's action centered on it but it is also the metonymic site of the novel's gesture towards an ordinary subjectivity. The blue veil separating the interior space of the press from the "front" parlor is in a way also the veil, of 'Maya', using which Nataraj maintains the illusion of "a lot of men working on the other side", the protagonist describes:

> *Between my parlor and the press hangs a blue curtain. No, one tried to peer through it.*[22]

Syed Mujeebuddin rightly observes:

> *It is through this subtle clustering of tropes that the novel effectively contains the emblematic import of the printing press as a symbol of modernity and progress. The repeated reference to "the original Heidelberg" (of the press next door) only reinforces the effectiveness of Narayan's figural transformation of the symbol.*[23]

The parlour itself where the best seat is the dubiously anglicized nomenclature "Queen Anne Chair' offered to those who have the owner's respect and affection is only the 'front" where people came to rest and get "ideas for bill reforms, visiting cards, or wedding invitations."[24] This Westernized hospitality by an Indian host is a pervasive mentality of a subjugated Indian society as a whole. Significantly, "the topography of the press is similar to that of a temple mirroring the inner and outer sanctums, only the twice born having access to the inner santum."[25]

Vasu's rough encroachment into this space is resented as he came forward "practically tearing aside the curtain, an act which violated the sacred traditions"[26] of Nataraj press. Though before Vasu, people only with good culture were known to gather around the parlour. People from different schools of thought and profession were having a nice pastime there sitting and chatting for hours. Be it: "a poet who was writing the life of God Krishna in a monosyllabic verse."[27] Or, Mr. Sen, "the journalist, who came to read the newspapers on … Table, and who held forth the mistakes Nehru was making."[28]

Nataraj also seemed to be very happy with his on-going life at office and at home. R.K. Narayan underlines the true essence of an Indian family — a united family, a rare thing that happens only in India.

> *All the four brothers of my father with their wives and children numbering fifteen, had lived under the same roof for many years. It was my father's old mother who has kept them together, acting as a cohesive element among members of the family. Between my grandmother, who laid down the policy, and a person called Grand Auntie, who actually executed it, the family administration ran smoothly.*[29]

And Nataraj's family background is absolutely religious. With reference to his father, Nataraj comments:

> *As he grew older my father began to spend all his time sitting on the 'pyol' on a mat, reading 'Ramayana' or just watching the street.*[30]

But Nataraj's chirruping life settled among his family members and friends went on a different track. Destiny and his own weakness and 'feebleness' forced him to mount on a tiger. His settled life became unsettled when one day the 'man – eater' of the title Vasu, a bullying taxidermist, bursts into his premises. From the moment he first appears, Vasu infringes upon the 'sacred traditions' of Nataraj's Press by going through a blue curtain that separates the inner sanctum — and with it Nataraj's sense of private space — from the little room at the front of his shop that he calls his "parlour" a public space where he entertains his customers. "In doing so, Vasu almost tears the curtain, an act of symbolic penetration which anticipates all his subsequent behaviour."[31]

Vasu himself lifts the curtain of doubt and puts forth his agenda:

> *You think I have come here out of admiration for this miserable city? Know this; I'm here because of Mempi Forest and the jungles in those hills. I'm a taxidermist. I've to be where wild animals live.*[32]

This is, of course, added up with a sarcastic though powerful remark of Nataraj, "And die."[33]

Vasu's wit falls short to understand it; Vasu is so sure about Nataraj of being the sort of what R.K. Narayan loves to call 'a frog of the well'. In one scene Vasu throws up his arms in vexation and acclaims:

> *You know nothing; you have not seen the world. You know only what happens in the miserable little place.*[34]

The above proclamation of Vasu definitely airs the Western prejudices of thriving authority on themselves for anything new and 'scientific'. And when "Vasu takes over Nataraj's 'attic', without Nataraj ever really agreeing to the arrangement and uses it for his work as a taxidermist the typical Indian Brahmin Nataraj is horrified to find that the room has been 'converted into a charnel House' by a murderer of innocent creatures'.[35] And, Nataraj has almost surrendered before the situation,

> *Stag-heads, tiger-skins and petrified feathers were going to surround me forever and ever. My house was becoming a Noah's Ark, about which I had read in our scripture classes at Albert Mission.*[36]

So Nataraj is faced with a crisis heterotopia within his protected inner space. Vasu's appropriation of the attic is clearly a psychic as well as a physical invasion, particularly since it violates Nataraj's belief in 'ahimsa'.

What Vasu exactly represents is open to debate. He claims to have a 'scientific outlook'. That is opposite of Nataraj's sentimentalism and he clearly symbolizes the incursion of an outside force (perhaps, Western and hundred per cent non-Indian) into the Malgudi cosmos. Vasu did not pierce only through a curtain but he pierced through a culture also. However, he adopts an 'American Style', which Nataraj feels he has "picked up from crime books and films".[37] "Whether this force should be seen as epitomizing modernity generally or more specifically either Western encroachments or the intrusion of another part of India into the south remains a matter for speculation and by the end of the novel Narayan will have pointed readers in completely different directions."[38]

Nataraj tells the readers that he is not mercenary, since although 'sordid and calculating people'[39] have considered him a fool for not taking the opportunity to rent his parlour out, he has preferred to keep it as a kind of command space where passersby with aching heel can rest. The tone is delicately poised, but of a kind that suggests irony to many Western readers. The novel, in fact, opens with this description.

> *I could have profitably rented out the little room*
> *in front of my press in market Road, with a view*
> *of the fountain. I was considered a fool for not*
> *getting my money's worth out of it. But I could not*
> *explain myself to sordid and calculating people.*[40]

R.K. Narayan through his mouth-piece Nataraj makes his intention very clear that his world least bothers about sordid and calculating people', because these are two things Indians are not meant for.

From the moment when Vasu first appears, he is described in terms that suggest that he is a demonic force, and as the tale unravels, it becomes clear that he is being associated with the 'rakshashas'. His taxidermy provides a direct challenge to Nataraj's belief in the sanctity of life and this is underscored by various mythological references.

When Nataraj visits the attic he is shocked to discover the carcasses of various animals including a cat that has frequented his press, a tiger poached from the forest and a stuffed cow. He is, however, most disturbed to see Vasu working on a dead eagle and the full extent of his repugnance emerges as he tries to convince Vasu that the bird is the sacred 'garuda', the messenger of God Vishnu. Here is an example of Nataraj's desperation to make him understand what a 'garuda' stands for:

> *You have no doubt excelled in giving it a right*
> *look, but, poor thing, it's dead. Don't you see that*
> *it is a 'garuda'?"*

"What if it is?"

'Don't you realize that it's sacred? That's the messenger of God Vishnu? [41]

Further, Nataraj expresses his fear:

I shivered slightly at the thought and the way his mind worked. Nothing seemed to touch him. No creature was safe, if it has the misfortune to catch his eye.[42]

The detail directs attention to a number of Krishna-Vishnu analogies that permeate the text, possibly even informing the choice of blue for the colour of the curtain that separates the inner world of Nataraj's press from his parlour. Later in the novel what seems as though it will be the climatic episode of the novel, Nataraj feels that he may have to act, in direct opposition to Vasu's view of preservation, as a Vishnu-like preserver of life. One of his friends is a poet, who is writing an epic about the life of Krishna, an incarnation of Vishnu, in monosyllabic verse, and during the course of the action the poet arrives at the moment of the hero's marriage to Radha. To celebrate this, it is agreed to hold an elaborate ceremony, centered on an elephant, in conjunction with the annual spring festival at the local Krishna temple. Worried that Vasu, who has been quick to grasp the commercial possibilities of a dead elephant will try to kill it, Nataraj initially feels that he must act as the elephant's protector, but then remembers a mythic tale that suggests otherwise and this braces up his natural inclination towards inaction. In the tale the elephant Gajendra is saved from a crocodile's jaws through the intervention of Vishnu who gives Gajendra the strength to save himself. When he remembers this, Nataraj is able to persuade himself that the problem will solve itself without his having to lift a finger; and when he falls prey to a seemingly psychosomatic illness, this is exactly what happens.

The two characters, Nataraj and Vasu, are very obviously foils to one other and at one point Nataraj calls Vasu 'a perfect enemy'. Vasu sets himself up as 'a rival to nature'[43], while Nataraj champions 'the Natural' and the balance is weighed in favour of the aspects of brahminical Hinduism that Nataraj represents, though not unequivocally or uncomplicatedly so.

Nataraj likes one thing most in him, that is, his being a 'man of word' and Nataraj admits:

> *He was a man of his word. He had said that he never wasted his time. I could see that he never wasted either his time or his bullets.*[44]

But very often Nataraj finds himself standing in sharp contrast to Vasu:

> *I had been brought up in a house where we were taught never to kill. When we swatted flies, we had to do it without the knowledge of the elders. I remember particularly one of my grand uncles, who used the little room on the 'pyol' and who gave me a coin every morning to buy sugar for the ants, and kept an eye on me to see that I delivered the sugar to the ants in various corners of the house. He used to declare with approval*

from all others 'you must never scare away the
crows and sparrows that come to share our food;
they have as much right as we to the corn that
grows in the fields.[45]

Whereas, Vasu owns no family. The interplay between Vasu and Nataraj also indicates a contrast between two diametrically opposed attitudes to life each shown to be disastrous in its own way, between the demonical, self-centered egotism of Western Vasu and the ineffectual self-effacing altruism of Nataraj, between the temerity of Vasu and the timidity of Nataraj.

For Vasu, everything in the external world must
subverse his own interests: other people, society,
human considerations — all exist to feed to his
egotism. Such an attitude to life is fraught with
obvious dangers for both the individual and
society; such self-centeredness must inevitably
end in self – destruction, for true to its nature it
must generate from within itself the forces which
destroy it.[46]

The description of the rakshasha fits Vasu perfectly in all respects. His very appearance is 'rakshasha' like 'A large man about six feet tall', he has a 'bull neck', 'a tanned face', a 'hammer fist', large powerful eyes under thick eyebrows, a large forehead, and a shock of unkempt hair 'like a black hat'. His clothes loud and 'gaudy' (red check bush shirt and field – grey trousers") are all of a piece with his appearance, so is his vehicle, a jeep which he drives at breakneck speed, Nataraj aptly describes him as 'the prince of darkness'. His movements are as mysterious as his activities in the jungle. "I challenge any man to contradict me"[47] is his motto.

At the same time Nataraj's altruism is as extreme as Vasu's egotism. It makes him unworthy and unbusinessman- like in his own profession. His rival, the owner of Star Printing Press, has an original Heidelberg machine and Nataraj is more proud of it than the owner himself. His salesmanship too is extremely poor. Narayan writes:

> *If business rests upon the principle that you make*
> *people buy things they don't need by high pressure*
> *salesmanship, Nataraj's way of doing business*
> *is most unorthodox. When Vasu wants five*
> *hundred visiting cards printed Nataraj suggests*
> *that he get only one hundred so that they keep*
> *fresh. When KJ places a big order for labels for*
> *aerated bottles, Nataraj must neglect it since he is*
> *busy with printing the poet's book, free of cost.*[48]

On the other hand, Vasu is a 'man of business' and he cannot afford to waste his time. Nataraj himself admits:

> *I admired him for his capacity for work for all*
> *the dreadful things he was able to accomplish*
> *single handed ... short of creating the animals,*
> *he did everything.*[49]

Nataraj at the same time, compares Vasu with 'the thorns of a bush' and himself as a prey or victim to it.

> *Sastri, you know the old proverb that when your*
> *cloth is caught in the thorns of a bush, you have*

to extricate yourself gently and little by little,
otherwise you will never take the cloth whole? [50]

To the readers' comfort, Sastri being an orthodox Sanskrit semi-scholar, appreciated this sentiment, set it off with another profounder one in Sanskrit which said that to deal with a 'rakshasha' one "must possess the marksmanship of a hunter, the wit of a pundit, and the guile of a harlot."[51]

Vasu, a triple M.A., knows about Indian constitution and its 'fundamental rights' loopholes. Vasu's inhumane behavior and stubborn attitude and rude irony make him stand much against the Indian moral and ethical values. When Nataraj asks about his 'permit' he comes up with the most idiotic and insensitive response: "the tiger didn't mind the informality."[52]

The relationship between Nataraj and Vasu is markedly unequivocal; Nataraj is the weak and Vasu the strong. Perhaps it is for this reason that Nataraj both tears and admires Vasu. Vasu himself does not seem to care much about Nataraj, riding rough shod over his feelings and much else besides. Nataraj cannot do anything when Vasu walks into the attic and takes it over. Syed Mujeebuddin makes a very significant remark:

Significantly the narrative here seems to allegorize the colonial takeover of India. Vasu having first come to do business, like the West, stays back and takes over the entire attic over the press. Nataraj lets him stay through a mixture of feelings: fear, compassion, and a spirit of hospitality. Furthermore, Vasu's proclivity towards hunting also hints at the habits of the colonial masters. Significantly enough, we are

> *made to note repeatedly, that Vasu prefers the*
> *"Queen Anne" chair so much that it is referred*
> *to as "his chair" for the rest of the narrative.*[53]

Clearly it is resistance that the novel seems to be figuring through its tropes. The novel's chief concern is with Nataraj's relation with Vasu and the means that he employs to cope with the rude disruption of his placid life. Interestingly, Narayan's depiction of Nataraj's meek Hindu and Vasu's demon correspond with the roles that Ashish Nandy in his important work on colonialism in India, *The Intimate Enemy*, ascribes to the colonized Indian and the colonizing British. Nataraj possesses what Nandi describes as the quintessential quality of the Hindu, "the passive, 'feminine' cunning of the weak and victimized, surviving other pressures by refusing to overplay his sense of autonomy and self respect *and who* in his non-heroic ordinariness … is the archetypal survivor."[54]

On the other hand the oppressor Vasu possesses what Nandy calls the "'Dionysian aspect of the modern west. The demonic self or "asura prakriti".[55]

Vasu's demonic creed, like the attitude of the colonizing British seems to be well described in the following 'slokas' (verses) from the Gita:

> *I wanted his, and today I got it. I want that: I*
> *shall get it tomorrow. All these riches are now*
> *mine: soon I shall have more. I have killed this*
> *enemy. I will kill all the rest. I am ruler of men.*
> *I enjoy the things of this world. I am successful,*
> *strong and happy. I am so wealthy and so nobly*
> *born. Who is my equal?* [56]

The bullying Vasu pretends to be a man of scientific outlook. He hates sentimentalism:

> *Shall I tell you what the matter with you is? You are sentimental: I feel sickened when I see a man talking sentimentally like an old widow. I admire people with a scientific outlook.*[57]

He also claims himself to be a 'broad-minded' person:

> *You allow your mind to be carried away by your own phrases. There's nothing terrible in shooting ... he used to tell me the way to be broad – minded is to begin to like a thing you don't like. It makes for a very scientific outlook.*[58]

Like Ruth P. Jhabvala's characters in *Heat and Dust*, he mocks at certain Indian idiosyncrasies especially those associated with long-cherished beliefs and rituals:

> *If you are a real philosopher and believe in reincarnation, you should not really mind what happens. If one is destroyed now, one will be reborn within a moment, with a brand – new body. Anyway, do you know why we have so many melas in our country? So that the population may be kept within manageable limits. Have you not observed it? At Kumbh Mela, thousands and thousands gather, less than the original number go back have —cholera, or small pox, or they just get trampled. How many temple chariots have run over the onlookers at every festival gathering?*[59]

Besides this demonic figure Vasu has got powerful connections also. Evil forces corrupt others easily as in the British Raj many of our valiant fighters and 'rajas' were corrupt and were involved in resoluting their family feuds. Vasu is conscious of his influences and connections:

> *Inspector ... I will complain against you for trespass and... I'll wire to the Inspector – general and the Home Minister. You think you can fool me as you fool all those wretched bullock- cart drivers and cobblers and ragamuffins whom you order about. Whom do you think you are talking to?*[60]

When Nataraj comes to know about Vasu's intention to kill Kumar, the temple elephant, he does everything he could to prevent the catastrophe so much so that he stretched his 'capacity for patience to the utmost in the cause of "God and Country"[61] until he could cope no more. Amidst the suffocating crowd at the temple feast he gets into a daze and lets out a terrific cry which drowned the noise of children, music, everything:

> *Oh! Vishnu!... Save our elephant, and save all the innocent men and women who are going to pull the chariot. You must come to rescue now.' Unknown to myself, I had let out such a shout that the entire crowd inside and outside the hall stood stunned, and all activity stopped.*[62]

The intense invocation of God does not go unheeded, for the "asura prakriti" (demonic nature) of Vasu is destroyed in the classical Hindu fashion, through the agency of 'maya'. 'Maya' as the female principle and a temple dancer, after Narayan's last novel *The Guide*, makes an appearance here again in *The Man – Eater of Malgudi*. For it is Rangi, the temple dancer and town prostitute, who is instrumental in the destruction of Vasu. Rangi here corresponds with Mohini of the original legend, who was the cause of the demon's death. Having broken his cot in demonstrating his strength, Vasu has to do without his mosquito net and sleep in the chair. But his abhorrence of mosquitoes compels him to depend on Rangi to keep them off him, but while fanning the sleeping Vasu Rangi herself dozes off. As a direct consequence of Rangi's negligence, Vasu Kills himself while trying to slap away the mosquito that lands on his head. Sastri, Nataraj's assistant, sums it all up at the end:

> *Every demon appears in the world with a special boon of indestructibility, yet the universe has survived all the rakshashas that were ever born. Every demon carries within him, unknown to himself, a tiny seed to self-destruction, and goes up in thin air at the most unexpected moment. Otherwise what is to humanity?* [63]

Throughout the novel, we can easily see that Nataraj is always discomfited and cowed down by Vasu's domineering presence and desperately tongue-tied in response to Vasu's banter. But all through the novel he is depicted as having a certain amount of resilience and self-possession that is never shattered except at one point of time. When Nataraj saw Rangi at first, his imagination set him on fire and he finds himself battling and balancing on a precarious balance of the Western flesh versus the Eastern spirit:

> *My blood tingled with an unholy thrill. I let my mind slide into a wild fantasy of seduction and passion. I was no longer a married man with a child and home. I was an adolescent lost in dreams over a nude photograph. I knew that I was completely sealed against any seductive invitation she might hold out for me, but, but I hoped I would not weaken....When I tiptoed back to my place beside the grille, there she was, ready as it seemed to swallow me up wholesale, to dissolve within the embrace of her mighty arms all the monogamous chastity I had practiced a whole life time ... I found her irresistible.*[64]

At the end, his world seems to be shattered. His friends thinking him a murderer shun him and a number of visitors at his press dwindle. As he says towards the end:

> *This was the greatest act of destruction that Man – eater had performed; he had destroyed my name, my friendships, and my world. The thought was too much for me – hugging the tiger cub, I burst into tears.*[65]

However, Sastri returns to the press, signals a positive note in the novel's conclusion, sparkling the hope that others would return too. The demon destroys itself and Malgudi having passed through a difficult time, now settles down to its routine.

The description he gives of a traditional village community somewhat isolated from the main stream of modern life by the sixty miles that separate it from the nearest railway station, the three miles that separate it from electricity, and the criss – cross streets that separate it less than hundred houses from each other, is quite apt. This suggests that "the West has made deep inroads into the common man's life in Malgudi in respect of not only the geographical aspects of the town but also of the steady erosion of the traditional way of life and rise of the new values necessarily accompanying the contemporary cultural upheaval."[66]

This 'rise of new values necessarily accompanying the contemporary cultural upheaval', is quite apparent when Malgudi becomes a chronotope, in which "national time becomes concrete and visible."[67] His Malgudi evokes "national peculiarities" like Nataraj's daily visit to the river for a bath early in the morning at exactly the same time, the opening and closing time of the press, the over-loaded transport buses

> *...an old dump, rigged up with canvas and painted yellow and red. It was impossible to guess how many were seated in the bus until it stopped at stop and the passengers wriggled and jumped out as if for an invasion...outnumbering the flies...* [68]

Or, the matter of possessing a car in 1960s or 70s India was a thing attached with the social status (perhaps, nowhere else such mentality has ever survived); we can see how the bus conductor had then "developed a wholesome respect for

(Nataraj) as member of the automobile fraternity…prepared to overlook …unbuttoned shirt and disheveled appearance and ticketless condition."[69]

R.K. Narayan has very subtly indicated the prevailing 'inequality before the law' – a sort of Indian culture much against the impartial Western society who can even impeach their President, and even in the modern "shining" India of the twenty first century, BMW owners are too powerful to disown any law. Here, they travel with or without a ticket- who cares.

R.K. Narayan also does not forget to bring out the inner desire of the majority of Indian bachelors who always surf for 'a dutiful wife' on different matrimonial portals as those of one like Mahout's wife discussed in the novel. This special drive for 'a dutiful wife' happens only in India as the Western world has already falsified the family institution. Had it not been the case, Oscar Wilde would never have played the pun 'Divorces are made in heaven' in his *Importance of Being Earnest*. Vasu, here, is a pseudo- representative of such 'live-in'-societies of the west who believes that "only fools marry and they deserve all the trouble they get… if you like a woman, have her by all means. You don't have to own a coffee estate because you like a cup of coffee now and then."[70]

A. Hariprasana has rightly stated:

> *His equating woman with coffee and drink is not a mere instance of his self- congratulating 'wit'. He proves as good as his word and has no inhibitions in this regard. Nataraj is "taken aback at the number and variety of women that he brings to his room for this pleasure.*[71]

No doubt, Nataraj, after observing his licentious life style, is bound to utter:

> *I was mistaken in thinking that Rangi was the only woman. I had only to stand there between seven and eight in the morning, and it became a sort of game to speculate who would be descending the stairs next. Sometimes a slim girl went by, sometimes a fair one, sometimes an in between type, sometimes a fuzzy-haired woman, some mornings a fashionable one who had taken the trouble to tidy herself up before coming out.*[72]

Further, we find R. K. Narayan anticipating those many NRIs who serve in multinational companies possessing a green card citizenship but fly over to India at least once as a Siberian bird to 'have a wonderful woman…. (who) won't eat her food unless' her husband is 'back home, even if it is midnight'.[73] And, many of the Indian husbands, like Nataraj in the novel, are still fond to be tied up with a 'mom'-like figure who really feel 'weak… might eat all the burns in the world, but without a handful of rice and the sauce… wife made… could never feel convinced that (they) had taken any nourishment.'[74] But in return, they do not forget to maintain the sublime character of maintaining chastity which the west has dropped long back in the Mediterranean Sea. In India, the Indian wives observe rituals like 'karwa chauth' but their 'eternal' partners are also supposed to be loyal to their 'unselfish' wives. When Nataraj, a personification of the typical Indian husband, lets his "mind slide into a wild fantasy of seduction and passion"[75] when he was struck by the bewitching beauty of Rangi he himself confesses to have gone off the roots.

The Indian readers pray to save him from his possible tragic fall. When Nataraj is observed controlling his unreined passion, the long cherished Indian culture and expectations from the successors of Lord Rama was saved.

Indian modesty and humbleness, another typical Indian peculiarity, has been further reflected in the initial chapters. In India, not only Khushwant Singh's grandmother (refer to his essay *The Portrait of a Lady*), has inherited and promoted the long cherished culture of feeding ants and stray dogs but our Nataraj also does the same. But at the same time, there is a ten percent 'posh' India who is often heard to lambast her own countrymen, that too, ruthlessly:

> *More people will have to die on the road, if our nation is to develop any road sense at all.*[76]

And, they believe that the weaker majority of India is 'spineless'.[77]

Vasu is not an Oxford graduate but he is triple M.A. and he tries to get into the Westerners' shoes. Here goes R.K. Narayan's excellence as an exquisite craftsman. He has made a contrast of black and white – Vasu and Nataraj. While Nataraj has been taught 'never to kill' and to 'feed (ing) sugar to ants', Vasu's ruthlessness and indiscriminate slaughtering of animals and birds, set him apart as utterly anti-social and anti-cultural. As A. Hariprasana points out:

> *Vasu's isolation and alienation is also underlined by his occasional use of the American style of speech.* [78]

It is this ambivalent attitude and his honesty in putting down that Narayan reveals his characteristic genius. India is a wonderful country with a civilization stretching across several millennia. The joint family has survived for centuries; even "the title chosen for the novel indicates among other things... the implications of the family theme, perhaps these two characters could be taken as representing two opposed attitudes to the family, Nataraj the traditional and Vasu its radical opposite."[79]

Nataraj is shaped and stamped by his family and ancestry, and is steeped in the life of Malgudi unlike Vasu who is rootless. The impressionable years Nataraj has spent in the joint family have actually shaped his outlook. His tendency to be accommodative seems to have been the result of living in a joint family. Basically he is gentle, normal, a devoted husband and father. He has willingly practised monogamous chastity all his life. The attraction he feels for the temple dancer and prostitute, Rangi, later in the story, is only a momentary distraction caused by tension and overwork in press.

For an analysis of the family theme in this novel a study of Vasu's character is of particular importance because he is not just a misfit in the family like Raju and Rosie of *The Guide* and Daisy of *The Painter of Signs* but he is the very negation of it; he is everything that Nataraj is not. Nataraj is deeply rooted, Vasu is an uprooted. Nataraj adheres to the Eastern values; Vasu goes for the Western 'scientific outlook'. For Nataraj, marriage is divine, for Vasu "drink is like marriage. If people like it, it's their business and nobody else's."[80]

Today, the Westerners are known for grooming their 'in vitro–babies' at different Child Care centers. Likewise

Vasu seems to possess no sincere concern for children and would often scare them away. When Nataraj's son Babu used to come to the Press, he virtually orders him "now, go away, boy".[81]

Vasu also represents many of those Westernized Indians who study literature just for the social status or fashion but they 'never read poetry' as they have 'no time' for it.[82] We can also doubt on his Indianness during the ritualistic celebration of the wedding of the divine pair of Radha and Krishna, which is the temple festival in which the entire Malgudi community participates, Vasu alone is a solitary exception. "No family, no society-which cherished these ideals can afford to accommodate such a man as Vasu, nor can he with his bloated ego, with no ties of any kind, with no sense of responsibility or obligation to anyone ever remain within the confines."[83]

In fact, religion lays its heavy hand on the social life of Malgudi. If we take the case of Kumar, it is not just an ordinary elephant, but a temple elephant. It might be especially mentioned that elephants are so much a part and parcel of the temple scene in South India that they are considered equal to the divine. In the year 1982, the death of the Guruvayoor temple elephant Keshavan virtually occasioned a State-wide mourning in Kerala[84]. The Trichur temple of Vadakkunathan is well – known for its Pooram Festival in April - May when two processions of 15 elephants, each starting from different points, meet near the temple gates to the accompaniment of night-long fireworks. It is this deep religious sanctity attached to the temple elephant that causes Nataraj's anxiety and concern for the life of Kumar.

O.P. Saxena writes:

> *Only those who have emotions know what it is to suffer. Vasu has no emotion, no sense of crime on his conscience.*[85]

He has no cultural consciousness, too. Kumar's survival is the survival of religion in Malgudi and Vasu is all ignorant of this fact. For this westernized man of 'scientific outlook'

> *...there's nothing terrible in shooting. You pull your trigger and out goes the bullet, and at the other end there is an object waiting to receive it. It is just give and take.*[86]

And, it is no wonder to find out his idiotic point of view which goes like this:

> *Science conquers nature in a new way every day; why not in creation also? That's my philosophy.*[87]

The above statement of Vasu has the resonance of the new Western group of Social scientists who claim themselves to be the *possibilists*.

The novel here mimics and subverts the narrative of colonial discourse that characterized the native as unheroic, comic and effeminate, full of guile and unfaithful till the last – which is the Kiplingesque picture of the dichotomous, feminine East and the masculine West – and a harping of the slogan of "never the Twain shall meet". What Narayan's fiction attempts to do is to show resistance not on the level of power but on the cultural and psychological front.

> *Nataraj is endowed with submissive qualities*
> *usually discomfited and cowed down by Vasu's*
> *domineering presence and desperately tongue-*
> *tied in response to Vasu's banter.*[88]

Syed Muzzubuddin further quotes Simon who writes:

> *Malgudi becomes for Walsh not only 'a Metaphor*
> *of India. Whatever happens in the one happens*
> *in the other' but also a metaphor for 'everywhere',*
> *for the reader, as he says, 'begins to believe,*
> *whatever happens there happens everywhere.*[89]

The material of Narayan's novels broadens out from the family to the community and the nation and one notices that modernity is slowly but surely seeping deeper and deeper into it. The East- West theme is thus unavoidable. But in R. K. Narayan, as O.P. Mathur believes:

> *This theme has not been presented in terms of*
> *a vast social, economic or political conflict, nor*
> *in terms of a philosophical confrontation: its*
> *dimensions are ethical, so deep and unobtrusive*
> *that one might easily miss it altogether. Narayan*
> *gives us the feel of life itself which is neither all*
> *white nor all black but the grey, twilight world of*
> *allotropy - a life quivering hesitatingly between*
> *tradition and modernity, East and West,*
> *inextricably individuals.*[90]

It is a cliché that the changes that have come over our world in the last half century are far beyond anything that took place in all the millions of years before. Weapons have been invented which can destroy mankind in a few seconds and men have landed on the moon. Changes in Indian social life in the same period have not been less sensational. "Age -old rites have been put aside, undoubtedly never to return. Narayan's novels preserve for an anthropologist or social historian many features of a world fast receding."[91]

References:

1. O.P. Mathur. *The West Wind Blows through Malgudi. Perspectives on R.K. Narayan.* ed. Atma Ram. Ghaziabad: Vimal Prakashan, 1981. pp.35- 36.

2. An interview with R.K. Narayan by Sunil Saxena. *Probe.* Sept. 1987, p.37.

3. William Walsh. *Sweet Mangoes and Melt Vinegar: The Novels of R.K. Narayan. Indo-English Literature: A Collection of Critical Essays.* Ed., K.K. Sharma. Ghaziabad: Vimal Prakashan, 1977. p. 123.

4. Ashish Nandy. *At the Edge of the Psychology.* Delhi: Oxford University Press, 1980.p.58.

5. William Walsh. *A Manifold Voice.* London: Chattor Windus, 1964. p.22.

6. D.S. Philip. *Perceiving India through the works of Nirad C. Chaudhuri, R.K. Narayan and Ved Mehta.* New Delhi: Sterling Publications, 1986. p.97.

7. Quoted from M.M. Mahood. *The Colonial Encounter.* New Jersey: Rowman and Little Field, 1973. p. 94.

8. Ramesh Srivastava. *What is So Great in R.K. Narayan. Perspectives on R.K. Narayan,* op. cit., p. 201.

9. As quoted in O.P. Mathur's *The West Wind Blows Through Malgudi,* op. cit., p.36.

10. *ibid.,* pp.35-36.

11. E.M. Verma. *Some Aspects of Indo-English Fiction.* Delhi: SAL, 1984. p.135.

12. Professor C.D. Narasimhaiah. *The Swan and The Eagle.* Simla: 1969, p.58.

13. R.K. Narayan. *Next Sunday.* N. Delhi: Orient Paperbacks, 1965. p. 8.

14. O.P. Mathur. *The Modern Indian English Fiction.* N. Delhi: Abhinav Publications, 1993. pp. 78- 79.

15. H.M. Williams. *Indo Anglian Literature, 1800 – 1970.*N. Delhi: Orient Longman, 1976. p.50.

16. R.K. Narayan. *The Man-Eater of Malgudi*. Madras: Indian Thought Publication, 1968. 17th Reprint 2003. pp. 75-76.

17. *ibid., p.* 76.

18. Richard Cronin. *Imagining India*. N. Delhi: Macmillan Press, 1983. p.73.

19. R.K. Narayan. *The Man-Eater of Malgudi*. op. cit., p.7

20. *ibid.,* p. 7

21. *ibid.,* p. 7

22. *ibid.,* p. 8

23. Syed Mujeebuddin. *R.K. Narayan's The Man-Eater of Malgudi: Problematising the Nation. Indian Fiction On English,* Eds., P. Mallikarjuna Rao, M. Rajeshwar. N. Delhi: Atlantic Publishers and Distributers, 1992. p. 77.

24. R.K. Narayan. *The Man-Eater of Malgudi,* op.cit., p. 7.

25. Syed Mujeebuddin. *R.K. Narayan's The Man-Eater of Malgudi: Problematising the Nation, Indian Fiction In English.* op.cit., p. 77.

26. R.K. Narayan. *The Man-Eater of Malgudi.* op. cit., p. 16.

27. *ibid.,* p. 7.

28. *ibid.,* p. 8.

29. *ibid.,* pp.11-12.

30. *ibid.,* p. 12.

31. John Thieme. *R.K. Narayan.* Manchester: Manchester University Press, 2007.pp.114– 115.

32. R.K. Narayan. *The Man-Eater of Malgudi.* op. cit., p.19.

33. *ibid.,* p. 19.

34. *ibid.,* p. 19.

35. *ibid.,* p. 54.

36. *ibid.,* p. 58.

37. *ibid.,* p. 31.

38. John Thieme. *R.K. Narayan.* op.cit. p.115.

39. *ibid.,* p. 7.

40. *ibid.,* p. 7.

41. *ibid.,* p. 53.

42. *ibid.,* p. 53.

43. *ibid.*, p. 52.

44. *ibid.*, p. 53.

45. *ibid.*, p. 54.

46. M.K. Naik. *Twentieth Century Indian English Fiction.* Delhi: Pencraft International, 2004. p. 53.

47. R.K. Narayan. *The Man-Eater of Malgudi*, op. cit., p. 17.

48. M.K. Naik, *Twentieth Century Indian English Fiction.* op. cit., p.54.

49. R.K. Narayan, *The Man-Eater of Malgudi*, op.cit., p. 73.

50. *ibid.*, p. 75.

51. *ibid.*, p. 75.

52. *ibid.*, p. 49.

53. Syed Mujeebudin. *R.K. Narayan's The Man-Eater of Malgudi: Problematising the Nation.* op. cit., p.79.

54. Ashish Nandy. *The Intimate Enemy: Loss and Recovery of Self under Colonialism.* N. Delhi: Oxford University Press, 1983. p.111.

55. *ibid.*, p.78.

56. *ibid.*, p. 78.

57. R.K. Narayan. *The Man-Eater of Malgudi.* op.cit., p.134.

58. *ibid.*, p. 134.

59. *ibid.*, p. 149.

60. *ibid.*, p. 150.

61. *ibid.*, p.131.

62. *ibid.*, p. 139.

63. *ibid.*, pp.182 -83.

64. *ibid.*, p.121.

65. *ibid.*, p. 180

66. O.P. Mathur. *"The West Blows Through Malgudi". Perspectives on R. K. Narayan.* ed. Atma Ram. Ghaziabad: Vimal Prakashan, 1981. p.27.

67. Homi Bhabha.ed., *"Disseni Nation: Time, Narrative and The Margins of Modern Nation". Nation and Narration.* London: Routledge, 1990. p.310.

68. R. K. Narayan. *The Man-Eater of Malgudi.* p.41.

69.　*ibid.*, p.42.

70.　*ibid.*, p.34.

71.　A. Hariprasana. *The World of Malgudi: A Study of R.K. Narayan's Novels.* N. Delhi: Prestige, 1994. p.79.

72.　R.K. Narayan. *The Man-Eater of Malgudi.* op.cit., pp.108-109

73.　*ibid.*, p.99.

74.　*ibid.*, pp.40-41.

75.　*ibid.*, p.158.

76.　*ibid.*, p.33.

77.　*ibid.*, p.33.

78.　A. Hariprasana. *The World of Malgudi: A Study of R.K. Narayan's Novels.* op. cit, p.78.

79.　*ibid.*, p.76.

80.　R.K. Narayan. *The Man- Eater of Malgudi.*p.34

81.　*ibid.*, p.20

82.　*ibid.*, p.24

83.　A. Hariprasana. *The World of Malgudi: A Study of R. K. Narayan's Novels.* op. cit., p.80

84.　In reference to the news published in *The Hindustan Times,* Nov.20, 1982

85.　O.P. Saxena. *Glimpse of Indo-English Fiction.* N. Delhi: Jainsons Publications, 1985. p.288

86.　R. K. Narayan. *The Man-Eater of Malgudi.* op. cit., p.176.

87.　*ibid.*, p.15.

88.　Syed Muzzubuddin. *"R.K. Narayan's The Man-Eater of Malgudi: Problematising the Nation in Indian Fiction in English".* op.cit., pp. 80-81.

89.　*ibid.*, p.74.

90.　O.P. Mathur. *The Modern Indian English Fiction.* N. Delhi: Abhinav Publications, 1993. p.87. *italics* are mine.

91.　O. P. Saxena. *The World of R. K. Narayan.* op. cit., p.335.

CHAPTER - IV

THE FOREIGNER

The 27ᵗʰ January, 2010 edition of the *Hindustan Times* had this opinion of Rajesh Ahuja:

> *Thirteen top musicians and eighteen prolific singers feel a tad short in rewriting history. 'Mile Sur Mera Tumhara', the anthem that entered millions of households – and hearts – through Doordarshan in 1988, has now been given a contemporary twist. Only that 'Phir Mile Sur', the new version that was first aired on TV on January 26, is disappointingly inclined towards Bollywood, feel members of music fraternity.*

> *Singer Javed Ali of 'Delhi 6' and 'Jodha Akbar' fame says the song lacks "Indianness". He further adds that, "in the process of modernising it, the makers have killed its soul.*

Surrender Oberoi, or Sindi Oberoi or Sindi, the protagonist of Arun Joshi's *The Foreigner* also resembles that modernized remix number 'Phir Mile Sur', who despite being influenced by Indian philosophy inscribed in *The Gita* and the *Upanishads*, does not possess a typical Indian soul, throughout the novel, save the last few pages (where he seems to be parroting the Indian philosophies only to realize its real meaning at the very end).

Sindi knows about the 'detachment' but not about the 'non-attachment' the guiding principle of the Holy Gita. Sindi errs in taking 'non-attachment' for 'detachment'.

Arun Joshi is primarily a novelist writing in a contemporary context. His novels are structured in the native socio - cultural situations. His novels are concerned with the moral and spiritual problems of the Post-Independent Indian with the exposure of the foreign education system. His heroes more usually suffer from spiritual vacuum, up rootedness, evils of Materialism, identity crisis and loss of faith in social values. They grow out of alienation and a sense of non-belonging. They are the youths, intellectuals and artists. They are members of the alienated group of the Indian Society. His Sindi Oberoi, Billy Biswas, Ratan Rathore and Sow Bhaskar face the predicament, torture and agony. They are the contemporary urban elite journeying through the confusion of the present time. While penning down this chapter I recall Jack an NRI participant of ZEE TV Reality Dance Show 'Dance India Dance 2'. During one of his vote appeals his pressure of being a 'foreigner' and the 'sense of insecurity' could easily be discerned in his voice:

> *Sir, please vote for me and accept me as an Indian. There in Norway, people call me an outsider; here in India, you people consider me as an Outsider, but this is my earnest plea that please consider me as one of you.*

Though Sindi's cry in *The Foreigner* is not that audible the resonance of the above plea may be felt clearly here:

> *And what country had I represented? Kenya or England or India?*[1]

As a study in cross- cultural dilemma, *The Foreigner* has been compared to *The Bostonians, The Americans* and *The Ambassadors*. The working of the personal and the human problem against the background of the cultures follows the same delicate pattern as of Henry James. According to the *Journal of Indian Writing in English:*

> *It is not only novel with a fine artistic vision. (but) marks a definite improvement over all other novels in English on the East-West muddle.*[2]

The Foreigner is, in the main, the study of "an uprooted young man" living in the latter half of the twentieth century, who looks out frequently for randomly drifting life. Sindi, a Kenya born Indian of mixed parentage, feels uprooted and lost like "a foreigner anywhere" and endeavours all along not to get involved with anybody or anything (as he wants to live without desire and attachment) until he at last gets to know what detachment actually means.

Sindi, the protagonist, himself muses over his "foreignness" and up-rootedness:

> *I wondered in what way, if any, did I belong to the world that roared beneath my apartment window. Somebody had begotten me without a purpose. Perhaps I felt like that because I was a*

foreigner in America. But then, what difference
would it have made if I had lived in Kenya
or India or any other place for that matter? It
seemed to me that I would still be a foreigner. My
foreignness lay within me and I couldn't leave
myself behind wherever I went.[3]

Sindi bears no trait to be called an Indian. Sindi who
had his early education in England goes to America for
his doctoral degree in mechanical engineering. There he
meets Babu and their friendship begins. He also comes in
contact with June with whom he begins to live intimately
and continues his passionate affair with her for quite a
long time. Unlike an Indian, earlier in England, he had
"amorous relationships with Anna and Kathy as well. But
all his relationships fizzled out like an ill packed crackers"
because he "couldn't pay the price of being loved."[4]

Sindi is indeed a perfect foreigner not only to the two
cultures between which he shuttles. He was an orphan
both in terms of relations and his emotional roots. He was
brought up by his uncle settled in Kenya, after the death of
his parents in a plane crash near Cairo. In a way he was as
near to these cultures as he was far from them for his mother
was a British and his father an Indian. O.P. Bhatnagar very
aptly remarks:

It is this mixed belonging which gives him the
perspective of looking at the situation on the
human rather on the Jamesian cultural plane.
He is better placed and poised than any of the
heroes of Indo-English or Anglo-Indian novels
in his analysis of the situation.[5]

His casuality in relationships is definitely an alien feature. Far off from the Indian roots his causality has forced him to deny the reality and permanence of things and life. Unlike a typical Indian, he claims:

> *I don't want to get involved. Everywhere I turned*
> *I saw involvement.* [6]

To glorify his fear he preferred to call it by the much-flaunted Indian virtue of "detachment". All the same he revelled and indulged in sumptuous sex in England and America with Anna, Kathy, Judy, Christine and June. Much in the 'human live-in relationship'- style, he established a sort of 'detached' relationship with them having no sincere bond of commitment. Like many foreigners, especially Westerners, he also does not believe in marriage. For him

> *…marriage was more often a lust for possession*
> *than anything else. People got married just as*
> *they bought new cars. And then they gobbled*
> *each other up.*[7]

Sindi appears to be a bundle of paradoxes before us. This confusion and conflict in him is nothing but a by-product of his being a foreigner. He does not want to marry, yet he only wishes to possess, and that to, a married woman. About his relationship with Cathy he reveals it in one of the conversation:

> *"Did you love her (Kathy)?"*
> *"No, I had only wanted to possess her,*
> ……………………………………

Did she leave you?
"She had to leave me, she was married."[8]

All this was a clever cover for Sindi to shy away from involvement, commitment and action. Against the background of his pompous philosophy of detachment and the pose of "living without desires" he makes love to a series of women (Anna, Kathy, Judy, Christine and June) but with June he is exposed with his hypocrisy, cowardice, vanity and stupidity. June loved Sindi not to leave him alone. She was free, frank, uninhibited, generous and humane. "She knew what soothed, solaced and pleased Sindi. She therefore gave of herself abundantly to him. But when he refuses to marry her she turns to his friend Babu, who characterizes the typical Indian fantasies about the much glamourized dreamland of America."[9]

Sindi and Babu both are like two sides of a coin. Sindi is a foreigner-Indian. Babu is an Indian-foreigner. Sindi is an anglicized version of an Indian who is all brain, Babu is an Indianised version of a foreigner who is all blood. Sindi is fed up of his American world as according to him:

> *America is a place for well-fed automatons*
> *rushing about in automatic cars. I'd go mad if*
> *I had to do that.*[10]

Babu couldn't see why Sindi was 'so against America'. Sindi comes up with an honest advice to Babu:

> *"Listen, Babu", I said, "don't do anything in*
> *hurry. Women are desirable creatures but they*
> *can also hurt you. We all make use of each other*

> *even though we don't want to. In your part of*
> *the world you marry only once in a lifetime".*[11]

Babu takes America to be "a wonderful country." He would rather never 'go back to India' if he had the choice. He sees America as a paradise of free-sexers and argues with Sindi,

> *What is the good of coming to America if not to*
> *play around with girls?* [12]

Exhibiting the image of an indefatigable half-baked Casanova abroad, he wants 'to make more American friends" and not "to mix with Indians all the time". He also begins to find that Indians are so underdeveloped as compared to them. He utters:

> *Sometimes I wish I had been born in America.*
> *Not that I have been anything against India but*
> *there is nothing to beat America.*[13]

Actually, Babu's apparent love for America or say, Western outlook is very much Indian as one tenth of the Indian population who belongs to the upper class family, loves to go abroad, at least for higher studies. This is the upper class Indian psychology to mock at their own underprivileged countrymen and brood over anything English. For them, 'progressive' means, anything western-oriented.

On two different occasions we can see what actually the term "progressive" stands for, especially in the psyche of the 'anglicized' Babu whose 'id' is basically Indian but his 'superego' goes for the 'western' outlook. That is why he results in a spilt personality. At one instance, when June mocked at his father for being terrible, Babu replied sullenly:

> *He is not terrible… He is just orthodox. My sister is very modern. She has very progressive views on these things.*[14]

At another instance, when June asked him if they ate doughnuts in India he replied:

> *"Only upper class Indians do."*
> *"Why? Are they very expensive?"*
> *No. They are not expensive.*
> *But the lower class people are just not progressive.*[15]

But Babu's "progressive" – foreigners is only a borrowed term. He himself has no choice. As a typical Indian 'obedient' son, he is not prepared to go on and drape himself in a Western outfit. It is quite visible when he says vehemently:

> *I think it (America) is a wonderful county. I would never go back to India if I had the choice."*
>
> *"Why don't you have a choice?" June said. "My father would never agree to it," he said mournfully, "I'm an only son, you see", he added with a touch of pride and regret.*[16]

Babu is such a character in the novel whose feet is all grounded in the Indian soil but he wishes to pluck western flowers, and that too to retain it forever. It was only a Westernized but sensible Sindi who could sense

Babu's 'Indianness' even in his body language which was all pervasive:

> *We (Babu, June and Sindi himself) finished our coffee and doughnuts and then went for a drive in June's car because Babu had said he wanted to see the snow. June wanted me to drive. Babu insisted on sitting in the back seat. When we finally coaxed him to sit in the front he clung self-consciously to the door so he would not touch June.*[17]

From the above scene, we could easily figure out two things, first, Babu is consciously trying to wear a western outfit though he is not comfortable with it, and second at the sub-conscious level he is an Indian while Sindi is sub-consciously a Westerner while he is consciously an Indian.

Mohan Jha aptly observes that Babu has innocence and simplicity but not the seriousness and toughness of experience as one thinks of his childhood's moralistic training. Ever since his childhood, he has been fed on the hygienic diet of morals but he does not "apply himself to his pursuit with the seriousness that is expected of him".[18]

Babu was sent to America for his higher studies. Sindi, the analyst, feels it was not so much for Babu as for his father's needs and social prestige because in an Indian family a son is considered to be a proud possession. Sindi tells Sheila:

> *He (Sheila's father) sent Babu to America so he would come back and add that much more weight to your family's social status – He could*

talk to friends at the club about his foreign-returned son.[19]

But in America Babu is a misfit in the absence of his father and sister. There are plenty of Babus who find themselves unable to cope with this sudden change in the cultural ethos. And, this is what echoes in one of the scenes:

> *Is it true, professor, "said a woman somewhere behind me," that many Indian students in America feel very lost?" she hesitated for a moment. Some of them even commit suicide?*[20]

C. Malathi Rao admits:

> *Babu with his dependence on his father, his craving for his friends, his ignorance of American patterns is a square peg in a round hole.*[21]

In contrast to Babu, Sindi is purely a global man. He knows the tension and pressure and unbelongingness of a global man; he is a cosmopolitan; he has no roots; he bears no flag. He lives in a world which is well-depicted in his own words:

> *As I moved, the language changed until each layer seemed to have its own tongue. It was like switching a radio from one alien wavelength to another. Here and there, I picked up a word in French or a phrase in Spanish but they didn't convey much, I had ceased being curious about other people's conversation.*[22]

The dance floor where he faced such a situation is actually symbolic of his cosmopolitan world where the horizons of the globe meet and people lose their identity so easily. His monologues sound louder:

> *So what about the world? I was born an Indian*
> *and had been spat upon; had I been a European,*
> *I would have done the spitting. What difference*
> *did it make? I would still die and be forgotten*
> *by the world.*[23]

Sindi is, in fact, an explicit example of a cultural allotrope. Sindi's parentage and early life made him the ideal "foreigner", the man who did not belong anywhere. He was born in Kenya, of an Indian father and an English mother. Both of them died in an air crash near Cairo long ago so that he had no recollection of them and it was as if they never existed for him. He was brought up by his uncle in Kenya who also died later. He had his early education in Kenya and later in England and finally in America. Thus he was not an African because neither of his parents belonged to Africa. He was not an Englishman because his father was Indian. To America he was not in anyway attached:

> *It is much sterilized for me. Much too clean and*
> *optimistic and empty.*[24]

And he had not seen India till he was 26. Even his coming to India was not by deliberate choice. It was decided by the flip of a coin. Thus he was one who did not have roots anywhere in the world.

*I wondered in what way, if any, did I belong
to the world that roared beneath my apartment
window. Somebody had begotten me without
a purpose and so far I had lived without a
purpose... Perhaps I felt like that because I was a
foreigner in America. But then, what difference
would it have made if I had lived in Kenya
or India or any other place for that matter! It
seemed to me that I would still be a foreigner. My
foreignness lay within me and I couldn't leave
myself behind wherever I went.*[25]

He felt he was a misfit who did not belong to any place
and his words and behaviour created the same impression in
all those with whom he came in contact. Very early in her
acquaintance with Sindi, June remarked: "I have a feeling
you'd be foreigner anywhere".[26] And, Mr. Khemka told
him sometime after he came to India: "... you don't belong
here."[27]

Sindi, the cynical, alienated young man, belongs to a
prolific genre, both in life and literature. "What way I fly
in Hell; myself am Hell" – this seems to be the cry of the
uprooted angry young men of the modern age. Among
the tragic legacies of the British Raj in India is the class of
Indian intellectuals – anglicized greatly in their outlook
and way of life and, at the same time, without their roots
fully cut off from the soil of their motherland. They are
a completely alienated lot. Sasthi Brata is one such "herd
abandoned dear". In his "bold and irrelevant" autobiography
My God Died Young; he has uninhibitedly laid bare the
tradition – bound society in India. He is equally critical in
his accounts of the West, especially England and America.

He complains that the British rule in India produced men like himself who can neither feel nor identify themselves with their own people nor accept "the glare, the steel-muscle concept of human life" in the western countries."[28]

Arun Joshi's first novel *The Foreigner* centers on a youngman Sindi Oberoi who, as Meenakshi Mukherjee aptly observes, "is an alien everywhere physically as well as metamorphically."[29]

Amidst all these issues, one thing is clear that this cultural allotrope Sindi is unbiased, without any prejudices. Sindi and even June know better that Americans are not "very congenial towards foreigners." It is here that Arun Joshi explores the cleavage, the prejudices and illusions of the east and the west.

The author reveals through Ms. Blyth how Indian poverty becomes the subject of laughter and derision in America. He also brings forth the snobbish and patronizing attitude of the Americans in their charities they bestow on India. In the cultural stampede Ms. Blyth once remarked:

> *One thing I don't like at all about Hinduism is their nonsense about idols. It just isn't human.*[30]

The author also picturises the Gandhian non-co-operation movement being mocked at in America. Sindi rightly questions Ms. Blyth:

> *And what use have you made of your extra height and extra years? You carry heavier guns and have a longer time to make each other unhappy, that's all. Can you call that achievement?*[31]

Sindi and his readers are astonished to know why June told him to keep her relation with Babu a secret. She, in fact, "didn't like June having affairs, and certainly not with non-white foreigners."[32]

Against this social and cultural milieu lies the personal problem of Sindi, June and Babu. If Babu's hair-line morality is indiscreet, Sindi's detachment is unwise. While Babu is incapable of making resolutions, Sindi does not make them because the pain of breaking them is unbearable. "They wore the two aspects of the same psychology — one foolish, the other unwise. One was under-controlled, the other over-controlled. Both were basically cowards."[33]

Babu's *id* is 'Indian' his superego is 'English'. Sindi's *id* is 'Western'; his superego is 'Indian'. Sindi, therefore, ponders over his detachment and objectivity, not realizing that objectivity is just another form of vanity. Detachment either in the West or in the East is mistaken for inaction, but now he has begun to see the fallacy in it. Detachment consists of right action and not an escape from it. Even in India he sees a kind of fakeness about life, its vanities and its money-grabbing morality saps away all that is human. At one place we hear Sindi telling Mr. Khemka:

> *Your morality was nice for India, it didn't work in America.*[34]

Sindi knows it better that "the codes of morality differ from country to country. Girls do certain things in America that women would never do (in India). ... (but this) doesn't mean that they are wicked".[35]

Not only Sheila but her brother Babu also feels that Sindi is "a perfect example of an Indian who pretended to be a foreigner and behaved as one.'[36] But readers feel that it is Babu who is a perfect example of an Indian who pretended to be a man with Western ways and 'broad-minded' and tried to behave as one but failed miserably. Like most of the Indians, "he talked very politely to a foreigner."

To Mr. Khemka and his daughter Sheila, June is a foreigner who cannot be happily married to Babu as she does not know the language, the customs, the traditions, and the religion of India. Sindi laughs at the Indian brag of tolerance and says,

> *Foreigners don't fit in our homes because we don't want them to fit in.*[37]

Sindi scoffs at the sex-centered morality of India when Sheila accuses June of not being virtuous on the grounds that she is not virgin:

> *So you think one of these Marwari girls is really superior merely because of a silly membrane between her legs?*[38]

Whereas the fact remains that she finds no fault with the tax-evasion morality of Mr. Khemka. Sindi thus finds himself as much a foreigner in India as he has been in America. O.P. Bhatnagar opines:

> *The spatial development of the novel … reaches the depths of human problems of exploring the peculiar predicaments in which they are placed beyond their geographic-historico -socio-cultural existence.*[39]

Usha Pathania shares the opinion with him. She says:

> *The irony of Sindi's predicament is that though*
> *labeled as an Indian, he is an outsider, a stranger,*
> *a foreigner in India too.*[40]

Sindi is a child to none. A stranger to the world of filial relationships, he learns about four families, directly or indirectly. Sindi's first exposure to the filial situation is with Mrs. Blyth's family at Boston. Mrs. Blyth is a divorcee who lives with her only daughter June. June loves Sindi, a student at Boston. Her father's memory is alive and she yearns for a father.

The two American families stand in direct contrast to their two Indian counterparts. Both the foreign families are economically well to do and matriarchal in nature. In Mrs. Blyth's family, the husband has divorced and left. Karl's father is dead. Whereas June, Blyth and her mother and Karl love to meet foreign students and take interest in them. June admits:

> *Yes, By and large, I like meeting people from*
> *different countries, especially people from Asia.*
> *They are so much gentler and deeper than other….*[41]

Sheila, a member of a powerful family of Khemka in India, has her own reservations on this issue:

> *"A foreigner just doesn't fit in our homes."*
> *"Why? Why not?"*
> *"They don't know the language, the customs.*
> *Their religion is different."*[42]

In Karl's family, we come across with bewilderment a big difference between the western and eastern way of life. Karl's narration reveals everything, including the difference in our cultural values:

> *There were a number of things. I was always hungry, for one thing. It was terrible after the war. Then I hated the way my stepmother brought lovers home after my father died. And one day when she got drunk and tried to seduce me, I left.*[43]

That is why the West has almost become fed up with everything. They have become hopeless. Morose. Mental unrest. Karl's desperation is not only his own but he echoes the entire West:

> *Fed up with many things. Fed up with the way we pretend to have forgotten the past and yet all the time we are looking for an opportunity to revive it. Fed up with puerile demonstrations of love. Fed up with my own self-importance.*[44]

In contrast to it, the ethos of an Indian family laden with moral teachings and discipline are reflected in Babu's letter addressed to his sister:

> *I have bad news for you, Didi. For weeks now I have been wondering how to break it to you. I am getting married. I have gone through weeks of turmoil before reaching this decision. At last I have found enough courage to marry the girl*

*I love. And yet sometimes at night I wake up
with Father's raving image before me and all my
strength drains out of me.*[45]

Now among Indian families which have been presented
through Mr. Khemka and Muthu; once again a contrast
has been drawn. Mr. Khemka's richness symbolizes the
"westerly Indians" and Muthu's poverty stands for 'easterly
Indians". Mr. Khemka's family is rich and educated. Muthu
is poor and lowly.

Sindi as a Westerner, finds himself baffled on his own
discovery of India. Sindi notices the kind of life the affluent
in India are leading:

*The house was old and single storeyed with a
magnificent lawn that contrasted beautifully
with the red gravel of the drive. I looked at …
the richness of Mr. Khemka's drawing room …
Plush carpets, low streamlined divans, invisible
lighting, bell buttons in every corner, and
sculpture.*[46]

Sindi realizes that Babu was brought up amid all these
material luxuries. Later when he has lunch with Khemka,
he finds the lunch room "furnished as luxuriously and
tastefully as the drawing room."[47]

Contrasted with this is Sindi's visit to Muthu's family
towards the end of the novel which makes him aware of
the poverty amidst which these people live. On the one
hand are the Khemkas who have "three houses in Delhi
and a villa in Mussoorie" on the other is Muthu, a low
paid employee in Khemka's office, who lives in a one-room

tenement with a dozen other people. This makes clear the population explosion and overcrowding in India amidst poverty and hunger and disease. The appalling condition of Muthu's large family makes Sindi aware of "accumulated despair of their weary lives".

On the one hand, there are the guests of Mr. Khemka:

> *Old men grown fat with success, came with their plump wives. They drank and then they had gorgeous dinners. They talked of money and how to make more of it. They left the impression that they could buy up anybody they wanted.*[48]

On the other, we readers along with the protagonist Sindi, are shocked to our very core when Muthu narrates the tale of misery of his life.

> *It becomes difficult to remain calm when you find so many children going hungry most of the time.. I wouldn't worry so much if I could at least be sure of food for these people.*[49]

Sindi is deeply touched by the squalor of the place and the wretchedness of Muthu's lot. "Earlier, he had sympathized with the laborers and indicted Mr. Khemka for exploiting his workers."[50] His accusations are quite audible:

> *It is you who have swindled those miserable wretches in rags who push carts on your streets and die at twenty five. It is you who have been telling lies and fabricating documents first so that you could air-condition this ostentatious*

> *house and throw gigantic parties for the horde of*
> *jackals who masquerade as your friends.*[51]

This conflict and tension of Sindi is not his own alone. This frustration in him is a by- product of his "socio-economic and cultural" gap. Neither Sindi nor his creator Arun Joshi is the first one to undergo such mental agonies. Basically, the process of modernization that started after Renaissance in the West exerted its influence on the Eastern mode of life as a consequence of the encounter between England and India. Whatever be the historical or political reasons, once the Indian mind came to know the Western style of life and its guiding principles, it was lured not only to adopt it but also to re-examine its own almost forgotten achievements of the past just as Krishnan the protagonist of R.K. Narayana's *The English Teacher* (1945) expressed his discontent with the British education which as he said, "makes us morons, cultural morons."[52]

Along with Sasthi Brata and R.K. Narayana's Krishnan, another vain seeker of a home, a refuge, for the tortured soul is V.S. Naipaul. After a brilliant school and college career in his adopted country, West Indies, he went to England where he spent eight years, marrying an English girl. Inspite of all this, he felt like an alien in England – he describes himself as having achieved the Buddhist ideal of 'non-attachment'. He came to India the home of his ancestors to discover his identity. But this voyage of discovery proved a thorough failure as we see from his travelogue *An Area of Darkness*. He was a Brahmin – cum – Englishman in India. Like Sasthi Brata and Naipaul "Sindi felt like an alien, a foreigner in whichever country he went – Africa, England, America or India."[53] He also tried to find out the meaning of "non-attachment" but initially he took it for "detachment". At first he appears to be a man completely cut-off from his spiritual roots. This is evident from one of his responses to Sheila. When Sheila asked about June Blyth's beauty, he snapped:

> *Tall and slim, with blonde hair and large blue eyes.*[54]

And he himself states,

> *I described her like an automobile light grey with a radio and heater, or red over black with white sidewalls.*[55]

Sheila couldn't hold her desperation; she asked again, this time with a caution to be more precise:

> *"I meant inside", Sheila said, pointing to her breast where the soul is supposed to reside.*[56]

This makes clear that Sindi who claims to have attained the Geeta's sutra of "detachment" is absolutely fake. A man who is devoid of the concept of the two types of beauty - inner and outer may certainly misunderstand the message of "non-attachment" taking it for "detachment."

For him "marriage was more often a lust for possession than anything else. People got married just as they bought new cars."[57] And just like buying new cars he kept changing female partners in his life. The principle that guides him is anything but the "non-attachment". Perhaps Joy Abraham tries to trace his inner framework:

> *When one comes closer Sindi is threatened with the fear of the loss of his identity. D.H. Lawrence's Paul Morel is a case in point. In his* Sons and Lovers, *Paul seeks to confirm his identity through his relationship with Miriam. Happily he loves her keeping a distance in between them. When Miriam turns out to be possessive Paul feels his self is threatened. I can only give you friendship- it's all I am capable of – it's a flaw in my make-up.*[58]

Against this philosophy of detachment and the way of living without desires Sindi loves a series of women but June exposes his hypocrisy, vanity and stupidly. Falling in love with her, Sindi himself admits, "It is difficult to be a saint."

She loves him not to live alone. She is free, frank and humane. She knows how to soothe, solace and please him. She gives too much of her to him as "she wanted to be used to someone." At times, she seems to be more genuine than Sindi. After all, she is a woman who crosses all boundaries deep within her centre.

When Sindi comes to India and, as the manager of the Khemka's firms, gets closer to Babu's sister, Sheila, it is by constantly talking to Sheila about Babu and on reading Babu's letters to his sister that Sindi realises his Indian 'id' of love for humanity. Only then he could discover the disastrous consequence of alienating the 'self' from the 'roots'. "It is Sheila's solemn and controlled sadness, now and then coming to the fore during their conversations, that makes Sindi gain the human perspective and understand the meaning of familial relationship in the Indian context."[59] Sheila is right when she comments upon Sindi's attitudinal changes:

> *You may be a wise man and I might admire*
> *you for your wisdom. But you forgot how long*
> *it has taken to get where you are. And all the*
> *destruction that you've caused in the process.*[60]

In *The Foreigner* Joshi has moved from Boston to New Delhi. *In The Strange Case of Billy Biswas*, he moves from New Delhi to Satpura Hills in Madhya Pradesh. The two geographic locations represent two different cultures – the sophisticated and the primitive. Billy's unconscious self drives him to renounce the monotonous respectability of his high middle class society and seek his roots in the company of primitive tribe. The sophisticated Meena represents New Delhi's anglicized ruling – class immersed in the phoney materialism whereas the primitive Bilasia represents the Satpura hills.

A certain awareness of man's rootlessness and the consequential loneliness and anxiety is the keynote of Arun Joshi's unique vision of predicament of the modern man in a contemporary Indo-English fiction.

Arun Joshi's *The Foreigner* deals with the life of Sindi Oberoi, in search of his roots and the meaning of life. Sindi was a perfect foreigner. He was not only a foreigner to the two cultures between which he shuttled but also to his soul. He was an orphan both in terms of relations and his emotional roots. In a way he was as near to these cultures as he was far from them, for his mother was a British and his father an Indian. According to O.P. Bhatnagar:

> *It is this mixed belonging which gives him the*
> *perspective of looking at the situation on the*
> *human rather on the Jamesian cultural plane.*
> *He is better placed and poised than any of the*

heroes of Indo-English or Anglo-Indian novels
in his analysis of the situation.[61]

Sindi's observations are keen and these help to make us understand 'what is that undefined 'Indianness'. Perhaps 'Indianness' is skin-deep:

Soon after, Babu entered the lobby twirling his hat self-consciously. Rounding a corner, he bumped into a young girl and apologized profusely.. He wore a dark blue suit with enormous trouser cuffs. It enhanced his good looks, but the Indian stitching lent him a strictly non-Western appearance.[62]

It was through over - westernized 'Surrender' only that we could find out the difference between Indian and Western stitching.

Sindi's contradictions regarding Americans are also well spread out and quite audible in different situations. At one place we hear him stating: "Americans are a pretty good people on the whole".[63] But just after a minute, he seems to change his attitude:

While in America, Babu, don't fall in love. It does nobody any good.[64]

When June came to know about Sindi's impression about American girls, she got a little hot under the collar.

They (American girls) should be all right except that they behaved so much like boys ... American

> *girls did their hair like boys, they dressed like boys*
> *and they bullied you around.*[65]

While just in contrast he possesses absolutely a different and esteemed outlook for Indian girls. What he could see in Sheila is quite noticeable:

> *I watched her go into the house. Her step had*
> *the unusual grace that only Indian girls have.*[66]

And finally he could reach his roots, his Indian roots when his heart is all enveloped with sympathy for all Indian women, known world - wide for their endurance.

> *She was getting my shoes from under the diwan*
> *and as I watched her arched back. I was filled*
> *with a sense of sympathy for all Indian women*
> *who always had their back arched, stooping to*
> *someone's service.*[67]

Coming once again to Babu, Sindi's cultural contrast and counterpart, we can say he is an Indian to the core. While remembering his sister, he became nostalgic and 'homesick' – a typical trait of homebound Indians. "Tears of homesickness glistened in his eyes"[68]

Sometimes it takes us high and on an absolutely different platform while peeping into 'India' through his eyes.

> *I had read much of inequality in India.*[69]

Listening to this we, as a reader, get food for thought whether, Sindi is correct or the Preamble of our Indian constitution which promises for "EQUALITY, of status and opportunity and to promote it among them all."[70]

His second impression of India is equally interesting as many people had seemed maniac to him. He also discovered that,

> *Somebody wanted to know the best university of econometrics in America. Somebody else asked about scholarships. It always came down to that. In India everything ended in seeking money.*[71]

Not limiting to this, Sindi's observations are so minute. He is also conscious about our 'over –politenesses towards foreigners. Commenting on Babu, he generalizes the things:

> *Like most of us he talked very politely to foreigners.*[72]

Sindi, being a foreigner, is also fed-up with the typical Indian habit of unending chats,

> *You found them* (Indians) ... *discussing, discussing, discussing. I think Indians discuss things more than any other people.*"[73]

Sindi is fed up with Indian parks and its forte:

> *There are no lovers in Indian gardens. Only little heaps of humanity lay here and there trying to snatch a few hours' sleep.*[74]

And perhaps these everything including the death of his beloved June and Babu made him yell:

I hated everything that was Indian.[75]

But after listening to Babu it absolutely becomes a moot-point for all of us - who is right whether Sindi who could see India like this or it's Babu who claims to Sindi: "No, never, You are an Indian, yet you are so terribly ignorant of India."[76]

But we cannot trust Babu because he himself could never know and remained ignorant of this America. America stood much against his cultural values, emotional requirement and intellectual make up. He collapsed. He succumbed to his Indian emotionality and morality.

How powerful Mr. Khemka's claim was, say for example,

India is working towards a new age, an age in which each man will be equal to another.[77]

Sindi did not ponder upon this promise of equality. Rather he could see the "Slumdog Millionaire"-type scenes:

The sky had begun to clear ... In the slums across the street, bundles of soggy humanity shuffled out of their huts and spread their miserable rags to dry... Full-breasted women, their things naked under wet saris, scurried back and forth like animals quarreling over small bits of tin. Naked children rolled in the filthy pools, squealing with delight ...

Bright red buses of the Delhi transport undertaking sloshed through the mud splattering pedestrians with grime. In spite of the rain

> *they were full; in India things are always full*
> *whatever the circumstances. A horde of hawkers*
> *had appeared from nowhere making a brisk sale*
> *of rotting fruits and gluey sweetmeats that passed*
> *well with slum-dwellers.*[78]

Seeing all this Karl's short but a zillion pound valuable
statement finds an everlasting echo:

> *You Indians and your mealy mouthed philosophies.*[79]

Arun Joshi is one of the younger Indo-Anglian novelists
who excel in their themes and techniques and in their
explorations of psyche. He presents the aspects of Indian
life so skillfully that it becomes universal in creative smithy.

East-West encounter is a theme exploited for the study
of possibility of shifts in attitude; but the conclusions drawn
from the experiment in international living are as varied as
the temperaments of novelists.

> *If Raja Rao (*The Serpent and The Rope,*1960)*
> *and Kamala Markandaya (*Possession, *1963)*
> *thought Indian genius was too self-conscious and*
> *profound to establish any sensible communication*
> *with the West, R.K. Narayan (*The Vendor of
> Sweets, *1967) found the Indian circumstances yet*
> *unfavuorable for the transplantation of western*
> *values into Indian soil, and Bhabani Bhattacharya*
> (Shadow From Ladakh, *1966) envisioned the*
> *possibility of the amalgam of the two: the soulful*
> *East absorbing the technical know -how and the*
> *pragmatic wisdom of the West.*[80]

Arun Joshi has tried to explore that possibility through Engineer Sindi, the protagonist of *The Foreigner*.

The present social system of India is very well exposed by the novelist. Lying, hypocrisy, bribery, drunkenness, womanizing and unfair distribution of money pinch the heart of the writer. The various problems have also come to light in the course o the novels, and the problem of unemployment, the growth of education, population explosion housing problem, etc. are some of them.

Sindi Oberoi, an Indian Kenyan, who returns to India after years in the West finds himself incapable of achieving any emotional involvement with the milieu of his racial origin. He finally gets over his inner pricks and mental pressures, and the hope of a successful, cheerful life brightens him up with the realization (which is well-depicted by the Vision Studio on the cover page 'a fish in the water pot') that his despair "that had so long enveloped my (his) being like a fish is surrounded by water. And like a fish, I (he) had always been unaware of it …. an uprooted young man living in the later half of the twentieth century who had become detached from everything except himself."[81]

We are also surprised and happy at the same time with his come back and alongwith Sheila we also ask this lost Indian overwhelmingly:

I didn't think you would come back.[82]

And yes this is our Indian hospitality that we always consider our guest our god and we never forget to offer him something. Let us also finish this cultural treat with Sheila's offer:

Shall we have some tea?[83]

References:

1. Arun Joshi. *The Foreigner*. Delhi: Orient Paperbacks, 1993. p.43.
2. The blurb of *The Foreigner*
3. Arun Joshi, *The Foreigner,* op.cit., p. 55.
4. Madhusudan Prasad,ed. *An Anthology of Critical Essays.* New Delhi: Sterling, 1982, p. 52.
5. O.P. Bhatnagar. *"The Art and Vision of Arun Joshi". Response: Recent Revelations of Indian Fiction in English.* ed., Hari Mohan Prasad. Bareilly: Prakash Book Depot, 1983. p. 250.
6. Arun Joshi. *The Foreigner.*op.cit., p.60.
7. *ibid.*, p. 60.
8. *ibid.*, p. 61.
9. O.P. Bhatnagar. *The Art and Vision of Arun Joshi*, op.cit., p. 253.
10. Arun Joshi. *The Foreigner,* op. cit., p.100.
11. *ibid.*, p. 100
12. *ibid.*, p. 80
13. *ibid.*, p. 80
14. *ibid.*, p. 79
15. *ibid.*, p. 81
16. *ibid.*, p. 78
17. *ibid.*, p. 80
18. Mohan Jha. *"The Foreigner, A Study in Innocence and Experience". The Fictional world of Arun Joshi.* ed., R.K. Dhawan, New Delhi: Classical, 1986. pp. 173- 74.
19. Arun Joshi, *The Foreigner,* op.cit., p. 51.
20. *ibid.*, p. 44.
21. C. Malathi Rao. *The Foreigner: Arun Joshi.* Literary Criterion, 8 (4), 1969, pp. 76- 77.
22. Arun Joshi. *The Foreigner,* op. cit., p. 26.
23. *ibid.,* p. 26.
24. *ibid.*, p. 45.

25. *ibid.*, p. 55.

26. *ibid.*, p.29.

27. *ibid.*, p.39.

28. K. Radha. *"From Detachment to Involvement: The Case of Sindi Oberoi". The Novels of Arun Joshi,* ed. R.K. Dhawan. New Delhi: Prestige, New Delhi, 1992. p. 112.

29. Meenakshi Mukherjee. *The Prospect: The Twice Born Fiction* New Delhi: Heinemann, 1971. pp. 202 – 03.

30. Arun Joshi, *The Foreigner,* op.cit., p. 62.

31. *ibid.*, p.88.

32. *ibid.*, p.73.

33. O.P. Bhatnagar. *"The art and Vision of Arun Joshi". Arun Joshi: A Study in Fiction.* ed., N. Radhakrishnan. Gandhigram: A Scholar Critic publication, 1984. p. 33.

34. Arun Joshi. *The Foreigner,* op. cit, p. 119.

35. *ibid.*, p. 51.

36. *ibid.*, p. 130.

37. *ibid.*, p.52.

38. *ibid.*, p.52.

39. O.P. Bhatnagar. *Arun Joshi's* The Foreigner. The Journal of Indian Writing in English, I, No. 2, July 1973, p. 13.

40. Usha Pathania. *"Having and Being: A Study of The Foreigner". The Novels of Arun Joshi.* Ed., R.K. Dhawan. N. Delhi: Prestige, 1982, p. 139.

41. Arun Joshi, *The Foreigner,* op.cit., p. 29.

42. *ibid.*, p.51–52.

43. ibid., p. 25.

44. *ibid.*, p. 25.

45. *ibid.*, p. 25.

46. *ibid.*, pp. 11-12.

47. *ibid.*, p.14.

48. *ibid.*, p. 16.

49. *ibid.*, p.188.

50. R.K.Dhawan. *The Fictional World of Arun Joshi.* N. Delhi: Prestige, 1992, pp.14-15.

51.	Arun Joshi. *The Foreigner,* op. cit., p.180.

52.	R.S. Singh. *Indian Novel in English, A Critical Study.* New Delhi: Arnold-Heinemann, 1977. p. 16.

53.	K. Radha, *"From Detachment to Involvement: The Case of Sindi Oberoi". The Fictional World of Arun Joshi.* ed., R.K. Dhawan. N. Delhi: 1986 p. - 184.

54.	Arun Joshi. *The Foreigner,* op.cit, p. 49.

55.	*ibid.,* p. 49.

56.	*ibid.,* p. 49.

57.	*ibid.,* p. 60.

58.	Joy Abraham. *"The Foreigner: A Study in Technique",* *The Novels of Arun Joshi.* ed.,R.K. Dhawan. N. Delhi: Prestige, 1992. pp.146 – 147.

59.	V.N.Rajendra Prasad. *The Self. The Family And Society In Five Indian Novelists.* N.Delhi: Prestige,1990. p.113.

60.	Arun Joshi. *The Foreigner.* op. cit., p.182.

61.	O.P. Bhatnagar, *"The Art and Vision of Arun Joshi",* op.cit., p. 250.

62.	Arun Joshi. *The Foreigner,* op.cit., p. 18.

63.	*ibid.,* p. 19.

64.	*ibid.,* p. 20.

65.	*ibid.,* p. 32.

66.	*ibid.,* p. 53

67.	*ibid.,* p. 183

68.	*ibid.,* p. 20

69.	*ibid.,* p. 16

70.	The Preamble, *The Constitution of India*

71.	Arun Joshi. *The Foreigner,* op. cit. p. 43.

72.	*ibid.,* p. 86.

73.	*ibid..,* p. 115.

74.	*ibid.,* p. 115.

75.	*ibid.,* p. 175.

76.	*ibid.,* p. 77.

77.	*ibid.,* p. 38.

78.	*ibid.,* p. 40.

79. *ibid.*, p. 67.
80. R.S. Singh. *Indian Novel in English: A Critical Study,* op. cit. p. 164.
81. Arun Joshi. *The Foreigner,* op. cit., p. 164.
82. *ibid.*, p. 191.
83. *ibid.*, p. 191

CHAPTER - V

THE COFFER DAMS

Kamala Markandaya, one of the leading Indo-Anglian novelists, has written ten novels: *Nectar in a Sieve, Some Inner Fury, A Handful of Rice, A Silence of Desire, The Nowhere Man, Procession, The Coffer Dams, The Two Virgins, The Golden Honey Comb* and *The Pleasant City.* To quote O.P. Saxena:

> *In each of these novels there are two cultural worlds set in opposition to each other. These cultural worlds belong to two distinct races of Indian and Europeans, they cannot merge.*[1]

East-West encounter is the major theme of all Markandaya's novels. Having been brought up in India, her presentation of the East - West conflict, tension and culture, is characterized by her first - hand experience. This East - West conflict is presented on different levels, namely political, social, human, technological, cultural and artistic.

R.M. Verma rightly observes about her novels that they are the bi-cultural world of Kamala Markandaya without any partiality or favour either for the East or for the West. She brings out the various points of weakness and strength of both the cultures. She looks at the West through the eyes of the East and looks at the East through the eyes of the West. The setting may be England or India, city or village. She brings out clearly the barriers of arrogance, colour and cultural differences that keep the East and the West apart. She tries to bring about a reconciliation of the two. C.D. Narasimhaiah rightly remarks:

> *Generally her novels reflect her strong penchant for Indian values is against the spiritual impoverishment of the English society, but Indians are not spared. Actually her good men and women come from both cultures.*[2]

In *The Coffer Dams*, the East-West encounter is on the technological as well as the human level. On the technological level, the conflict is between the technological power and forces of nature represented by the turbulent South Indian river on which the dam is being built and also the heavy rains which try to hinder the task of the construction work. On the human level the conflict is between the arrogant British officers under their leader, Clinton and the poor hill tribesmen working as labourers.

> *Kamala Markandaya has depicted with discernment the impact that the West has created on the Indian mind during the British regime (1857 – 1947). Sophisticated families of Westernized Indians, ultra-modern woman, orthodox grannies, swamis, scientists, artists and prostitutes – all are authentically portrayed in her fiction.*[3]

Her major theme has been the cultural clash of the two modes of life, the western and the oriental and the consequent actuation of the painful process of modernization. This clash is all exhibited when Clinton replies to a query of Helen if there be no line drawn, at which one stops?

> *No lines are possible.... Whatever the departures or deaths, the suicides in baths of repentant water, one would continue.*[4]

In *The Coffer Dams,* Kamala Markandaya treats a new aspect of cross – cultural interaction by depicting the conflict between technological power and the forces of nature symbolized by a turbulent South Indian River. On the human level, the conflict manifests itself in the form of hostility between the sophisticated British technicians and the hill – tribesmen of India, who have been dislodged from the site of the dam and who worship the river as a veritable god:

> *Sometimes when the rains failed there was no river at all, only a trickle that did not percolate through to the shallowest irrigation channels of their parked fields. At other times, the land was inundated; they saw their crops drowned beneath spreading lakes, their mud-huts dissolved to a lumpy brown soup and carried away on the flood tide. At both times they prayed to God, they never blamed him. It was their fate.*[5]

It depicts the uneasy relationship between the two. The dam and the river assume symbolic significance:

> *One world view against the other: the mechanical*
> *versus the mystical.*[6]

The Indian river, dark and turbulent, is willful and irrational, unpredictable and uncontrollable like the unconscious. For the tribal people, it has a metaphysical character; the Western technicians understand it only in terms of its strata, flow and course. When turned wild, Nature respecting no human designs, flouts all the sophisticated computations. The symbolic meaning can be stretched a little further. Mackendrick, who runs the show, is compelled to consult the tribal chief and learns the secrets of the river's behaviour. The prophecy of the chief, unambiguously suggestive of Delphi's Oracle, comes true. The turbulent river subsides and the dam is saved. The denouement also suggests that technology may possess the tools to build a dam but it does not have the wisdom to ensure its preservation. The symbolic meaning can be stretched still further in that "the construction of the coffer dams symbolizes man's joint efforts on the international level to control the turbulent river, symbolic of wild nature."[7]

The novel depicts the scientific and technical superiority of the West.

> *The country was full of foreigners – Americans,*
> *West Germans, the Russians fresh from their*
> *triumph at Aswan, the immense successful*
> *undertaking of taming the Nile, the Dutch with*
> *their ancient knowledge of dam – building, the*
> *brilliant achievement of the Zuider Zee and the*
> *Delta plan behind them – all of them eager,*
> *in greater or less degree, to gain a foothold in*

*an expanding sub-continent of vast commercial
potential.*[8]

The story revolves around a dam to be constructed over a turbulent hilly river in India. As it has been described by the author:

> *The Great Dam, it had come to be called: not by
> him...... but by people of the Maidan and the
> Malnad, the plains and the hill – country people,
> who had watched with awe the precipitate birth
> of a town in the jungle.*[9]

Clinton, middle – aged engineer, is a partner of a dam building firm in England, the ramifications of which have become international. The people of his native land see him as a man of wealth and property but "he saw himself only as a builder, a man whose conceptions of concrete and steel his highly polished and perfected technical skills could translate into reality."[10]

The central character in this novel is again a woman, but the action takes place against a background which is unusual for Markandaya, a world of gigantic construction. The project brings in the usual retinue of foreign experts and their families including Helen, Clinton's wife and Millie Rawlings, the chief engineer's wife. Clinton incarnates the township ideals of ruthless efficiency and concentrates on the challenging assignments which are all clear from his discussion with Mackendrick:

> *'Hope there won't be trouble!'*
> *'Only from our men," Mackendrick grimaced.*

> *They hate the place by night, it twists their guts.'*
> *'I can't think why'*
> *'Well. Strange places do have an effect'.*
> *'They've been out here a year,' said Clinton,*
> *'Two years, some of 'em" one can scarcely call it a*
> *strange place." Mackendrick shrugged 'Is India*
> *ever anything else?"*[11]

On the other hand, his young wife Helen looks around for a few moments of relief in the "tribal wilderness". Helen is absolutely awe - stricken and overwhelmingly charmed by the bewitching Indian beauty as the author writes:

> *Its density, the rampant furious growth, affected*
> *her in a way that the ordered charm of a*
> *restrained civilization would never do. After a*
> *little she opened the door, and stepped out into*
> *the blackness where the shadows of the first trees*
> *fell and deepened the night.*[12]

She has boundless curiosity about the country and its people and her rapport with them puzzles and irritates her husband. "He (Clinton) had his work: what had she?"[13] This became his curiosity. Also Clinton is very often found wondering "… of the glib communication she had established with a people who presented to him only the blank opacities of their total incomprehension."[14]

Helen's flexibility and inner desire to get mingled with the Indian culture is quite soothing and deserve our due reverence for her being 'the East-ward Westerner':

> *Nobody speaks their lingo: none of the workers.*
> *Except Bashiam, he's one of the tribe, and*
> *Krishnan, he's gone to some plains to learn*
> *it, heaven knows why… and Helen of course.*
> *Clever gal, picking up a dialect so quickly. Done*
> *it in months, most people would take years.*[15]

Helen is, in fact, a superb example of that cultural allotrope who adopts other cultures out of deep regard and sagaciousness to accept others. Her outer outfit is that of the west and inner self carries the softness and humbleness of the east. Whereas her contrast Bashiam is opposite to her in sex as well as race; but he appears to be handling an imported machine of the west, that is, a crane, moving on in the "westward ho" – spirit on the path of development, helping to construct a new India with dams which had got a sobriquet of "modern temples of modern India" by late Pt. Jawahar Lal Nehru. Bashiam, here, represents the whole tribal community of modern India who are on the verge of tasting the flavor of westerly development, not merely by hunting inside the jungle, blaming their ignorance and illiteracy but with their pro-active participation in it. That is why, Bashiam, a hilly tribesman, has been depicted not as an ordinary but a dexterous, highly skilled Crane operator. In him, the readers could see the 'will and passion' of jungle to move from antiquity to modernity. Bashiam, if taken as a geographical figure, seems to represent a 'buffer zone' between two different states. He is, in fact, a cultural allotrope, who embraces a 'white mem Saab' without easterly prejudices and inhibitions.

Clinton is conditioned by memories of the colonial past, while she has no such inhibitions. She can be compared with Mrs. Moore of E.M. Foster's *A Passage to India* as both have intuitive admiration for Indian beauty and want to see the real India. Despite the difference in age, both are sensitive and emotional, and there exists an incompatibility between Helen and Clinton and Mrs. Moore and her son Ronnie Heaslop, the city magistrate, as both men have a rational and practical outlook towards life. Their mystic nature and their intuitive response to things Indian, stand in contrast to the highly scientific, relational and matter of fact - outlook of Clinton and Heaslop.

> *Clinton and his wife are thus portrayed with diametrically opposed attitudes to life. They represent two extremes, the former absolutely incapable of communicating with the natives, the latter achieving almost total identification with them.*[16]

Helen finds fulfillment in building bridges of understanding, while Clinton finds satisfaction in constructing the coffer dams. She is able to perceive the vastness of tradition that sustains the tribal people. To her, the tribals are not "black opacities… total incomprehension?" but live, feeling men and women.

The novelist also does not forget to highlight Helen's ideology about the Indian natives. When she was once intrigued by her husband whether it was her age that she carried no blocks, she had laughed.

> *It's nothing to do with age. … just think of them as human beings, that's all …. You've got to get beyond their skins…. It's bit of a hurdle, but it is an essential one.*[17]

Helen has the capacity to look beyond the skin. Others simply do not have. Perhaps it was because of what Helen believes that "it's something to do with being born in India"[18] in her previous life.

The "prestigious project" of the dam brings the British technicians closer to the primitive world of the native Indians:

> *There was a coffee club and a soft – drinks stall and a tin shack where they showed the films that the Madras Picture Corporations sent up by truck ... Clinton's Lines, the men called them.*[19]

Also, "the men...had had time to carry their Englishness into the jungle with them."[20]

The novel poses the problem: Does the dam really bring the alien races together or does the collaboration of the East and the West help in bridging the gulf between the two cultures? Ramesh Chadha does have a pessimistic answer to this question:

> *The dam becomes a symbol of modern technology, a sanctuary under which men may unite. The dam is the centre of the novel around which all the characters assemble. The dam takes shapes out of the British brain, supplemented by Indian 'need, conception, money, flesh and blood and bone'.*[21]

In fact, the joint venture does not unite them in the real sense of the term and they remain like "an ill-sorted bundle of sticks that stood or fell together."[22]

Perhaps, Markandaya wants to bring home the point that all attempts at the superficial level – social, political, technological – are inadequate to bridge the gap unless the urge to change is prompted at the level of human understanding. The conflict of human relationships assumes complex and multi-sided dimensions when Clinton's partner – friend Mackendrick differs from him in his attitude towards the coolie labour and surmises: What is there in the Indian air that includes disharmony even between close associates as they are? There we have Rawlings who considers "Indians… an excitable breed, a quality that diminished rational behaviour."[23] While Mackendrick "had no strong feelings either way, but he was not walled off from the feel of the country. Anyone, he knew, who adopted the panoply and pomp of an English archbishop would find himself heartily jeered in any Indian town."[24]

Wrapped up more in a form of bundle of questions, the distrust and dissonance is all clear when Rawlings confesses his resentment and distrust before Clinton:

> *Are you just going to hand her over to jungle Johnnies?... Yes I know some of 'em pretty good…. But the real know how? You think it comes in two years? Or ten? Our chaps, it's in the bone. This let you, never know which way they're going to jump…I wouldn't trust one of them farther than I could throw him. That goes for Bashiam especially.*[25]

As the action of the novel advances, layer after layer of discord in human relationship is revealed. The British technicians are jealous of other Western technicians – Americans, West Germans, Russians – who are getting a foot hold "in an expanding sub-continent of vast commercial potential."[26]

Millie Rawlings, the wife of the chief Engineer, looks down upon other European women as she tells Das, Clinton's Indian cook, in her forthright manner:

> *Only a few left now. The memsahibs, I mean. Not the ones from Russia and Sweden and Salford, they're there all right, inheriting our earth …. I mean the real mems like us, dearie, there's precious few of that breed left. When it's extinct, they'll follow.*[27]

Even the British officers are divided by differences in their attitude towards the Indians. The Englishmen of the older generation, who have basked in the glory of the British rule in India, find it difficult to understand how the younger men are able to adjust with the natives of new India. Mackendrick envies "younger men like Bailey and Lefevre who despite rebuffs rubbed along with the new India better than he or his generation could hope to do."[28]

While working together on the same project, the British and the Indian technicians remain hostile to each other and are unable to appreciate the opposite point of view. Krishnan, the leader of the engineers, deputed by the Indian Government, disagrees with Clinton on the construction program of the dam and, finding the latter indifferent, feels bitterly hurt:

> *Brush off like flies, he thought, hurt and insult like splinters under his skin, despise us*

> *because they are experts and we (Indians) are*
> *just beginning. Beginners he repeated bitterly;*
> *barred from knowledge and power as from the*
> *secrets of a master guild; and the memory of those*
> *neglectful years lay in deep accusing pools in his*
> *mind. But it's over now... Our day is coming.*
> *The day when they will listen to us.*[29]

On the other hand, the British like Mackendrick "sighed not for the old days, which he did not lament, but because he did not feel in tune with the new .... Somehow one no longer belonged in India – the reserved place in it was gone. Was it also, he wondered, because one no longer came by right as an owner, but strictly by invitation only."[30]

Though in conflict with each other, both the British and the Indian officers look down upon the tribesmen and shun their company. They even snub the presence of Bashiam, the local technical hand and call him a primitive or "Jungly Wallah". Even to his own tribesmen, Bashiam was "an outsider detribalized" and sometimes, without undue agonizing, he acknowledged the truth of it. But he also "knew in his bones that, however, detribalized he might be, birth and upbringing within the tribe gave him race knowledge and instincts that could never be acquired by the real outsiders, those who had never been inside."[31]

And, even Clinton feels about Bashiam something out of the line:

> *Of them all, only Bashiam clung to his*
> *reservations. He was not like the others, a product*
> *of technical training colleges that were being*
> *urged into being up and down the country....*[32]

Even the other Indians kept him apart, a stranger in their midst, calling him 'Jungly wallah', a man of the jungle. A primitive just come down off the trees. The irony of Bashiam is that the Englishmen and Hindu alike looked down their fine Aryan noses and covertly spurned the aborigine.

Rather, Helen makes Bashiam conscious of his 'status'. How can we simply ignore the intense dialogue which ran between them:

> *"Do you know what they call you behind your back?"*
> *'Jungly Wallah! he said at once without hesitation'.*
> *'Do you know what it means'*
> *'A man of jungle.' 'An uncivilized man'.*
> *'What it really means!' she said cruelly, 'is someone who doesn't count. Someone who gets kicked around and doesn't do anything to stop it."*[33]

Though, Bashiam was 'detribalized' and his 'roots were attenuated', he was the perfect stuff that Helen expected from India as she "wanted someone local, someone whose breath and bones had been formed in these hills – not for introduction and entrée', which she could manage quite well by herself, but for interpretation,…and eventually found what she wanted virtually on her doorsteps in the person of Bashiam."[34] And Helen was so touched from within when she realized that "it was simply that one expected people like Bashiam a backward people to be content with natural things like hills and woods and a waterpump or two."[35]

The British officers recruited labourers from among the tribals but had no sympathy for them and made no effort to befriend them or adjust to the local environment. To Clinton, the local people appear "a tribe whose outstanding characteristic is the severe retardation of its civilization"[36] and who present to him "only the blank opacities of their total incomprehension."[37]

Parallel to Clinton's character, Bashiam, the aborigine crane operator has rejected the old traditional way of life for modern technological existence. Bashiam's positive assertion in favour of the on-going development reveals that the planners have infected the germ of development amidst the 'marginalized junglees' also. He asserts (with conviction that the old way of life held nothing for him) to Helen:

> *Machines are to me what they are to your husband... only more. They have given me another way of life.*[38]

His is a precarious position. For his education and modern scientific outlook, his own men disown him and he is looked down upon by the British personnel as a native "junglee" which, according to Helen, means "someone who doesn't count". It is in Bashiam that Helen finds a guide to the heart of the tribal world. And, it is because of their understanding of each other, not neglect or isolation, that they eventually develop kinship.

Bashiam also felt that,

> *It was more to do ...with the divergent channels they had carved for themselves — he the skilled and competent technician away from his jungly*

wallah tribe, she the No. 1 memsahib who refused to bear the memsahib's load.[39]

Bashiam often thought about Helen that

She was not like the other memsahibs, even those latter day ones, whose outlook barred them from allowing their interest to be sparked by anything.[40]

At the same time, Helen definitely takes Bashiam as "the jungly prophet"[41]. Helen puts it:

Look at me. I've never been a memsahib. You're not some kind of freak to me. We're alike, we're freaks only to the caste we come from, not to each other.[42]

Helen is presented to stand for the West's desire to understand the East, and Bashiam, with his obsession with the machine and technological progress, cut off from his traditional moorings, is supposed to represent the predicament of the modern youth of India. Helen desperately tries to understand the East and her cry is quite audible:

Can't you care? Don't human beings matter anything to you? Do they have special kind of flesh before they do?[43]

Sometimes, Helen's empathy makes Clinton unnerved too. It reaches to the level of bewilderment:

Clinton, bewildered, face to face with forms of violence he had not suspected in his wife, had

> *nothing to say…The country's affecting her…it's*
> *getting on her nerves.*[44]

Helen genuinely sympathasizes with the unprivileged deprived Indians. This is all evident in her following discussion with Clinton:

> *"They're rattled around like seas in a tin."*
> *'They should be used to it by not.'*
> *'But now it's worse. The nights are. They feel it more.'*
> *'They'll get used to it. People do when they have to."*[45]

Rama Jha rightly remarks:

> *Helen of* The Coffer Dams *is an apter illustration of the East – West encounter in the post – colonial India.*[46]

The tribal-cum-rural world of India not only fits in the structure of the novel, it becomes an integral part of the pattern and enriches the significance of the theme. Though backward, the tribesmen have the advantage of close familiarity with the local surroundings. They understand the changing seasons and can predict rain and cyclones by the mere smell of the soil. Their headman foresees when the rains will stop and the fury of the demoniac river abates. They are not frightened by the wildness of the jungle like the British technicians who cannot sleep at night and who "hate the place at night, it twists their guts."[47] The tribal headman is full of forebodings. He is afraid that before the great Dam is finished "the man eater (the river) will have its flesh... a score or more before they bend the river."[48]

For Clinton, the completion of the dam, according to the agreed schedule, is the main thing. What the tribals think or feel is nothing to him. He is armed with his blueprints, time schedules and statistics, But Bashiam and even Krishnan know better how the monsoon in India and the behaviour of the rivers cannot simply be taken easily. Nature in India is not to be lightly treated. Rochelle Almeida writes:

> *Bashiam is in the happy position of having other educated Indians fight for his interests and leading the labourers in a strike; but he himself is a simple aborigine, in awe of white skins, a victim of colonial exploitation, treated as cheap labour, easily dispensable. The task of getting him a better deal falls to Krishnan, an educated, professional Indian who is in a better position to bargain with his English employers. Bashiam's role of the underdog arouses Helen's sympathy. Since she, too, is a victim of her husband's brutal harshness, the two of them become team-mates in their shared sorrows and stick together providing mutual solace – though temporary to each other.[49]*

While the Indian female protagonist in the Indo-English novel is usually depicted as an idealized being, the European women on the contrary are seen negatively as mean and unkind, secure in her position of racial superiority, the consort of the White ruler.

To understand the reason for this, one must examine the forces that brought the white woman (commonly referred to as the Memsahibs) to India. These are related to the development of colonial zeal. The white woman's world in India was a luxurious, an idle one, her demands attended to by a plethora of servants. It was punctuated by leisure - time events like Club Dances and sessions at Whist. Disdainful of native Indian culture, these women made no attempts to understand or appreciate its differences. They preferred to recreate the feel and an ambience of English life in the most remote regions of India also, for example, the Rawlings' bungalow, "always well lit, was a blaze of light when they gave their parties. The company's labour mustered in strength to watch the display, gathering in bunches around the flood and fairy lights strung about the compound in intriguing pattern. Bob Rawlings was proud of his lighting effects."[50]

To Millie, "they were essentials to gaiety in an area of darkness"[51] and she saw the lovely lights, and averted her eyes from the intense blackness they created beyond the illuminated circle.

While studying the 'memsahib' as a type – figure in Indo –English fiction, Kai Nicholson quotes Michael Edwards:

> *They tended to bring with them the English prejudices of the time. Their attitude, generally speaking was Christian and narrowly so… The women had little to occupy their minds. Their life was a tedious social round, but they did have gossip.*[52]

The figure of the Memsahib occurs very prominently in Kamala Markandaya's works. Millie Rawlings in *The Coffer Dams*, Caroline Bell in *Possession*, the arrogant anonymous

Memsahibs in *A Handful of Rice* to whom Ravi must deliver the finished garments, and Lady Copeland in *The Golden Honeycomb* are examples of this sort of English women.

Mrs. Millie Rawlings came across as singularly disagreeable. She takes every opportunity to express her scorn for her 'native' servants, and openly derides Indian customs and culture. Her invective is not only directed against India, but Indians as well:

> *Never trust these blacks. That's my motto and I stick to it.*[53]

Harish Raizada calls her a "remnant of the old tribe of *'Memsahibs'*"[54] and points out that she likes lot of booze, "coffee parties, shooting jaunts to the nearest town that boasted of a civilized club that possessed a dance band, a bar, and imported one armed bandits."[55]

Millie Rawlings dislikes Helen because she is aware of Helen's sympathy for the aborigines and because Helen never hides her dislike of the snooty, sophisticated 'Memsahib' who hampered Indo-British relations by her misplaced snobbery and false sense of racial superiority. Millie Rawlings is good example of the kind of woman Paul Scott writes about in attempting to analyze why Indo-British relations were so difficult to achieve:

> *Certainly no one was more adept at making an Indian feel like something crawling from under a stone than the Memsahib, and she it was who, creating a home away from home and solemnly observing the rites of Camberly in the heart of Mudpore, ensured that the Raj should never*

> *develop along lines that could lead to an English*
> *sense of identity with India.*[56]

Helen's special characteristic of 'creating a home away from home' reflects her adaptability and capacity to bring out the behavioral changes according to time and place. For her, be it Camberly or Mudpore - there is not much difference. If Bashiam is a "buffer zone" between two cultural spaces, she is the "twilight zone" of time.

There are, of course, some exceptions to the stereotyped image of the Memsahib' found in the Indo-English novel: Helen in *The Coffer Dams*, Mrs.Bridie and Mrs. Pippa Pearl in *Pleasure City*. In creating them Markandaya seems to want to be fair to the British. From the start, Helen is sympathetic not just to Bashiam, but to all the Indian workers. Seeking to escape from her husband's bigoted clutches, she forms an alliance with Bashiam who distrusts her advances, categorizing her with other women of her kind. When Helen asked Bashiam if she was wrong, he replies:

> *"only don't be sorry afterwards", he said, thickly,*
> *'because — I've only been sorry before."*
> *She (Helen) cried, 'feeling and feeling, and*
> *stopping. And starting again and again, and*
> *never finishing.'*
> *'Finish this time,' he said hoarsely, and covered*
> *her.'*[57]

This affair ripens from casual sex to deep concern (if not love) for the other's well being. Helen is all heavy with the feeling of unbelongingness to the Bashiam's world. She misses him at the level of her senses also. Her affiliation with Indian values lie at sub - conscious level, her love for Bashiam is its unconscious manifestation. She is attached from within, though she is not authoritative about her emotional bondage with India and its roots. She has the sense of insensitivity of the hard metallic Western world. When Helen couldn't smell the rain, she laments:

> *"But you can and I can't," she said. "I wish I could. But my senses have been blunted. ...Our world...the one in which I live. Things are battened down in it. Under concrete and mortar, all sorts of things. The land. Our instincts. The people who work in our factories, they've forgotten what fresh air is like. Our animals – we could learn from them, but we are Christians you know an arrogant people, so we deprive them of their rights. Then they don't know about sunshine or rain either... We've cut off ourselves from our heritage. We've forgotten what we knew.*[58]

Helen's deep concern for Bashiam and his whole people is quite apparent when she almost inflames the sentiments of Bashiam the moment he expresses his remorse:

> *"There used to be a village where the bungalows are... where our bungalow is.. 'A tribal village'.*
> *'A small settlement, yes.'*
> *'When they were told to go, they went',*
> *'Yes'*
> *'Without protest. Just got up and walked away, like animals'.*
> *'I suppose you could put it like that.'*[59]

Since beginning she approaches on a different platform. Her concern is too genuine. Her frustration is visible. Her soliloquy reverberates:

> *These people, 'these' people…. But these people aren't different clay; they are like me, like people like me. What is for me is for them, there's no other kind of yardstick that's worth anything…*
> *It was their land. They didn't want to leave it, they were persuaded.*[60]

In this, she shows her characteristic sense of British fair play – something conspicuously absent in the other British 'Memsahibs', though they pride themselves on being British. This is not just because Bashiam is her lover, but because his condition makes him vulnerable to exploitation and he has no one to prevent him from this happening.

Like the Memsahib, the 'sahib' or Lord cloistered himself from the Indian 'hoi polloi' and built an exclusive life for himself far from the contaminating influence of the 'natives'. In her essay entitled, *Kamala Markandaya: Indo-Anglian Conflict as Unity* Joan Adkins points out that the "British element" in Indo-English fiction appears as "industrialist and his workers; the British missionary; the British doctor, the British nobility and the British educated Indian, with his new ideas of nationalism, democracy and socialism. Representative of this vein of writing is Kamala Markandaya, an Indian writing in English about Indian problems."[61]

"The British Industrialist and his workers" is seen twice in Markandaya's novels – in the figure of Clinton Mackendrick and his team of English engineers in *The*

Coffer Dams, and in Herbert Boyle of *AIDCROP* who works with Toby Tully and the other site-developers on 'Shalimar' in *Pleasure City*.

Rochelle Almeida writes,

> *In* The Coffer Dams, *the character of Clinton contrasts immensely with that of Kenny* (Nectar in a Sieve) *or Richard* (Some Inner Fury). *Clinton has all the makings of a tough and ruthless taskmaster who is out to exploit cheap Indian labor.* [62]

The deaths of several Indian labourers are viewed by him complacently; he knows that replacements are easy and that his work will get done. Clinton's attitude is well revealed in the following statement:

> *We could sack the entire coolie labour force overnight and have a queue a mile long by morning if we wanted and they know it. Organized casual labour – it's almost a contradiction in terms.* [63]

"Organized causal labour", while Clinton uses this oxymoron he better knows the Indian paradoxes- a country, rich in resources but Indians - the poorest humanity breathing on the globe.

Clinton even refuses to waste time retrieving the drowned corpses and giving them a decent burial. According to Clinton, acclaiming a decent burial is nothing more than a 'sane belief' as it can easily be sensed in one of his exasperated response to Helen:

> *'Are these sane beliefs….beliefs of sanity, to which*
> *I am asked to ponder?*[64]

And he does not seem convinced by Helen's argument, that they are beliefs and one *does* not 'walk over graves wearing jackboots'.

Later, when writing his report on Bashiam's death he absolves himself and his company of all responsibility and conveniently puts it down to an accident.

Ramesh Chadha very aptly remarks:

> *Markandaya exhibits her skill in the delineation*
> *of the minor characters as well. Mackendrick is*
> *portrayed as a man with the widest sympathies*
> *for India.*[65]

Mackendrick understands the complex of the Indian engineer Krishnan and tries to place the racial tension in historical perspective:

> *Mackendrick glanced at the Indian with*
> *something like sympathy. In a way he understood*
> *better than either of the Englishmen – the pulsing*
> *jealousy and the pride that a poor nation could*
> *feel and transmit to its nationals;, the pride of*
> *an ancient civilization limping behind in the*
> *modern race called backward everywhere except*
> *to its face and underdeveloped in diplomatic*
> *confrontation.*[66]

Then, we have Clinton's chief assistant, Rawlings, and his wife Millie who uphold the myth of racial superiority.

Among the Indians, Krishnan has been portrayed as mistrustful and always on his guard; he moves swiftly to counter the western techniques of seduction, persuasion and coercion. As the author writes:

> *He (Krishnan) brooded,…his subtle brahminical mind delicately picked up and dissected the Western techniques of seduction, persuasion, and coercion. It was the new guiding trinity, as piety, gunboats and the way of Christ had been the old.*[67]

And

> *Like Rawlings he had no patience for amiable weaklings… his vision …saw no place for them in the power game that the world was playing. Strength; one spoke only from strength. The west understood no other language.*[68]

During the construction of the dam, two accidents take place. The first is the death of Bailey and Wilkins and work is suspended to give them a "decent Christian burial". In the second, when the charges of dynamite are laid to split the rock and make the river turn as required and flow over its new bed, something goes wrong, the warning signals do not work, the blast itself is premature, and forty men, most of them tribals, are killed. Two of the dead are caught in the river. The dead bodies cannot be recovered because a boulder has jammed them. While Mackendrick and others debate about the possibilities of recovery of the corpses, Clinton ruthlessly suggests:

> *Rather than delay the work, the bodies could be*
> *incorporated into the structure.*[69]

The suggestion infuriates the workers and gives rise to racial conflict. The Indian workers insist that the bodies be recovered. Under their leader, Krishnan, they threaten to strike. They quote the precedents when the bodies of the two British workers were recovered and work remained suspended for two days. Krishnan reminds Rawlings and the other English officers of the callous difference in their treatment and tells them that it should be "a simple matter of equality the same done to us as to you."[70]

The points have been made effectively and the episode displays the novelist's perfect understanding of racial tension. Clinton has no option but to yield and Bashiam is asked to operate the newly repaired crane to lift the boulder and release the trapped corpses. Driven by a fatal instinct, Bashiam does the job. The crane being defective falls across the land and water and involves Bashiam in its fall. He barely escapes death, and although not his old self, he hopes to be employed again. Helen charges her husband pointedly:

> *He (Bashiam) was not told and could not know,*
> *since it was a concealed defect (in the Crane).*[71]

Clinton's reply is: "I did not wish to destroy", but when Helen asks him if he is sure, he does not reply. This gives rise to two questions: has Clinton out of jealousy, laid the trap? Clinton could have averted the possible danger by not giving him permission to operate the defective crane but instead of preventing Bashiam, he simply asks him: "Do you wish to go on?"[72] So that he may not be accused afterwards.

When Mackendrick reminds Clinton that it is against safety regulations to operate without the safe load indicator, he had a callous response:

"He knows what he is doing"[73]

In the end, when Clinton writes his report he does not mention the faulty lugs, which proves that he has a guilt conscience. The second question is: has Bashiam, out of a vague sense of guilt, half deliberately walked into the trap? It is not loyalty to his tribe that makes him volunteer to haul the jammed bodies off the rock; he instead "would have withdrawn (notwithstanding his people, and obligations through them) but that the shadow fell that was Clinton's, whose wife he had taken, to whom a debt was owed."[74] If this second question really carries some truth Ramesh Chadha opines that through her portrayal of the Clinton - Bashiam relationship, Markandaya has poignantly brought out the temperamental differences between the West and the East... the West is calculative and rational, whereas the East is emotional and sentimental[75], he is not at all wrong.

Far from presenting only the theme of East-West encounter or the problem of industrialization, the novel goes beyond "these stereotype themes to present a larger than life abstraction – man's indomitable will that stops at nothing to gain its goal. *The Coffer Dams* is about Howard Clinton, a builder with a steel will who drives every one – himself most ruthlessly of all – into completing a preoject."[76]

Clinton is single – minded in pursuit of his goal and is determined to put his strength against the "formidable natural hazards of the scheme" of building a dam across the untamed river, and nothing is going to prevent him, not the unreliability of rail and road transportation, not the rebelliousness of the workers, not even the savage fury of the monsoon. He is impersonal to the point of inhumanity. His obsession with his work results in the loss of his capacity for a whole gamut of emotions. He is an example of the Western pragmatist with no care for humanistic concerns in professional works. In one scene:

> *Clinton frowned. But what weight if any… could attach to the words of a people who worshipped birds and beasts and probably snakes, decking the forest with scruffy hutches which they knocked up out of driftwood and crammed with leaves and flowers for their deities?*[77]

His apathy for social upliftment is also quite resonant in the following statement:

> *"What's the good of telegrams? Half these johnnies can't read!"*[78]

Also, he feels like "the country's getting (him) down."[79] Hence, the individual element in his personality is greatly weakened. His disciplinary action of cutting everyone's pay as penalty for pilfering his callous decision to incorporate the bodies of two tribal workers in the dam and his stubbornness in refusing to allow for human failings such as physical and mental fatigue and, in the end, his refusal to breach the coffer dams though there is danger of the whole tribal village being washed away, are some of the glaring examples of his indifference to human pain and suffering. As against Clinton, Mackendrick has been portrayed as an ideal man, a counter- balance to Clinton, combining the qualities of hard work and leadership with considerable leniency. He is perspective enough to understand the various complexes nurtured by the Indians; compassionate enough to feel touched by every mishap suffered by others. As Mackendrick is observed here in introspective mood:

> *In a hundred years... In a generation, less, they've been sprung from Stone Age into space age.*[80]

Or, Mackendrick appears too amiable when he reflects on the death of his teammates:

> *How maudlin one became about dying in a foreign land.*[81]

And, it is true that "Mackendrick had no strong feelings either way, but he was not walled off from the feel of the country."[82]

Clinton is, whereas, not a stereotype, he is an individual motivated by a kind of ambition that transcends the material. Clinton personifies the forces of ambition and Ḥelen personifies the forces of humanitarianism. Clinton and Helen are two distinct personalities standing poles apart and pitted against each other. Helen at one point thinks:

> *It was as if they were walking on different levels: he on the flyover, she on the underpass.*[83]

The author's final identification is with Helen. Emotionally, Helen cannot subscribe to Clinton's view, but intellectually she can. That is why she can understand his preoccupation with his work. Both are strong characters, fiercely independent, both hate superficialities, scorn formalities, ignore conventions and are impelled by a sense of higher abstraction. Their concrete goals are different but the inner force is the same. Helen intellectually knows it from "the noxious emotional cauldron that Britain the ruler and India the ruled had kept on the boil throughout the term of an imposed overlordship, to the humiliations of being an underdeveloped and pauper nation."[84]

Also,

> *History, for her (Helen) still lay largely between the covers of a book… It was only now, lodging on Indian soil, that the first intimation came that between them Howard Clinton, and Krishnan, and Bashiam, Rawlings, and Mackendrick as well, were illuminating the pages.*[85]

As to ignore conventions and formalities, Helen wishes to leave for an Indian excursion without any European colouring. She wishes to be plain, unwritten with any prejudiced scribbling over the sub-conscious zone of her mind:

> *Helen's initial excursion to the up- river village had been alone. This was partly intentional for she liked keeping her first impressions uncluttered, her visual images free of tags like interesting or charming that the formulae of conversational exchange might slung round their necks.*[86]

Helen seems to be absolutely awestricken and overwhelmingly charmed by the bewitching Indian beauty:

> *Its density, the rampant furious growth, affected her in a way that the ordered charm of a restrained civilization would never do. After a little she opened the door, and stepped out into the blackness where the shadows of the first trees fell and deepened the night.*[87]

Helen was warned "not to drink their polluted water, reminded her they were in tiger country."[88]
And,

> *Occasionally when he (Clinton) wanted her (Helen) and she wasn't there he wished she was more like them (Indian tribe) ubiquitous, conformist and predictable.*[89]

And no doubt, Indian climate is, too soothing for her. She herself accepts,

> *It must be the climate. It agrees with me.*[90]

Then, there is Bashiam, tribal by birth and upbringing but trained in the urban industrialized world. Rather than Clinton's antithesis, he is his alter ego. He too is fiercely independent, an outsider to his class, is impelled by super-human abstractions. He speaks and acts exactly like Clinton because, as Helen notes, the dam means as much to him as it does to Clinton. Both Bashiam and Clinton live by and for their principles. Once Bashiam had revealed his philosophy when intrigued by Helen:

> *Machines …have given me another way of life.*[91]

The old way of life held nothing for him.

Further, the author, along with Bashiam, is conscious of the fact:

> *He (Bashiam) knew he no longer belonged in the tribal huts of birth.*[92]

It is not loyalty or love or material ambition that moves them to take up challenges, but principles. For Clinton, the coffer dams have to be built before the monsoon, and he does every thing that has to be done to complete them:

> *There were indeed no limits, no frontiers which he would not cross or extend so long as the power lay with him…*[93]

As Mackendrick observes:

> *…he seemed to miss out somewhere on the human level.*[94]

And Helen also accuses him of being inhumane:

> *"Don't human beings matter anything to you? Do they have to be a special kind of flesh before they do?"*[95]

The dams, nearly complete, face the threat of being destroyed by the oncoming monsoon. Clinton wants to complete them at any cost. The rains have already started in the upper reaches of the mountain range leaving them four days in which the last pillar of cement is to be erected. Four days of round- the -clock work would complete it. But suddenly, an accident takes place in which 40 workers are killed, two of them jammed between boulders. The arrogance with which Clinton at first refuses to respect the Indian sentiments of the native workers is symbolic not only of the Western push in technology but also of their double standard. In the earlier accident, in which the victims were British, the bodies were retrieved. At that time Krishnan had said:

> *They (Hindu scriptures) teach us that the body is nothing, it is the spirit that matters.*[96]

But now he is the leader demanding equal treatment for the dead Indians, Clinton does not think that their demand is reasonable:

> *I do not understand such preoccupation over something which is lifeless and irrelevant when there is so much at stake.*[97]

There are two ways of looking at the incident. One is that Clinton is a dehumanized monster and the other is that there is really too much at stake. To Clinton, the dam is the living embodiment of man's indomitable Will, and since Will is the power that keeps man above chaos and the degradation of human weaknesses, the dam has to be saved whatever the price.

Clinton himself knows that the final responsibility is his, not Bashiam's. It shows how the public image is different from the private in Clinton's code of conduct. Bashiam goes ahead, shuts off the safety load indicators and releases the bodies by making the crane lift a weight too heavy for safe functioning. Then the jib breaks and Bashiam is crushed hip downwards in his driver's cage. Clinton writes his report making no reference to the faulty lugs. But his conscience tears him apart. It becomes an encounter with himself in which he sees his own guilt as an object. Helen also accuses him of having withheld that part of information from Bashiam. She reiterated,

> *He was not told, and could not know, since it*
> *was a concealed defect.*[98]

Again this has been interpreted in two ways by many critics – Clinton has withheld the information not because the builder in him has pushed him to clutch at the last straw, but because the jealous husband in him has wanted the lover to risk his life. But I perceive it in different perspective. Clinton's behavioral pattern can simply be a by- product of a Utilitarian society in which Clinton had got his nourishment. No wonder, Helen drifts away from Clinton because he lacks certain qualities which she thinks are essential in a human being. The novel leaves the three characters severed from each other: Bashiam, still strong, husbands his strength so that he can start again where he has left if off, Helen glowing with "some gaiety of spirit" and a wholeness of vision, and Clinton standing over the coffer dams "where formidable ribs rose bleached and clean in the washed air above the turbulent river."[99]

Each has paid a heavy price but each has won a victory in his or her own way.

With the death of the unnamed tribal chief and the clearing of the sky, the parallel plots coalesce into a unified one. Helen, who has gone through an awareness of all possible layers of social intercourse, ends her affair with Bashiam, now a helpless cripple and returns to Clinton. Here, Helen does not seem to be a baron of post-Simone de Beauvoir world, rather her morality and sublime character goes back either to the Victorian England or the contemporary Indian society. She is also to move away as the project has been completed and Bashiam, after recovery would also move on to some other project elsewhere in the country. In response to the question about his future plan Bashiam replies,

> *'I shall go too,… there are many projects. It is a big country.'*[100]

The plot finally makes us aware of the great depths of a seemingly ordinary tale: the construction of a dam, an Indo-British project, and the liaison of an English woman with a tribal crane operator, the skillful way in which Markandaya weaves a conflict of sensibilities and attitudes makes it more than a tale of racial prejudice, a pulsating record of human suffering and cultural consciousness against the backdrop of the formidable elements of Nature.

Like her earlier novels, this novel also has three facets, namely, a personal story, a wider conflict, and a social background. Here, the focus is on Helen who is caught between two radically different systems of values, beliefs and attitudes. It is her story around which are woven the stories of her husband, Clinton and the wider social circle of the British technocracy.

The structure of the novel is built against the Indian backdrop so that the confrontation between the Eastern and Western values is poignantly brought about and the handling of the situations is effectively authentic and clearly relevant to the theme of the novel. Just like *Heat and Dust* by Jhabvala, *The Coffer Dams* centers on a European couple in India. Both the men, Douglas Rivers and Clinton, are responsible officers, always busy with official duties. Olivia and Helen, sensitive and emotional by nature, suffer form alienation and seek some moments of relief in the company of nature. Olivia falls in love with the Nawab and Helen with Bashiam. Olivia's love affair results in her pregnancy, and leaving Douglas, she goes to live with the Nawab, whereas Helen's love affair results in her disillusionment. Both the men are insensitive to their wives' feelings. They believe that they should mechanically follow the ways of the older generation.

> *Follow established custom… and behave like the other women on the station do.*[101]

Both want their wives to be conformists. They do love their wives and try to keep them comfortable, but they hardly realize that their company may also be essential for them. Rather than treating them as individuals, they treat them as "objects" and wish to see them nicely dressed and impatiently waiting for them, primarily because they are high officers ruling over the subordinates and treat their wives also as such.

> *As India is not their motherland, they are not rooted in the cultural heritage of India. Olivia*

> *and Helen are both non-conformists and want to*
> *have their own way. The male protagonists are*
> *conservative and do everything according to the*
> *traditional way.*[102]

Unlike their husbands, they have inquisitive minds and are keen to learn about Indian culture and traditions. For this, Olivia takes the help of the Nawab and Helen that of Bashiam. Helen goes to the jungle all alone and sometimes in the company of Bashiam, and Olivia goes to the shrines of Baba Firdaus in the company of the Nawab. These men act as their guides to India and show them round. These women's frequent meetings with their guides lead to their intimacy and they develop relations which bring them sorrow and suffering. Indeed, in both these novels sex becomes an instrument of disaster.

Both the female protagonists like India and their lovers. Olivia loves Douglas and comes to live with the Nawab and lives in India for the rest of her life. Helen also likes India. She remarks, "It must be the climate. It agrees with me."[103]

In the end, Helen goes to see the chief of the natives, leaving Clinton alone; she cannot accommodate with her husband's views. The final meeting between them is dramatic and suggestive:

> *Clinton and Helen stood face to face unable to*
> *accept each other's views.*[104]

Each heroine feels (like Mrs. Kaul in *A Backward Place*, like "a bird in a gilded cage." Naturally, they cannot be happy together. Thus, the two novelists attempt to explore "the anguish of human and personal in the modern society."[105]

The two novels describe "the breakdown of a traditional social orders, thereby, highlighting the alienation or isolation between one individual and another in marital relations, in family life, in the society at large."[106]

It is a story not merely of Clinton versus the Indians or Clinton versus Helen, who has identified herself with the Indian sensibility. It is, in fact, a clash between the East and the West, and all the theories of individualism, materialism and technology stem from the West; the East cannot but twitch at the continued indifference to the values of human relationships in the race for progress.

Again and again, this is what Markandaya tries to voice: the human sensibilities are important, that the cultural castings do not make any difference to the importance of human relationships.

Undoubtedly, Kamala Markandaya brings out the various points of weakness and strength of both the cultures. She looks at the West through the eyes of the East and looks at the East through the eyes of the West. The setting may be England or India, city or village. She brings out the barriers of arrogance, colour and cultural differences that keep the East and the West apart; she tries to bring about a reconciliation of the two. C.D. Narasimhaiah rightly concludes:

> *Generally her novels reflect her strong penchant for Indian values as against the spiritual impoverishment of the English society, but Indians are not spared. Actually her good men and women come form both culture.*[107]

The Coffer Dams in some ways a revision of Kipling's *The Bridge - Builders*, once again explores the possibility of bridging the gap between the two modes and cultures, and once again comes up with a primarily negative response.

From the start, we see Howard Clinton as an arch realist and pragmatist, who has no sympathy for the mythic, spiritual propensities of the local people. Mackendrick is passionate about the mythic beliefs of the natives who were going to be displaced due to the building of the dam.

Several incidents and crises involving Anglo-Indian relations put Clinton and Helen on opposing sides, initiating a rift between husband and wife that comes to symbolize the ever-widening gulf between the British and the natives (with Helen as defender of the natives' rights) that, in the end, threatens to destroy the very project itself. But in this opposition very subtly lies the element of cultural allotropy. Although, Helen and Clinton both belong to the same part of the globe, their response to Indian culture is quite different. Clinton, being adamant fuelled by his false pride, is unable to be modest towards the native folks and his 'guilt consciousness' of his exploitative venture is merely a skin-deep concern whereas Helen loves to wear skin-tight Indian morality. She has accepted the Indian culture in its totality along with its language.

Bashiam, on the other hand, enamoured as he is of Western machines and of the Western mode of realism, has chosen to cut himself off from his tribe and their mythic, spiritual base. He is thus doubly an outcast, both from his tribe as well as from the people he works for. But, can we not see undercurrents of his Indian 'id', in his actions, which is world acclaimed for its hospitality? Bashiam - well exposed to the western development - becomes a cultural allotrope – doubly mis-identified.

The alienation of Helen and Bashiam from their communities is repeatedly stressed in the novel, obviously to convey the author's view that social rebels make it so in the East-West allotropy.

In *The Coffer Dams*, Markandaya thus goes into yet another sphere of race and culture contact, and lends weight to her skeptical attitude towards inter-racial and cross-cultural understanding by bringing to bear new explorations upon the subject of her study.

References:

1. O.P. Saxena. *Glimpses of Indo-English Fiction*. New Delhi: Jainsons Publication, 1985. p. 192.
2. As quoted in Jaydipsing K. Dodiya's *"East-West Encounter In Kamala Markandaya's Novels"*, *Indian Women Writers*.ed. R.K. Dhawan. New Delhi: Prestige, 2001. pp.56 – 57.
3. R.S. Singh. *Indian Novel in English: A Critical Study*. New Delhi: Arnold – Heinemann, 1977, p.136.
4. Kamala Markandaya. *The Coffer Dams*. Great Britain: Hamish Hamilton, 1969., p. 217.
5. *ibid.*, p.9.
6. P.S. Chauhan. *Kamala Markandaya: Sense and Sensibility*, Literary Criterion, 12, Nos.2 – 3 1976. p. 34 – 137.
7. Shyam M. Asnani. *Character and Techniques in Kamala Markandaya's Novel. Rajasthan University Studies in English*. 11.1978, p.72.
8. Kamala Markandaya. *The Coffer Dams*. op.cit., p. 10.
9. *ibid.*, p.8.
10. *ibid.*, p.8.
11. *ibid.*, p. 98.
12. *ibid.*, p.29.
13. *ibid.*, p.15.
14. *ibid.*, p.35.
15. *ibid.*, p.35.
16. Shyam A. Asnani. *East and West Encounter in Kamala Markandaya's Novels*. TRIVENI. 48, No. 4.January – March, 1980.p.23.
17. Kamala Markandaya. *The Coffer Dams*, op.cit., p.12.
18. *ibid.*, p.12.
19. *ibid.*, p. 7.
20. ibid., p.11.
21. Ramesh Chadha. *Cross – Cultural Interaction In India English Fiction*. New. Delhi: National Book Organization, 1988. p. 55.

22. Kamala Markandaya. *The Coffer Dams,* op. cit., p.152.
23. *ibid.,* p.18.
24. *ibid.,* p. 62.
25. *ibid.,* p. 93.
26. *ibid.,* p.10.
27. *ibid.,* p. 99.
28. *ibid.,* p. 62.
29. *ibid.,* p.19.
30. *ibid.,* p. 62.
31. *ibid.,* p. 80
32. *ibid.,* pp.22 – 23.
33. *ibid.,* p.48
34. *ibid.,* p. 44.
35. *ibid.,* p. 95.
36. *ibid.,* p. 35
37. *ibid.,* p. 35
38. *ibid.,* p. 46
39. *ibid.,* p. 81
40. *ibid.,* p. 81
41. *ibid.,* p.134
42. *ibid.,* p.136
43. *ibid.,* p.105
44. *ibid.,* p.105
45. *ibid,* p.104.
46. Rama Jha. *"Kamala Markandaya: An Overview". Perspective of Indian Fiction in English.* Ed., M.K. Naik. New Delhi: Abhinav Publication, 1985. p.169.
47. Kamala Markandaya. *The Coffer Dams.* op. cit., p. 98
48. *ibid.,* p. 73
49. Rochelle Almeida. *"Characters and their Indianness In the Novels of Kalama Markandaya." Novels of Kamala Markandaya.*eds. Nilufer E. Bharucha and Vrinda Nabar. Delhi: Vision Books, 1998. p. 334.
50. Kamala Markandaya. *The Coffer Dams.,* op.cit. p. 461.
51. *ibid.,* p. 61

52. Kai Nicholson. *A Presentation of Social Problems in the Indo-Anglian and the Anglo-Indian Novel*. Bombay: Jaico Publishing House, 1972. p.169.

53. Kamala Markandaya. *The Coffer Dams*. op. cit p. – 38

54. Harish Raizada. *"East – West Confrontation in the Novels of Kamala Markandaya"*. *Perspectives on Kamala Markandya*. Ed. Madhusudan Prasad. Ghaziabad: Vimal Prakashan, 1984. p. 61.

55. Kalama Markandaya. *The Coffer Dams*. op. cit. p.38.

56. Paul Scott. *The Raj*. New Delhi: Vikas Publishing House, 1974. p.84.

57. Kamala Markandaya. *The Coffer Dams*. op. cit., p. 136.

58. *ibid.*, p. 138.

59. *ibid.*, p. 48.

60. *Ibid.* p. 49.

61. *Journal of South Asian Literature*. Vol.- X, No. – 1, *Fall*, 1974. p. 91.

62. Rochelle Almeida. *Novels of Kamala Markandaya*. op. cit., p.346.

63. Kamala Markandaya. *The Coffer Dams*. op. cit., p. 54.

64. *ibid.*, p. 177.

65. Ramesh Chadha. *Cross Cultural Interaction in Indian English Fiction*. op. cit., p. 58.

66. Kamala Markandaya. *The Coffer Dams*. op. cit., p.18.

67. *ibid.*, p. 51.

68. *ibid.*, p. 51.

69. *ibid.*, p.163.

70. *ibid.*, p.179.

71. *ibid.*, p.195.

72. *ibid.*, p.185.

73. *ibid.*, p.188.

74. *ibid.*, p.183.

75. Ramesh Chadha. *Cross Cultural Interaction In Indian English Fiction*. op. cit., p. 59.

76. Uma Parmeshwaram. *"Native Alien and Expatriates – Kamala Markandaya and Balchandra Rajan". A Study of Representative Indo- English Novelists.* New Delhi: Vikas Publishing House, 1976.p.109.

77. Kamala Markandaya. *The Coffer Dams.* op. cit., p. 76.

78. *ibid.,* p. 73.

79. *ibid.,* p. 77.

80. *ibid.,* p. 54.

81. *ibid.,* p. 120.

82. *ibid.,* p. 62.

83. *ibid.,* p. 100.

84. *ibid.,* p. 43.

85. *ibid.,* p. 43.

86. *ibid.,* p. 41.

87. *ibid.,* p. 29.

88. *ibid.,* p. 25.

89. *ibid.,* p. 25.

90. *ibid.,* p. 65.

91. *ibid.,* p. 46.

92. *ibid.,* p. 47.

93. *ibid.,* p. 217.

94. *ibid.,* p. 63,

95. *ibid.,* p. 105.

96. *ibid.,* p. 113.

97. *ibid.,* p. 181.

98. *ibid.,* p. 195

99. *ibid.,* p. 222.

100. *ibid.,* p. 203.

101. *ibid.,* p. 78.

102. Ramesh Chadha. *Cross – Cultural Interaction In Indian English Fiction.* op. cit., p. 64.

103. Kamala Markandaya. *The Coffer Dams.* op.cit., p. 65.

104. R.S. Singh. *Indian Novel in English.* op. cit. p. 142.

105. Yudhishtar. *Conflicts In the Novels of D.H. Lawrence.* Edinburgh: Oliver Boyd, 1967. p. 45.

106. Vasant A. Sahane. *Ruth Prawer Jhabvala*. New Delhi: Arnold Heinemann, 1976.p. 25.

107. As quoted in Jaydipsing K. Dodiya's *"East West Encounter in Kamala Markandaya's Novel"*, op. cit., p. – 57.

Chapter - VI

HEAT AND DUST

To many of her readers, Ruth Prawer Jhabvala is equated with the silks and spices of *Heat and Dust* (1975). In appending her husband's even more exotic name, she has been able to overshadow her own alien origins and her Jewish descent is a surprisingly little known fact, especially in India, where it is enough that she is a westerner in Delhi presuming to comment on Indian country and culture. Nevertheless, perhaps by its very absence, it is central to her writing.

Ruth Prawer Jhabvala was born on May 7, 1927, in Cologne, to a Polish born father and German mother. She married Cyrus Jhabvala in 1951. From 1951 until 1975, she lived in India, but moved to New York City in 1975. She now holds a dual (British-American) citizenship. Her awards include the Booker Prize for *Heat and Dust* (1975), a Guggenheim Fellowship (1976), a Neil Gunn International Fellowship (1978) and a MacArthur Fellowship (1984).

Jhabvala was, in her own words, "practically born a displaced person." (Gooneratne) Her passage to India was an inversion of the immigrant's move from east to west, but while the country's poverty and corruption rankled with her sense of social justice (India remains for her a "great animal of poverty and backwardness" as she explains in *Myself in India*), she found life there "much closer to the Jewish world" and came across very Jewish attitudes towards, for example, the ritual of food, which often features in her writing. But even by marriage, Jhabvala was an outsider, since her husband was a Parsee, a member of a generally well - educated and prosperous ethnic group whose position in Indian society is not dissimilar to that of the Jews in Europe.

In *Myself in India* Jhabvala writes, "I'm absolutely passive, like blotting paper," explaining elsewhere: "Not really having a world of my own, I made up for my disinheritance by absorbing the worlds of others." Just as she captured the Anglo-Indian experience so comprehensively in *Heat and Dust*, so her many successful screenplays, including *Howards End* and A *Room with a View,* written for Merchant-Ivory (both of which won Academy Awards), evoke an England more English than it ever was.

Ruth P. Jhabvala has oozed out all her feelings through the characters- a part of her sub-conscious world. Her characters are voice of her inner world full of conflicts. Her characters are, in fact, her catharsis.

Major Minnies of *Heat and Dust* says in his monograph on the influence of India on the European consciousness and character that "one has to be very determined to withstand – to stand up to – India. And the most vulnerable are always those who love her best....one should never allow oneself to become softened by an excess of feeling."[1]

The novel studies the impact of India on the European consciousness, as it presents the experiences of two different generations unfolded mainly through the parallel love stories of two "softened" English women, separated by a span of fifty years. "It reveals that the essential nature of the impact has not changed, that the Western woman who loves India is equally vulnerable irrespective of her situation, that this country with its heat and dust affects the westerners in similar ways and that there is an essential continuity in spite of all the changes."[2]

The parallels between the stories of Olivia and the narrator are too clear to need a detailed analysis. In 1923, Olivia an English woman married to Douglas, an English ICS Officer, falls in love with the native Nawab of Khatm who is temporarily separated from his Indian wife Sandy. (She has always been called 'Sandy' - an anglicized version - though her real name is Zahira[3]). Fifty years later, Miss Rivers (the narrator), another English woman living with an Englishman Chid ('Chid' is an anglicized version of an Indian name "Chidananda" of an Englishman who adopted Hinduism during his stay in India), falls for Inder Lal, an English clerk whose wife also remains away for a length of time. The houses of both the Nawab and Inder Lal are looked after in the traditional manner by their mothers. A significant role in Olivia's life is played by Harry, the sick Englishman, who helps to bring her and the Nawab together.

While the latter story does not have an exact counterpart to Harry, Chid, who is mostly sick, and who, like Harry has finally been sent back to England, does embody many similar traits and functions. Again, just as the Crawfords, Minnies and Saunders constantly warn Olivia against the Indians, Old Missionary and the Europeans who have lived longer in India perpetually ask her to be cautious in this country. Major Minnies and Dr. Saunders have direct learning on this subject, as it is evident from the following passage:

> *Although the major was so sympathetic to India, his [monograph] sounds like a warning ... There are many ways of loving India, many things to love her for – the scenery, the history, the poverty, the music, and indeed the physical beauty of men and women – but all.... are dangerous for the European India ... finds out the weak spot and presses on it. It is there that India sucks them out and pulls them over into .... the other dimension... it is all very well to love and admire India – intellectually, aesthetically, ...sexually ....but always with a virile, measured, European feeling. One should never.... allow oneself to become softened (like Indians) by an excess of feeling because the moment that happens – the moment one exceeds one's measure – one is in danger of being dragged over to the other side.*[4]

Both Olivia and Miss Rivers find similar pictures of heat, dust, sickness, misery, poverty, dishonesty and deformity in India[5] and they are both entertained by their future lovers to the dance of eunuchs. Both the Nawab and Inder Lal think that they are faced with a lot of intrigues. "Both the English women first visit the shrine of Baba Firdaus in the company of their future Indian lovers who are accompanied by their friends and relatives. At the same shrine during the later visits, the love is consummated. In addition, there are many other minor parellels."[6]

Meenakshi Mukherjee writes that in *Heat and Dust* for the first time Ruth Prawer Jhabvala added "an extra dimension of time to her fiction – going back to the past for the confirmation of a pattern that she had traced so far only in terms of contemporary India."[7]

A more subtle version of this technique is to be seen in the film *The Autobiography of An Indian Princess* which James Ivory directed as mentioned above, and for which Jhabvala wrote the script. The parallel between the two stories (of Olivia's and the Narrator's) appears mechanical, but in the novel it is suggested more subtly. It is only slowly that the reader is made to realize that the surface might look different but deep down, the insidious change that India works on its foreign visitors remains unaltered.

How India metamorphoses the foreigner; is one of the themes of the novel. Even a typical Westerner like Olivia is also forced to reshape her attitude towards Indian culture. She advocates the Indian Culture:

> "… *it* is *their culture and who are we to interfere with anyone's culture especially an ancient one like theirs!*"[8]

Even if the whole lot of the Westerners cry along with Dr. Saunders:

> "*Culture! You've been talking to that bounder Horsham!*"[9]

We accept the fact that "*India always changes people*"[10] and there have been no exception as the narrator Ms. Rivers, too, confesses the truth.

The word "culture" is derived from the word "cultivate" which means to grow, to develop and to expand. Thus, growth of life according to set traditions and values of the land is the culture of the country. It is the sum total of the way of living built up by a group or groups of human beings and transferred from one generation to another. In brief,

> *Culture is the sum total of everything that is created, as modified through conscious or unconscious behavior of two or more interacting individuals.*[11]

The two central women characters, present the conflict of cultures at political and racial levels with emphasis on the difference between the past and the present. Olivia and the narrator – each very English in her own time, each allowing her India to captivate her. The dilemma of these two is the author's own as Jhabvala admits, "I don't know India". The leading problem for her is "to show how a European adapts to India."[12]

This adaptation is possible not by conquering but by getting conquered. That is why Olivia and the narrator stay back in India. Jhabvala employs the fictional flashbacks between 1923 and 1970 to bring out the cultural clash. The 1923 chunk of the novel seems to be superficially moving around a racio-politic conflict where the Douglouses, Crawfords, Saunders and Major Minnies make one group; the Nawab and his retinue the other; Harry and Olivia remain at the hinges as Orientals and occidentals both.

The first part of the novel shows the clash of personalities who belong to the two races and had a different cultural heritage. The Nawab had a dominating personality. None can resist him and his commands. Harry's impression of the

Nawab mesmerizes Olivia and when he informs her that the Nawab "most particularly wants (her) to come,"[13] Olivia's mind is psychologically conditioned. And, when she visits the Nawab's house for the first time, she feels that 'she had, at last come to the right place."[14]

It becomes apparent that Olivia liked India and its people, the restrictive influence of the British Raj is notwithstanding. She aspired to present a symbol of cultural unification and never subscribed to the opinion of other Europeans who say that they came to find peace but all they found here was 'dysentery'.

Jhabvala in the introduction to *An Experience of India* records three types of reactions of the Europeans to the Indian set - up. "The first stage is tremendous enthusiasm about Indian and everything Indian, the second stage that everything Indian is not so marvelous and the third stage that everything Indian is abominable.[15]

The narrator, an English woman in her twenties, who has come to India in the hope of finding out more about life led in India by her grandfather's wife, is at stage one. She accepts the sick and deformed citizens of Satipur as part of the landscape. Olivia, who is at stage one, accepts drumming and chanting as a part of Indian life whereas Harry begins to see "like brain fever and feels he cannot stand it another day."[16]

Mrs. Saunders is clearly at stage three; she nourishes sexual fantasies about her Indian servants and cultivates an abnormal fear of Indian sexuality. It is quite evident from the story she narrates to Olivia:

> *There was one lady in Muzzafarabad or one of those places – she was a lady from Somerset ...*

> *Her dhobi… was ironing her undies and it*
> *must have been too much for him. They're very*
> *excitable, it's their constitution. I've heard their*
> *spicy food's got something to do with it… they've*
> *got only one thought in their heads and that's to*
> *you -know – what with a white woman.*[17]

There are many other things which depict the cultural interaction very aptly. There are other facets also which attract and disturb Europeans about India. They feel intrigued over Indian's response to magical incantations, superstitions, Suttee system and sturdy- looking Sadhus.

It is not only Chid who has been fascinated by Indian spiritualism "after attending a lecture by a visiting Swami in London… In his case the original attraction had come through the Hindu scriptures."[18]

Even Indian superstitions have their own trademark and copyrights. It does not find place in any other country across the globe. And, it sets off the Westerners bewilderment especially when they find that even the figures like Begum, representing a progressive and an affluent society of India, very often puts her journey off for "either she's not feeling well or the stars are not right for journey or an owl hooted at the wrong time – it's always something or other and always at the last moment"[19] when everyone is all packed and ready. The erstwhile existing suttee system which was, indeed, barbaric caught the Westerns' attention in amazement. While describing the mental state of Inderlal's mother, Mrs. Rivers records,

> *…on certain days of the year, she and her friends*
> *come with sweets, milk and flowers to worship*

> *these widows who have made the highest sacrifice.*
> *She sounded really respectful and seemed to have*
> *the greatest reverence for that ancient custom.*[20]

Even the progressive ruler like the Nawab seems frustrated at times. The Nawab, on one occasion, shrugged in commiseration:

> *What is to be done, Mr. Rivers. These people will*
> *never learn. Whatever we do, they will still cling*
> *to their barbaric customs.* [21]

The East - West relationship is not a new theme in Indo-Anglian or Anglo - Indian or Indian English fiction; it is as old as the Indo-English relations. But "what is significant about *Heat and Dust* is that it deals with the experiences of two socially different Western generations in India".[22] It clearly demarcates and underlines the cultural changes through the dimension of time India has gone through, if any. But at the end of the novel, like the anonymous Narrator of the novel, we find ourselves back at the square one; the puzzle remains unsolved. But she emerges an expectant mother with a rich store of experiences. The narrator does not (and we should also do the same) interpret Olivia's India for us or evaluate Olivia's actions in moral or cultural terms. At best she tries to relive Olivia's experiences in an attempt at a better understanding of Olivia and India.

Olivia comes to India in the traditional role of a live partner to the sub-collector of Satipur, Douglas Rivers. She loves him deeply but gets bored just keeping at home with servants at her beck and call especially the condition in which she lives is suffocating:

The rest of the time Olivia was alone in her big house with all the doors and windows shut to keep out the heat and dust.[23]

Even her husband, Douglas feels the same when Olivia asked him very innocently what is wrong with her:

I told you: it's the heat. No English woman is meant to stand it. [24]

True that in India, "shortly before the monsoon, the heat becomes very intense."[25]

One finds it difficult to understand how an aesthetic and idealist as Olivia could fall for the Nawab. Perhaps, it was her love and fascination for India which lay deeply in her sub-conscious mind and that worked behind this attachment. In the presence of Douglas she reflects his virtues, loses touch with reality and rises to the highest plane of idealism. In the Nawab's company, she is a mere victim of his "magnetism" or "irresistible force of nature." She remembered how Harry had once told her "you don't say 'no' to a person like him."[26] And, found it to be true.

Conscience does not pose a problem for her. Sometimes it is super Ego that holds her ruins, at other moments Id takes complete possession of her. "Douglas and the Nawab are the externalization of her Super Ego and Id respectively."[27]

Jhabvala romanticizes Olivia's world with a highly colourful setting to suit her emotional temper and downgrades the narrator's world as a shoddy one. For Harry and Olivia, the experience of India is limited to the Nawab. With the Nawab entering her life Olivia had unconsciously given up playing the piano. Both Olivia and the Narrator became pregnant. But Olivia's Indian experience is abortive whereas the narrator's is enriching.

According to critics like Shahane, India is the real heroine of the novel. Jhabvala devotes most of the passages in the novel to a discussion of India and its effect on the Westerners. What is striking about these discussions and observations is that an outsider sees India from the inside. O.P. Saxena has rightly observed:

> *Jhabvala who seems to have been influenced by the Upanishads, the Gita, the teachings of Rama Krishna Paramhansa, of the Mother and of Ramana Maharishi does not spare a moment in satirizing the pseudo religionists, the fake swamis and the Bais of India. To Jhabvala, the places where they dwell are seats of corruption. Her young characters loudly proclaim that 'God does not need temples or priests, the ringing of bells, the clash of cymbals … He needs love and pure heart' (The House Holder, 131).*[28]

The people who continue to stay in India without fretting are presented as the real tough ones. Miss Tietz who has stayed on for thirty years is viewed as an unearthly person. Unless there is strong sense of duty or call of God it is impossible to pull on:

> *She has lived only in His will….. You can't live in India without Christ Jesus.* [29]

Douglous is certainly a seeker for whom India symbolizes the call for duty. Even the intimate moments, "flooded and shining in Indian moonlight", shared with Olivia bring happiness. The narrator herself is a seeker who claims to be interested in the simpler and more natural way of life as opposed to the materialistic West.

Mrs. Saunders's psychological inability to see anything good in India makes her an eternal sufferer. Mrs. Saunder could only see:

> ... (Indians) thieving, drinking and other bad habits. ... the filth in which they lived inside their quarters .... the whole town, the lanes and bazaars and ...their heathen temples?[30]

"Willy, let's go" – cry is absolutely western for them who, like Mrs. Saunder, cannot survive amidst the Indian slumdogs. She sees:

> There are crowds of people, some are sleeping – it's so warm that all they have to do is to stretch out, no bedding necessary. There are a number of crippled children (one boy propelling himself on his legless rumps) and probably by day they beg but now they are off duty and seem to be light – hearted, even gay. People are buying from the hawkers and standing there eating, while others are looking in the gutters to find what has been thrown away. [31]

Westerners like Mrs. Saunder cannot brave a country where there is "Hindu – Muslim riot", "small pox epidemics" and "several famines". It is ladies like Mrs. Saunders, Mrs. Crawford and Mrs. Minnies who, though they call themselves "old hens" and claim to lead "a cheerful and undaunted life" are the kind who follow the annual ritual ('April to September') of going to Simla to get themselves recharged with fresh lease of energy. That is their way of coming to terms with the physical reality of India, which is essentially all "heat and dust".

Jhabvala points out that though attempts are made on both sides, it is next to impossible to cross all cultural barriers. Even the narrator who feels absorbed by the society is happy to be with Inder Lal in the dark as darkness obliterates their differences. She narrates:

> *Inder Lal and I lie on my bedding on the opposite side, and it is more and more delightful to be with him .... I think he prefers to be with me when it is dark. Then everything is hidden and private between us two alone. Also I feel it makes a difference that he cannot see me, for I'm aware that my appearance had always been a stumbling block to him. In the dark... he let himself go completely... I don't mean only physically (though that too) but everything there is in him - all his affection and playfulness. At such times I'm reminded of all those stories that are told of the child Krishna and the many pranks and high spirited tricks he got up to. I also think of my pregnancy and I think of it as part of him.[32]*

Despite all social cordiality the Westerners have their preconceived notions about the East and vice-versa. This intersection of culture has been beautifully observed and described by the novelist:

> *The water channels intersecting the lawns*
> *reflected a sky that shifted and sailed with*
> *monsoon clouds.*[33]

Not only the poor wretched fellows of India but even the prejudiced Westerners spare not even the non-living entities like letters which connect people without any prejudice:

> *They (letters) always look as if they have been*
> *travelling great distances and passed through*
> *many hands, absorbing many stains and smells*
> *along the way. Olivia's letters – more than fifty*
> *years old – look as if they had been written*
> *yesterday. It is true, the ink is faint but this may*
> *have been the quality she used to blend with the*
> *delicate lilac colour and scent of her stationery.*
> *The scent still seems to linger. Chid's crumpled*
> *letters, on the other hand, appear soaked in all*
> *the characteristic odour of India, in spices, urine*
> *and betel.*[34]

The spiritual aspect of India is fictionally presented in the character of Chidananda. Jhabvala has absolutely no sympathy with the younger generation of the West that turns to the East in their search for answers. The Westerners are attracted towards them not only because the East has a message to give but also because they are tired of their material west. Some of them come to these so-called holy men and women "to lose themselves in order to find themselves." Hindu religion interests the Westerners. Jhabvala slightly refers to Christianity and Islam but deals at length with the Hindu guides of religion. O.P. Saxena is bold enough to notice that "the Swamis, the sadhus and the Bais of Jhabvala's novels are not always paragons of virtues and intellect or the embodiment of the pure spirit. They are sometimes an odd combination of worldly wisdom and other – worldly charm; they are of the earth, earthy."[35]

Jhabvala's contempt for "Eastward - ho" – runners are clearly revealed when she depicts venomously the European derelicts in A's Hotel, their heads full of lice:

> *...they just sleep on the street. They beg from each other and steal from each other. ... women and men, they've been here for years and every year that get worse. You see the state they're in. They are all sick; some of them are dying .... nothing human means anything here... they did look like souls in hell.*[36]

The entire message that she wishes to convey in a nutshell is that once you get disillusioned with your own culture, you are naturally attracted by anything that is exotic. Unless one has strong roots in one's own culture, it would be hard to observe the good in another culture. The spiritual quest of the modern west that starts owing to disillusionment with their own culture often results in a worse disillusionment. This is seen in the bitterness of the travelers who come in search of "peace and Universal love" fascinated by the "melting eyes" of a sage who talks about 'the oceanic love."

Chid with his "scraps of picked up spiritual love" is a caricatured version of such a spiritual seeker. He has not managed to overcome even simple temptations in life. There is no truth in him. He is dirty, rowdy and steals shamelessly. Jhabvala criticizes the gullibility of the people and points out how even a rationally sound person like the narrator could associate Chid's simple sexual needs with his wanting to use her as an instrument to reach a higher plane of consciousness through the powers of sex. The narrator is, though, conscious and charmed by the Indian mystical concept of sex and salvation, the Shiva Sutra and other things. She is amazed and describes Chid in detail:

> *He is always hungry and not only for food. He also needs sex very badly and seems to take it for granted that I will give to him the same way I give him my food …he admits that this is what he is doing—using me to reach a higher plane of consciousness through the powers of sex that we are engendering between us … I'm reminded of Lord Shiva whose huge number is worshipped by devout Hindu women. At such times it seems to me that his sex is engendered by his spiritual practices… that chanting of mantras… beads in hand on the floor of my room.*[37]

One wonders whether even she is a kind of Westerner who could be swayed into gullibility. The utter helplessness of Chid's condition in the end proves the possibility of "the European feeling the alienation and isolation of Western cities makes a myth of India which if indulged will result in greater alienation and in disintegration of personality."[38]

This is yet another danger a Westerner has to guard against in India. According to Meenakshi Mukherjee:

> *Chid demonstrates the entire gamut of attitudes*
> *from total adoration to absolute hatred which a*
> *foreigner can go through in his relationship with*
> *India.*[39]

Standing just in contrast with Chid, we have Harry, a representative of those European victims, who love India emotionally much against the Major Minnies warnings. Harry is overpowered by the heat of emotions and looks for an "oasis" all the time.

Paul Verghese feels that Jhabvala portrays the fake sadhus because it "enables her to attempt a satirical portrait of India and ridicules the pseudo – romanticism of Indians and the Westerners who are in love with India and come to India seeking spiritual solace."[40]

Almost on the same line, R.S. Singh puts forth his opinion:

> *Marital dissonance in various shades, familial*
> *clashes between the old and the new generations*
> *or the fallen state of spiritual mentors of modern*
> *India, all these situations finally help her project*
> *her own secret non – acceptance of the country*
> *of her adoption.*[41]

Jhabvala also takes pleasure in mocking at the orthodox caste system:

> *When Tikka Ram, a dacoit, is about to be hanged*
> *he cries "Are you a _____?" but could not*
> *finish because the hangman had slipped the hood*
> *over his face. The missing word was probably*

> *"chamar" — he was worried about the caste of the hangman who was performing this last intimate function for him. It was apparently his only worry at that moment of departure.*[42]

By giving the example of Tikka Ram, Jhabvala wants to depict the height of fanaticism so that even at the time of death they are not ready to set aside the idea of caste system which perhaps follows them even after their death and that really makes them a laughing stock throughout the globe. This fanaticism seems to be contagious as even some of the Europeans start believing in orthodoxy. Miss Tietz is one of them who believe that she will die according to the will of God because "You can't live in India without Jesus Christ."[43]

A European is also surprised by the concept of "marriages made in heaven" and match – fixing by horoscopes. We are told that Ritu's marriage to Inder Lal is arranged on the basis of tallying horoscopes. Once we are surprised to see that Inder Lal's mother herself considers the widowhood part as the best part of her life. Inder Lal does not say anything about Ritu's treatment and it seems as if he too is dominated by his mother.

Ritu is mentally upset and she is treated in a non-western manner. The narrator hears the cries of Ritu that is quite audible to the readers as well:

> *A few nights ago there was such a strange sound – a high – pitched wail piercing through the night. It didn't seem like a human sound.*[44]

Inder Lal's mother sprinkles a handful of rice over her in the manner as of doing some act of magic as she has orthodox ideas. But the narrator, as a true representative of modernity and Western outlook is just an anti-thesis to all these Indian stupidity and the orthodoxical complexities. When Inder Lal and the narrator go to the Hindu shrine which the priest "had fixed up for his own worship,"[45] she as a representative of modernity, does not accept the petals of flowers and rock sugar whereas Inder Lal accepts it. So, here Jhabvala has given the contrasting views of the Indians and the Westerners.

Jhabvala gives the orthodox views not only of the Indian people but also of the Westerners. Mrs. Saunders gives a loud shout when the servant comes in "wearing slovenly shoes."[46] Mrs. Saunders calls dirty names to the servant.

O.P. Saxena writes that servants of India can be put into two categories:

1. The servant of the pre-Independence period, and
2. The servant in Independent India.[47]

In the Pre-Independent India, the condition of the servants was as bad as it is today. They lived in filth inside the quarters. Their quarters "exuded muffled out incessant sounds".

The narrator, like a true spokesman of a European culture, is awe-stricken and comes close to her wild imagination when she witnesses:

> *The washerman could be seen through the arched doorway eating his food in his courtyard…. For the first time I feel the Hindu fear of pollution. I went home and bathed rigorously ringing myself over and over again. I was afraid.*

Pollution – infection – seemed everywhere; those flies could easily have carried it from her to me. [48]

The narrator empathizes with an affluent Indian family (Kitty's family) living in London who feels that,

India was, of course, home but was becoming so impossible to live in that they had to stay mostly abroad.[49]

And the narrator guesses it very right that once adapted to the western materialistic hassle – free cozy luxuriant life style one never wishes to come back to India like Kitty and her family as they find themselves unfit for the country:

I didn't meet him again after that one visit, and though I sometimes think of him here, it is difficult to fit him and Kitty in either at Khatm or at Satipur; or even what I saw of Bombay.[50]

Inder Lal, a true representative of middle – class literate section, is all conscious about this class – biasness or say, class – difference:

… by Western standards his house as well as his food and his way of eating it would be considered primitive, inadequate – indeed, he himself would be considered so because of his unscientific mind and ignorance of the modern world. [51]

And there is no doubt left that he himself often feels like laughing when "he looks around him and sees the conditions in which people are living and the superstitions in their minds."[52] Though much to his respite and consolation, Inder Lal is perplexed when he comes to know (as revealed by the narrator) the reason why the Westerners rush towards the east:

> *Many of us are tired of materialism of the West and even if we have no particular attraction towards the spiritual message of the East, we come here in the hope of finding a simpler and more natural way of life.*[53]

But what they get in return is physical illness, that too, without the guarantee of mental peace. Dr. Gopal, being a true and impartial commentator of Indian health and hygiene, very frankly admits:

> *Not only Westerners but even most Indians suffer from amoebic dysentery. They hardly know it, for they also suffer from many other diseases.*[54]

Further Dr. Gopal admits (be it his irony or satire, but the fact remains as it is):

> *Let us admit for the sake of our argument that we Indians are fit to live here – where also are we fit for? Well now it is like this that we have our germs and we have reserved these for ourselves only. For Indians only!*[55]

And this is what the narrator's neighbor at the Society of Missionaries had already cautioned him of in the very opening of the novel:

> *You've probably arrived, that's why you're so careless. Never mind, you'll learn soon enough, everyone does... You've to be careful with your food in the beginning: boiled water only, and whatever you do, no food from these street stalls. Afterwards you get immune.*[56]

The Westerners are also of the view that in India, the doctors are no good. Karim tells the narrator that they cannot stay in India because Kitty gets stomach problem, due to water and there is no proper doctor available. Harry also has the same views and calls the Indian doctor "Quacks"[57]. To Westerners, Indian hospitals seem like a hell, as if St. Peter is sitting at the entrance gate:

> *The patients sit in rows holding out bowls into which are thrown lumps of cold rice and lentils and sometimes some vegetables all mixed up together, Only, people who are completely destitute will accept this food and it is indeed served up with the contempt served for these who have nothing and no one.*[58]

There is no doubt that our Narrator finally adapts herself to the Indian condition of harshness flaring a patchidermal attitude. She has now been 'immunized'. She confesses:

> *I made my way from Dr. Gopal's office through the crowded hospital corridors. I kept having to step over patients lying on the floor. Now a new thought – a new word –presented itself to me, and it was this: that the old man was dispensable. I was surprised at myself. I realized I was changing, becoming more like everyone else. But also I thought that if one lives here, it is best to be like everyone else.[59]*

The readers also feel her compulsion to change and melt herself into the chiselers' "India – changes – people" – pot. She herself feels her helplessness:

> *Perhaps there is no choice: everything around me – the people and landscape, life animate and inanimate – seemed to compel me into this attitude.[60]*

While we can see the contrast is superbly established by the author. On one hand there are grief – stricken destitutes and on the other a symmetrical junk of the elite class:

> *The rich men all seemed to look the same: they were all fat, and wore spotless loose white muslin clothes, and shone with oil and jewellery.[61]*

This disparity at the economic level in India has been a genuine concern of the Westerners since time immemorial. Douglas and a whole lot of Europeans perceive them as a "pack of rogues".[62]

Ruth P. Jhabvala found herself tossed between the two worlds of her upbringing and of her permanent stay; her greatest problem was whether she should merge with Indian soil or stay as a European. The following passage from her autobiography *An Experience of India* beautifully highlights her inner conflict:

> *Should one try and become something other than what one is? I don't always say 'no' to this question. Sometimes it seems to me how pleasant it would be to say 'yes' and give in and wear a sari and be weak and accepting and see God in a cow. Other times it seems worthwhile to be defiant and European and all right be crushed by one's environment, but all the same have made sure attempt to remain standing. Of course this can't go indefinitely and in the end I'm bound to lose — if only at the point where my ashes are immersed in the Ganges to the accompaniment of Vedic hymns, and then who will say that I have not truly merged with India.*[63]

While at one end, "she wanted to be merged with India, at the same time, the thought of her Europeanness never left her"[64], says Syed Mashkoor Ali.

Olivia, the heroine of *Heat and Dust* suffers because she resigns to the glorious and glorified India of her illusion, because she chooses to spend the end of her days here; Chid is disillusioned because he, too, like Olivia, resigns to his illusion of spiritual India. But Major Minnies does not suffer because he never allows himself "to become softened by an excess of feeling", because he never chooses to pass his remaining days in India– where town seems a "communal dormitory".

But unlike Olivia, the narrator does not suffer. Though she is surprised to see people's habit of sleeping outside, the town seems to her a communal dormitory. In a symbolic gesture of merging with the Indianness of the city, the narrator drags her bed outside in the open space. As her intimacy with Inder Lal grows, the Cupid strikes, they tie strings; the narrator gets pregnant like Olivia. Unlike Olivia, the young narrator is determined to have her baby after which she hopes to go upto the mountains and join an Ashram. T. S. Anand's argument has worth in it:

> *Sex provides a flimsy meeting ground of two cultures; it creates a temporal and temporary relation. Olivia seeks merger into India through sex but remains to suffer. She does not return to England but stays in a house upon hills where she hoped to find the resolution of conflict of two cultures. But the same is not true of the young narrator, though it is not the intention of the author to suggest resolution through passion. The young narrator imbibes the spirit of the land, identifies herself with India and is determined to have her baby, unlike Olivia who consents to abort the child in her.*[65]

The inability of the Europeans to create lasting ties with the Indians and vice versa, their distrust of each other's intentions, their misreading of each other's motives, their prediction with their notions of ethnic superiority and above all their differing cultural modes and perceptions, all these factors inhibit a meaningful dialogue between them and all the proverbial gulf between the East and the West yawns at them, in spite of Ruth Prawer Jhabvala's stature as "outsider-insider".

Jhabvala, no doubt, sometimes finds herself a 'cultural eunuch'. Like Olivia, she also appears to ask "What is an hijra?"[66] And, the whole India with Nawab laughs at the question and replies, "I will show you." Perhaps, both Olivia and Ruth Prawer Jhabvala are answered.

Jhabvala is observant of the artistically exotic surface of India. Amongst the bizarre and exotic mysteries of India are the 'hijras', the practice of 'suttee' and the midwives who 'always know' when a women is pregnant. The mystery of a spirituality which contributes to a sexual prowess is another curiosity to the Westerner, as demonstrated through Chid:

> *At such times it seems ... that his sex is engendered by his spiritual practices, by all that chanting of mantras he does.*[67]

Meenakshi Mukherjee records:

> *The Anglo-Indian community of Satipur in Jhabvala's novel is almost an exact replica of the Chandrapur community of A Passage to India, with close correspondence between the collectors (Crawford in one case and Turton in the other), their wives, the civil surgeons and the magistrates. Douglas Rivers of Heat and Dust is a fictional reincarnation of Ronnie Heaslop... Jhabvala writes in a deliberately down –to - earth language emphasizing realistic details of*

> *incidents and objects underplaying the complex*
> *workings of human mind.*[68]

Jhabvala's conscious efforts in building up the climax are apparently evident in her ending the novel with climatic heavy rains, mountain peaks and snow which brings the novel to a full circle beginning with scorching heat and choking dust:

> *I'm impatient for it to stop raining because I*
> *want to move on, go higher up. I keep looking*
> *up all the time, but everything remains hidden.*
> *Unable to see, I imagine mountain peaks higher*
> *than any I've ever dreamed of; the snow ... it is*
> *luminous and shines against a sky which is of a*
> *deeper blue than any yet known to me.*[69]

Olivia's loneliness, big house, doors and windows shut, and heat and dust of the opening scene have been carefully paralleled by 'move on', 'looking up', 'mountain peaks', 'higher up', 'white snow', 'luminous', 'shining', 'deeper blue sky' and heavy rain of the concluding paragraph.

At the end of the novel the English seem to be packing their luggage and preparing to go back home – to sweet little England. "The Crawfords, even Harry and, of course, Chid are booked for their homeward journey. Ironically, the Nawab too, goes to London to lead a rather sedate life there."[70]

Nissin Ezekiel sees *Heat and Dust* as a Western pot-boiler, exploiting a well - tried formula, and with little attention to craft. In any case Jhabvala's fiction too often tries to take the shape of a classical English garden, even when her theme and setting, not to mention the strong undercurrent of her despair, would seem to demand an Indian wilderness or at least some less formal rectitude. Further he adds:

> Heat and Dust *did not raise any heat or generate any dust in England. It did both in India, partly because of the Booker prize which put on the novel the stamp of English approval, naturally without any concern for Indian sensibilities. The gulf between the two viewpoints seems unbridgeable.*[71]

Laurie Sucher taking what might loosely be called a "feminist" position, claims that it is the difference between Olivia and the narrator that is most significant. Olivia representing one kind of sexual mythology and the "emancipated" narrator, a quite different kind. In fact, V. A. Shahane is right when he rolls on the discussion with his argument that, "sexual appetite is most intricately compounded with religious or spiritual pursuit in *Heat and Dust*."[72]

R.F. Isar and Shantha Krishnaswamy criticized it as anti-India and viewed it as the epitome of the novelist's twenty three years itch in India. The merchant – Ivory film version of *Heat and Dust*, eight years later, let loose a fresh wave of outraged feelings in India. Eunice De Souza and Sunil Sethi, among others, felt that the film was racist in spirit and 'hallow at the centre'. However, *Heat and Dust* did find some admirers in India. Yasmine Gooneratne and Brij Behari Singh found much to appreciate in the book, and Anita Desai, in a spirited defence of the film, failed 'to see any trace of an anti-Indian stance', maintaining that "if any society was being criticized here it certainly wasn't the Indian one."[73]

So "heat and dust" become both the physical and emotional landscape in the novel. India as the cultural concept is the theme of the novel and we find Jhabvala's eagerness to cover as many aspects of it as possible, the physical aspect being one as it poses a great problem to the Westerners by affecting their very mode of behaviour. Jhabvala writes:

> *Only those who have lived through days of endless Indian heat know their effect on one's behaviour.... My western characters – who of course include myself – have reason to be appalled at the transformation to which they are being subjected. Alongwith their behaviour their most cherished principles and feelings seem to be changing.*[74]

Khuswant Singh believes that her perspective is certainly not that of an Indian, not even that of "an adopted daughter of India" as he calls her but that of a daughter-in-law, who vouchsafes to caution the rest of her kind. The anxiety that lurks behind seems to undermine the fictional pattern. The characters appeal less to us as persons but are either Britishers or Indian throughout the novel. The narrator in the novel speaks out in the very second page:

> *They are no longer the same because I myself am no longer the same. India always changes people, and I have been no exception.*[75]

And at one place Jhabvala writes,

> *I have lived in India for most part of my adult*
> *life. My husband is Indian and so are my*
> *children. I am not, and less so every year.*[76]

She has watched India change over the years, watched westerners come and go and feels that she writes as a westerner for the western audience, of what she has felt and experienced.

Of course, Olivia, and the other characters who wear English – attitude (regardless, of being a Britisher or an Indian) are typical examples of cultural allotrope along with the novelist herself.

References:

1. Ruth Prawer Jhabvala. *Heat and Dust*. G.B.: John Murray (Publishers), 1975. p.171.

2. Prashant Sinha. *"The Parellel Traingles: The Relation Between the Two Love Stories in* Heat and Dust *and the Form of the Novel"*. *Indian Women Novelists.* ed., R.K. Dhawan. New Delhi. Prestige. 1993. pp.138-39.

3. Ruth Prawer Jhabvala. *Heat and Dust*. op.cit., p. 32.

4. *ibid.*, pp.170–71.

5. In *Experience of India*, Jhabvala says that "The most salient fact about India is that it is very poor and backward".

6. Prashant Sinha. *The Parellel Traingles.* op.cit., p. 139.

7. Meenakhsi Mukherjee. *Heat and Dust: Journey's End for Jhabvala. Indian Women Novelists.* op. cit., p. 131.

8. Ruth P. Jhabvala. *Heat and Dust*. op.cit., p. 58.

9. *ibid.*, p.58

10. *ibid.*, p.2

11. P.A Sorokin. *Contemporary Sociological Theories.* New York: Harper and Brothers, 1928. pp. 441 – 42.

12. Gamini Gooneratne. *Silence, Exile and Cunning.* Hyderabad: Orient Longman, 1983. p. 213.

13. Ruth P. Jhabvala. *Heat and Dust*. op.cit., p. 38.

14. *ibid.*, p. 19.

15. Ruth P. Jhabvala. *Myself in India. An Experience of India.* London: John Murray, 1971. p.7.

16. Ruth P. Jhavbala. *Heat and Dust*. op. cit., p.– 129.

17. *ibid.*, p.119

18. *ibid.*, p.22

19. *ibid.*, p.74

20. *ibid.*, p. 55

21. *ibid.*, p.56

22. Premila Paul. *"Heat and Dust: An Alien Perspective". Indian Women Novelists.* ed. R.K. Dhawan, op. cit., p. – 67

23. Ruth P. Jhabvala. *Heat and Dust*. op. cit., p.14

24. *ibid.*, p. 117.

25. *ibid.*, p. 123

26. *ibid.*, p. 152

27. Premila Paul. *Heat and Dust: An Alien Perspective.* op. cit., p. 72.

28. O.P. Saxena. *The Spiritual Porn in Jhabvala's Novels. Glimpses of Indo-English Fiction.* Vol. II. N. Delhi: Jainsons Publication, 1985. p. 227.

29. Ruth P. Jhavbala. *Heat and Dust.* op.cit., pp.4- 5.

30. *ibid.*, p. 28.

31. *ibid.*, p. 4.

32. *ibid.*, p.140.

33. *ibid.*, p.143.

34. *ibid.*, p. 95.

35. O.P. Saxena. *The Spiritual Porn in Jhabvala's Novels.* op. cit., p. 227.

36. Ruth P. Jhabvala. *Heat and Dust.* op. cit. pp. 5 - 6.

37. *ibid.*, p. 63.

38. Bruce King. *Three Novels and Some Conclusions:* Guerillas, The Adaptable Man, Heat and Dust. *The New English Literatures: Cultural Nationalism In A Changing World.* London: Macmillan, 1980. p. 228.

39. Meenakshi Mukherjee. *"Journey's End for Jhabvala". Explorations in Modern Indo-English Fiction.* ed. R.K. Dhawan.N. Delhi: Bahri, 1982. p. 212.

40. C. Paul Verghese. *A Note On Esmond In India. The Journals of Indian Writing In English,* Vol. 2, No. – 4 (July, 1976) p. 33.

41. R.S. Singh, *Indian Novel in English.* New Delhi. Arnold Heinemann, 1977. p.150.

42. Ruth P. Jhavbala. *Heat and Dust.* op. cit., p. 178.

43. *ibid.*, p. 5.

44. *ibid.*, p.52.

45. *ibid.*, p.13

46. *ibid.*, p.27

47.   O.P. Saxena. *"Suffering Humanity in Jhabvala's Novels", Glimpses of Indo – English Fiction.* Vol. II, op. cit., p. 245.

48.   Ruth P. Jhavbala. *Heat and Dust.* op. cit., p. 110.

49.   *ibid.,* p. 98.

50.   *ibid.,* p.101.

51.   *ibid.,* pp. 95-96.

52.   *ibid.,* p. 96.

53.   *ibid.,* p. 95.

54.   *ibid.,* p.158

55.   *ibid.,* p.159

56.   *ibid.,* p. 3.

57.   *ibid.,* p. 103.

58.   *ibid.,* pp. 156–157.

59.   *ibid.,* p.112.

60.   *ibid.,* p.113.

61.   *ibid.,* p. 56.

62.   *ibid.,* p. 37.

63.   Ruth P. Jhabvala. *An Experience of India.* op. cit., p.51.

64.   Syed Mushkoor Ali. *Heat and Dust: An Assessment, Indian Women Novelists.* ed. R.K. Dhawan, op. cit., p. 92.

65.   T.S. Anand. *"Heat and Dust: An Evaluation of Cross – Cultural Conflicts", Indian Women Novelists.* ed. R.K. Dhawan. op. cit., p. 117.

66.   Ruth P. Jhabvala. *Heat and Dust.* op.cit., p. 123.

67.   *ibid.,* p. 65.

68.   Meenakshi Mukherjee. *Heat and Dust: Journey's End for Jhabvala.* op. cit., p. 180.

69.   Ruth P. Jhabvala. *Heat and Dust.* op. cit., p. 180.

70.   Hari Mohan Prasad. *Response: Recent Revelations of Indian Fiction in English.* Bareilly: Prakash Book Depot. p. 229.

71.   As quoted in Ram Lal Agarwal's *Ruth Prawer Jhabvala: A Study of Her Fiction.* Delhi: Envoy Press, 1990. pp. 75– 76.

72.   V.A. Shahane. *Ruth Prawer Jhabvala.* Delhi: Arnold Heinemann, 1976. p.133.

73.   Cited in Arun Chakroborty's *Ruth Prawer Jhavbala: A study In Empathy And Exile.* Delhi: B.R. Publishing Corporation, 1998. p. 203.

74.   Ruth P. Jhabvala. *Moonlight, Jasmine and Rickets.* The New York Times, 22nd April, 1975, p. 25.

75.   Ruth P. Jhabvala. *Heat and Dust.* op.cit., p. 2.

76.   Ruth P. Jhabvala. *Living in India.* London Magazine, Sept., 1970, p. 41.

CHAPTER - VII

ENGLISH, AUGUST

The theme of exile runs through most of the modern literature and one of its persistent concerns is to explore the possibilities of reconciliation between man and his situation. This sense of exile is, in fact, a by product of cultural amalgamation. Reasons may be many. But this issue assumes an immediacy of concern with all post - colonial literature as they are an outcome of an unequal dialectic between a violent and rapacious imperialistic culture and a subjugated though often rich and complex native culture. This dialectic has caused in the colonized societies large scale displacements, dispossessions and dislocations – social, cultural, linguistic and geographical – thus resulting in a crisis of identity and creating a sense of alienation. Stokely Carmichael in his essay, *Black Power* reiterates:

> *So what the West was able to do is impose its culture and it told everyone: 'we are better, we are civilized.' And because of its force, all of the non-white countries began to try to imitate Europe and to imitate its ways, and to try and copy it because nobody wanted to be uncivilized…..*
> *So that all other non-western people have been*

> *stripped of their own culture. They have been*
> *forced to accept a culture that does not belong*
> *to them.*

In the same discussion, he further writes:

> *And so messed up are the minds of people of*
> *colour around the world, that in eastern section*
> *of Vietnam today and in Japan certainly, women*
> *who have slanted eyes are cutting their eyes so*
> *that they can get round eyes to look like the*
> *west. Needless to say, what black people have*
> *been doing to their hair, especially females,*
> *they have been putting hot combs in their hair,*
> *straightening it, attempting to look like white*
> *people, because the West has defined beauty as*
> *that which was theirs - the white woman, who*
> *was supposed to be taboo.*[1]

Under all these circumstances the modern man has become a cultural allotrope. The invading colonizing power brings in its wake a whole complex of material and discursive practices which operate on a bipolar axis where the values of the colonized power are marginalized. The crisis of identity, as Bill Ashcroft et. al. suggest, is caused by "cultural denigration, the conscious and unconscious oppression of the indigenous personality and culture by a supposedly superior social or cultural model".[2]

Upamanyu Chatterjee's *English August: An Indian Story* raises the issue of identity in a post - colonial society and problematizes the issue by implicating the subject in a web of contradictory and opposing material and discursive practices. The focus of the novelist is to show the mental plight of the urban Indians like August who are victims of an alien cultural discourse which has been internalized by them in the course of their educational cultural nurturing.

Chatterjee offers a complex view of the post- colonial landscape where the protagonist roams around aimlessly and which is "familiar yet unknown..., seen countless times, but never experienced"[3]. Here in such given situation, exile and alienation seem to be an inescapable and inevitable human condition. While acknowledging the impossibility of retrieving a pure pre-colonial culture, Chatterjee rejects the view that the hybridized nature of a post- colonial culture is a valuable source of strength.

The protagonist of *English, August* suffers from an exorable sense of exile and this feeling of alienation is produced in him by an acute awareness of his colonial legacy, the two mutually opposed traditions he has been heir to. He also "search (es) in vain for any reflection of (him) self, like James Baldwin who tries to examine his own situation as an American Negro:

> *I know, in any case, that the most crucial time in my own development came when I was forced to recognize that I was a kind of bastard of the West, when I followed the life of my past I did not find myself in Europe, but in Africa. And this meant that in some subtle way, in a really profound way I brought to Shakespeare, Bach, Rembrandt, to the stones of Paris, to the Cathedral at Chartres and to the Empire Estate Building, a special attitude. These were not really my creations, they did not contain my history, I might search*

> *in them in vain for ever for any reflection of*
> *myself; I was an interloper. At the same time, I*
> *had other heritage which I could possibly hope to*
> *use. I had certainly been unfitted for the jungle*
> *or the tribe.*[4]

Born of a mixed parentage, his father being a Bengali Hindu and his mother a Goanese Christian, Agastya becomes a metaphor of the incursion of the native Indian culture by the Western culture. His uncle, Paltukaku calls him "an absurd combination, a boarding –school- English-literature education and an obscure name from Hindu myth."[5] He is named after a great Hindu sage, Agastya, but he is often asked by people like an engineer or Srivastava, "So! Agastya, what kind of name is Agastya, Bhai?"[6]

Srivastava, a Collector, represents a whole lot of urban educated Indians who have ceased to value their own traditions especially under the siege of the imperial western culture. We have lost the powers of naming, meaning and interpretation. These powers are appropriated by the "superior" western culture and any articulation of meaning is possible only under this new cultural framework. We are often reduced to asking questions like what kind of a name is it in and what does it mean? Their suppressed but persistent psychology to follow the western norms is what runs through the sub-conscious thoughts of a colonized culture. It is not surprising when 'Agastya's envy had then blurted out, he wished he had been Anglo-Indian, that he had Keith or Alan for a name, that he spoke English with their accent."[7]

Quite significantly his name from Agastya to August is appropriated by the western discourse. Gauri Viswanathan notes that "the English education was introduced in India with an object to achieve and maintain political domination through cultural hegemony, by discretely introducing western values and perceptions among the natives".[8] So confident was Macaulay of the success of the project that he wrote in 1836, "No Hindu who has received an English education, ever remains sincerely attached to his religion. It is my firm belief that if our plans of education are followed up, there will not be a single idolater among the respectable classes in Bengal thirty years later." Agastya, being half-Bengali, is a product of this English education and upbringing only. Not only that his friends call him the 'last English man' or just 'hey English' and sometimes even 'hello Mother Tongue' – illogical and whimsical ..... like most names selected by contemporaries"[9] but figure like Kumar, the S.P. Madna, who loves, to call him as "the English type"[10] because he can speak English more fluently than any other Indian language.

Agastya's tragedy concerning his name and identity reaches its climax when he, himself, is found confused what name he should be called by. He requests his friends: "and please call me Agastya, Or English, Or Ogu, or August."[11] His names seemed like aliases, for his different lives. And this compulsion of a modern man to live different lives at different occasions actually makes him a cultural allotrope. Although, this builds up a paradoxical situation. And nothing could be more paradoxical than this that many of us have become like Agastya's father. Agastya explains:

> *My father eats beef too. He's amazing ...... he eats corned beef sandwiches and wears dhoti and reads the Upanishad in Sanskrit.*[12]

For most of us today being 'Indian' stands for what Agastya claims:

> *I suppose being Indian means being born an Indian citizen and not wanting to change citizenship.*[13]

But this transformation from Agastya to August is not complete. It contains a lack, a gap, a void. Homi K. Bhabha suggests that due to the ambivalence of colonial discourse, the colonial authority in never total or complete. Calling mimicry as a trope of partial presence Bhabha says that "it masks a threatening racial difference only to reveal the excesses and slippages of colonial power and knowledge".[14] If Agastya is a product of English education, he also comes to question its authority. Many times he is confronted with the question what such irrelevances as Chaucer and Swift and Dryden are doing in the English classrooms of M.A. His professor at the College, Dr. Upadhyaya calls English in India a parody, a complete farce. He says:

> *At my old university I used to teach Macbeth to my M.A. English classes in Hindi. English in India is a burlesque... Now I spend my time writing papers for obscure journals on L.H. Myers and Wyndham Lewis, and teaching Conrad to a bunch of half-wits.*[15]

The ultimate irony of mis-appropriation of the English "book" is when Agastya discovers lines from Shakespeare's Macbeth quoted on a packet of sleeping pills - "the innocent sleep, Sleep that knits up the ravell'd sleeve of care" and, of course, his instant reaction was:

> *absurdity again, someone in Ulhasnagar has found some use of English Literature, most famous insomniac... thought .... this more interesting than L.H. Myres.*[16]

Agastya deliberately sets out to subvert the colonial value system by refusing to take its civilizing mission at its face value. Stokely Carmichael has expressed a similar view:

> *The West with its guns and its power and its might came into Africa, Asia, Latin America and the USA and raped it. And while they raped it they used beautiful terms. They told the Indians 'we're civilizing you, and we're taming the West. And if you won't be civilized, we'll kill you.' So, they committed genocide and stole the land, and put the Indians on reservations, and they said that they had civilized the country.*[17]

Agastya when asked to write an essay on "My Ambition", writes that his real ambition was to become "a domesticated male stray dog because they lived the best life. They were assumed of food, and because they were stray they didn't have to guard a house or beg or shake paws or fetch trifles or be clean or anything similarly meaningless to earn their food. .... A stray dog was free; he slept a lot, barked unexpectedly and only when he wanted to end got a lot of sex."[18] The author sets a contrast in the next lines:

*The class hadn't heard him, and had instead
yelled, 'He is lying, his only ambition is to be an
Anglo- Indian.*[19]

This is just a symbolic interpretation of what exactly the
protagonist thinks of the whites. It is quite contrasting to
what Dhrubo, Agastya's friend thinks of London. According
to him:

*London is 'nice', bits of it are like a 'washed'
Calcutta, and all Bengalis will love it, being
Anglophiles to their balls.*[20]

Agastya also realizes that this is a country where trains
are always late (as it had been fours hours late during
Agastya's journey to Madna[21]) and where people's identity is
not his personal behaviour but his chair or say, designation.
Agastya took it quite surprisingly that people never forget
to add his designation along with his name. 'IAS' almost
became his surname. People asked him, "Are you Mr. Sen,
IAS?"[22]

Stuck up with "Anchorlessness" - syndrome "glimpses of
Madna en route, cigarette- and- paan dhabas, disreputable
food stalls, both lit by fierce kerosene lamps, cattle and
clanging rickshaws on the road, and the rich sound of trucks
in slush from an overflowing drain, he felt as though he was
living someone's else life."[23]

Life in Madna assumes almost a surrealistic quality.
The language and ways of bureaucracy seems to increase his
bewilderment and sense of alienation. People often eye him
suspiciously when he says that he is an IAS officer as if the

IAS were a fixed signifier and its signified had some inherent intrinsic qualities. The IAS is only a post-colonial social and political construct within an elaborately designed hierarchy of power and it is only within this hierarchy that signifiers like IAS and IPS acquire meaning. Once outside this frame, even Srivastava and Kumar, the DM and the SP of Madna respectively, who are used to years of commanding, lose the aura. Shorn of the trapping of official power, they look ridiculous. "On the road Srivastava and Kumar looked a little odd, Agastya realized that he had never seen them walking. They looked like ordinary citizens who hadn't got rickshaw, one merely much fatter than the other."[24] Again, in Delhi when Kumar tells the taxi driver that he is an SP and Agastya is an IAS officer, the taxi driver in response, makes an obscene gesture at him and says, "This is what I think of you Government types."[25]

The bureaucracy, once the proud creation and instrument of the British imperialism, Agastya soon discovers, has become a travesty of its former self in the hands of its Indian practitioners. The author writes sarcastically:

> *But Indianization (of a method of administration, or of a language) is an integral to the Indian story. Before 1947 the collector was almost inaccessible to the people; now he keeps open house, primarily because he does a different, more difficult job. He is as human and as fallible, but now others can tell him so, even though he still exhibits the old accoutrements (but now Indianized) of importance- the flashing orange light on the roof of the car, the passes for the first row at the sitar recital, which will not start until he arrives and*

for which he will not arrive until he has been
ensured on the telephone that everyone else who
has been invited has arrived. In Madna, as in
all of India, one's importance as an official could
be gauged by, how long one could keep a concert
(to which one was invited) waiting. [26]

Bureaucracy, in its Indianized form, is all marked with jealousies, rivalries, one upmanship and false egos, where one's importance as an official is gauged by the fact as to how long one can keep a meeting waiting, where making a field visit means a night long orgy of drinking and watching are endless charades in which one incoherency is matched by the other. During the last part of his training when he becomes the B.D.O. of Jompanna, a backward tribal area, Agastya thinks that things would be somewhat different and he would eventually settle down to the job and "his restlessness would dissolve in action."[27] But two months at the job and Agastya feels as restless and confused as ever:

I feel confused and awful. Journey after journey
by train and jeep; just motion. Integration
Meetings, Revenue Meetings, Development. First
the job didn't make sense, and, I thought then,
when it does, I'll settle down. When it did, it
didn't help, I'd always be wondering, thinking
chaotically of alternatives, happy images of my
past mocking. Most of the time I felt guilty.[28]

Things are not helped either by his urban (read, western) upbringing and background. When Agastya wants to leave a good job of an IAS to work in a publishing firm, his father writes back to him in a letter:

> *My dead Ogu,….. 'This is what comes of living in a city and not knowing what the rest of India is like, or words to that effect….. It is true, however, that you have led so far, in Calcutta and Delhi, a comfortable big city life, wherein your friends and lifestyle have been largely westerised.*[29]

Not only professionally, but even socially and culturally Agastya feels alienated. Before coming to Madna, he has never had an experience of the provincial town. Places and people and events which had earlier been just names out of newspapers, suddenly assume a reality whose meaning and significance escape him:

> *Glimpses of Madna en route; cigarette and paan dhabas, disreputable food stalls, both lit by fierce kerosene lamps, cattle and clanging rickshaws on the road, and the rich round of trucks in slush from an overflowing drain; he felt as though he was living someone else's life.*[30]

This is his first impression of Madna, an impression which is going to haunt him for the remainder of his stay there. Unable to relate to the life around him, Agastya retreats to his own private world, the privacy of his room in the rest house where "there would be marijuana and nakedness, and soft, hopelessly incongruous music (Tagore or Chopin), and thoughts that ferment in isolation."[31]

Stuffed with marijuana trance, however hard he tries to live in the present, he is unable to shake his memories of the past which come flooding back to him. What the popular psycho-analyst Thomas A. Harris M.D. writes is quite significant to understand Agastya's psyche or his fused mental agony:

> *The brain functions as a high-fidelity recorder, putting on tape, as it were, every experience from the time of birth, possibly even before birth.*[32]

Agastya thinks that "he could even make do with Madna, if his mind would not burgeon with the images of Delhi, or of Calcutta, walks with Neera in the Lake Gardens, long chats about life and books and sex; and beyond that Singapore, where every thing was ordered, and Illinois, with its infinite varieties of ham. It was convulsing, the agony of the worlds in his head."[33] He longs to return to his old life and he even considers the possibility of giving up the IAS and joining a publishing firm.

Once back in Delhi, he gets no reprieve from the feeling of his alienation. He realizes that this is no solution to his problems; it is only exchanging one kind of bridle with the other. He soon discovers that the feeling of dislocation, restlessness and alienation are not his problems alone but of the whole generation which, to use his father's words, 'does not oil its hair'. Dhrubo, who has been to Yale for his Ph.D. and has as a job with the City Bank, feels that he has been living an unreal life and is tired of it. What he finds that "all those expense accounts, and false accented secretaries, and talk of new York and head office, and ...man in Hong Kong, it's just not 'real', it's an imitation of something elsewhere: …. And I wear a tie, … kiss the wives of my colleagues on the cheek when we meet…; listen to Scott Joplin and Keith Jarrett and on weekends I see a Herzog film, or a Carlos Saura, it's ….. unreal".[34]

Renu, Dhrubo's girlfriend who is now in Illinois, suffers from a sense of dislocation and wonders why she ever left India. Madan feels deeply ashamed of his sister who is going to Oxford on a Rhodes Scholarship and has acquired phony accents and manners.

Agastya, like his friends, comes to question the bases of the western metaphysics, the very worldview which has constituted him. This worldview creates an alien sensibility in him which produces a sense of estrangement from daily experience. Agastya disowns the western values but in this rejection is not implied a return to the pure pre-colonial past, because Agastya realizes that this return is neither possible nor desirable. He resigns his job and leaves in search of alternative values which would provide him with a stable identity. Torn up into pieces with the concept of 'sexiness in the mind' and 'as an Indian (one) should live the life of contemplation', his search ends, he must continue to remain in exile.

Skepticism as a mode of perceiving the incongruities of modern living is integral to the urban consciousness. And it is all pervasive in the first novel of Upamanyu Chatterjee – *English, August*. The protagonist here is an IAS trainee posted for a year in a small -town, Madna, where he is totally out of place with his mixed parentage and upbringing and an alienating English education and habits of the public school type. The sight of Madna deprives him more of his coherence. As Paltukaku loves to call him "culturally mongrels", we see Agastya's misgivings as the train takes him from Delhi to Madna:

> *Outside the Indian hinterland rushed by Hundreds of kilometers of a familiar yet unknown landscape, seen countless times through train windows, but never experienced — his life till then had been profoundly urban. Shabby stations of small towns where the train didn't stop, the towns that looked nice from a train window, incurious patient eyes and weather beaten bicycles at a level crossing, muddy children and buffalo at a waterhole. To him, these places had been, at best, names of newspapers, where floods and caste wars occurred, and entire Harijan families were murdered where some prime minister took his helicopter just after a calamity, or first before the elections. Now he looked out at this remote world and felt a little unsure, he was going to spend months in a dot in this hinterland.*[35]

Agastya joins the prestigious IAS profession, but his western outlook could never accept its idiocy. What Menon, an IAS officer, has scribbled in red ball point in the margin of the book *Heat and Dust*, in fact, reflects the modern psyche of the Indian bureaucracy which attempts to go for a paradigm shift during these years but in vain as Menon writes his comment:

> *Not necessary these days to wear sola topee. Relic of the Raj. The bureaucracy to be indianized.*[36]

Agastya thinks that though our 'babus' no more wear 'sola topee' the real development is still a distant dream. Though "development is as major a leitmotif in the Indian story as are the goulash of cultures.... but development would never be fashionable or glamorous in Jompanna (read remote areas). Jompanna was Indian oblivion; life for most was slow and unheroic there. No First Page politician had ever gone there, and the visits of those who had, had been quinquennial, to make the promises and gets the votes."[37]

Agastya, the protagonist, reveals that if "Indianization (of a method of administration or of a language) is integral to the Indian story"[38], it is nothing more than what he witnesses in his BDO Office:

> *The files were of flimsy by brown, or thick yellow paper.*[39]

Dipped in the western outlook carrying the flair of simplicity our hero is bewildered when he "find(s) the place for his signature, just above the stamp reading 'Block Development Officer, Jompanna' and a little cross by the side of the stamp, the cross plainly saying, Here, Idiot, sign here."[40]

After constantly going through such nightmarish experiences, Agastya also feels that "administration is an intricate business, and a young officer who lacks initiative cannot really be trained in its artifices. There is very little that he can learn from watching someone else. Agastya learnt nothing. For a very short while he worried about his ignorance, and then decided to worry it properly when others discovered it."[41]

Agastya's characteristic mode of reaction to the self-conscious forced conversation in social gatherings at the Collector's residence is usually an irrepressible flow of fabrications (his secret safety-valve). The more insufferable the situation, the funnier is his fabrication. Agastya's responses serve to underline the perfunctoriness of these conversations as in the interlude where Mrs. Rajan is holding forth to the Englishman and his wife. She nags unwillingly Agastya to force him to join the discussion on the word "Indian". But before letting Agastya present his opinion about 'being Indian' she thickens the topic by giving a hint in her statement:

> *I maintain that India is too fascinatingly diverse a country for the world to have any precise definition.*[42]

But the way Agastya snapped the answer reveals all how sincere the modern 'Cola generation' (as Paltukaku loves to call it) is about being an Indian and the bullish "Indian-ness":

> *I suppose being Indian means being born an Indian citizen and not wanting to change citizenship.*[43]

Agastya, a prototypal representative of a complete blend of two cultures, not only takes the question of nationality, too casually but he is also insincere about the religious sentiments of a country. Agastya is found to really like his friend's (Mohan) opinion, which reflects the true spirit of modern India:

> *'Some like Rohini, who thinks sex is dirty, will think all this is O.K. because 'it's a temple. Didn't Mrs. Srivastava tell you just now, you've an 'intellectual' attitude to temple?*[44]

Mohan disaffiliates those women who follow the dual nature and 'coward to disguise this hidden attachment with the shivalings'. There are innumerable Mohans in India now who have gone through the Freudian outlook, especially, regarding shivalings. What Mohan snaps out can never be simply ignored;

> *Oh, it's like a blue film. So, what if the cock is Shiv's, it's still cock. Come. Let's go.*[45]

This 'let go' attitude has a powerful expansion now-a-days in India. Religion is not a serious business now as new cultures have softened and diluted us a lot.

Though Agastya's utterances and thoughts in the novel may smack of condescension or flippancy to reader who do not belong to his class, regarded without bias, they become indispensable to the exposing of an absurdity from which he does not exempt either his own self or family and friends. Of course, he is an absurd combination. Religion was with him a remote concern, and with his father "it had never descended from the metaphysical".[46]

This religious and cultural disinterestedness is now a common feature, especially among the urban youths. They are standing on the cultural crossroads. They have become global. What Paltukaku had objections to are the original and genuine ones, usually posed by a big marginalized old generation of today. They opine that India is going through a phase of cultural bankruptcy. Paltukaku had warned Agastya's father while he was going to marry a Goan (Agastya's mother):

> *Your children will culturally be mongrels. The past makes us what we are; you will deprive them of coherence.*[47]

This lack of cultural coherence is actually our basic worry. We are confused, yet, strolling on the path of unknown destination. This has, at times, alienated us badly and we have become absurd combinations. Paltukaku's remarks have an everlasting echo:

> *You (Agastya) are an absurd combination, a boarding-school-English literature education and an obscure name from Hindu myth. Change your name officially, please, to any of those ridiculous alternatives that your friends have always given you.*[48]

The incongruous juxtaposition of character and life-styles and the widely fully situations it generates, build up the ethos of the small-town which can no longer be fixed in the fictional image of R.K. Narayan's Malgudi. The comic mode which presents the deviant behaviour of Malgudi character is an implicit endorsement of traditional norms. But Madna, like Mirpore, is symptomatic of urban India's inadequate involvement and perfunctory participation in 'tradition' as well as 'modernity'. In this context, it is interesting that in spite of obvious difference of class, status, age, character and situation; there is similarity in the perceptions of the small town reality as seen by Deven of "In Custody" and Agastya of "English, August" even though Deven is not an "alien-insider" as Agastya perhaps is, because of his parental background. Further, the non-constructive surroundings drive both to seek refuse in the world of imagination, which in Agastya's case is fused with his "secret life" (of marijuana, music, Marcus Aurelius among other things) in "hot dark rooms" of Rest Houses with "thoughts that ferment in isolation" — all "much more exciting and more actual than the world outside". For Agastya, this retreat into his secret life is the only defence he has. Pitting the small-town against the more congenial and familiar city (Delhi or Calcutta) helps define the inadequacy of attempts at being modern whether in the way of living or in the developmental programs of the government carried out by a not – too – clean or competent bureaucracy against the indigenous reality (tribal or other) of non-comprehension and distortion. And just that extra touch of grotesque is added to the post – colonial scene by the presence of Sita (passing off as married to John as a prudent measure against the small-town norms different from those prevailing in a city like Bombay) and of John- that "Englishman on the trial of a grandfather who had been mauled by a tiger two generation ago" and carrying the "family heirloom" the sola hat which his grandfather wore on his rounds and which the grandson 'dying to wear it' had brought in order to "look a pukka burra sahib."[49] Agastya's passage to 'Experience' involves coming to terms with a world 'infinitely bizarre'. The representation of this world through the medium of English, particularly congenial to the ironic mode, makes the comment on the post – colonial world more pointed. It may rightly be said of *English, August* that it is indeed "an

Indian Story" which is best told in English, but aptly only by an Indian.

The Metropolis, which as a point of reference in both *In Custody* and *English, August* brings out the constrictive atmosphere of the small town, in central to Amitav Ghosh's *The Shadow Lines*. The city acts as a catalyst in creating circumstances of change and growth offering to the protagonist, avenues of exploration not imaginable in a small-town. But in this city life comes out with a perpetual threat of a shabby existence to those who fail. The threat, however, is remote for the protagonist unlike in Sunil Gangopadhyay's "Pratidhwani", a Calcutta – based novel in Bengali, where the city becomes a challenge as well as an opportunity for the protagonist, young Siddaharta, whose passage to 'experience' involves painful encounters with reality.

The urban consciousness as it has manifested itself in Indian fiction in English is a pointer to its rootedness in the contemporary Indian reality. The complexities and pressure of urban living resist facile value judgments. "In India we treat our old parents and other people so well, they always stay with us, we don't send them to mountains."[50] Depletion of such values in urban – city life puts us into a deep introspection. Skepticism becomes a desirable mode of vigilance against phoniness of all kinds. Nostalgia for the past blurs perspectives in the present. A forward – looking acceptance of change involves revaluation of earlier ways of viewing the modern 'city' as alien presence and therefore an alienating force in the precincts of the village or even the small – town. R.P.Singh, in this context, has very aptly discussed alienation:

> *Alienation has a triple aspect – it is a process of estrangement from a natural socio-cultural context, it is a condition arising as a result of such an estrangement, and it is the subjective experience of being in such a condition in which powerlessness, meaninglessness, social isolation, normlessness and self- estrangement become the distinguishing marks of the alienated individuals.*[51]

Such an alienated individual like August is, in fact, a cultural allotrope.

Recent Indian fiction in English compels such a revaluation by registering alternative perceptions available to its urban consciousness. Till these alternative perceptions come, we should also wear a 'mystic' (not, mysterious) smile on our face alongwith Agastya:

> *The last false promises.... then last train journey. Opposite Agastya sat a bald man eager to talk about his stomach. To avoid him he opened Marcus Aurelius. 'Today I have got myself out of all my perplexities or rather, I have got the perplexities out of myself – for they were not without, but within; they lay in my own outlook.' He smiled at the page and thought, He lied, but he lied so well, this sad Roman who had also looked for happiness in living more than one life, and had failed, but with such grace.*[52]

References:

1.   David Cooper. ed., *The Dialectics of Liberation*. Great Britain: Penguin Books, 1968. pp. 157–158.

2.   Bill Aschcroft, Gareth Griffiths and Helen Tiffin. *The Empire Writes Back: Theory and Practice in Post – Colonial Literatures*. London: Rout ledge, 1989. p. 4.

3.   Upamanyu Chatterjee. *English August: An Indian Story*. London: Penguin Books in association with Faber & Faber, 1988. p. 4.

4.   James Baldwin. *Notes of A Native Son*. London: Michael Joseph, 1964. p.14.

5.   Upamannu Chaterjee. *English August: An Indian Story*. op.cit., p.129.

6.   *ibid.*, p. 15.

7.   *ibid.*, p. 2.

8.   Gauri Viswanathan. *Notes of A Native Son*. London. 1964. p 14.

9.   Upamanyu Chatterjee. *English August: An Indian Story*. op.cit., p. 2.

10. *ibid.*, p. 23.

11. *ibid.*, p. 259.

12. *ibid.*, p. 281.

13. *ibid.*, p. 10.

14. Homi K. Bhabha. *Of Mimicry and Men: The Ambivalence of Colonial Discourse*. 1984. pp.125 - 133.

15. Upamanyu Chatterjee. *English August: An Indian Story*. op. cit., p. 24.

16. *ibid.*, p. 96.

17. David Cooper. ed., *"Black Power"*. *The Dialectics of Liberation*. Great Britain: Penguin Books. 1968, pp. 156 –157.

18. Upamanyu Chatterjee. *English August: An Indian Story*. op.cit., p.35.

19. *ibid.*, p. 3.

20.   *ibid.*, p 93.

21.   *ibid.*, p. 5.

22.   *ibid.*, p.5.

23.   *ibid.*, p.5.

24.   *ibid.*, p.110.

25.   *ibid.*, p.146.

26.   *ibid.*, p.10.

27.   *ibid.*, p. 253.

28.   *ibid.*, p. 284.

29.   *ibid.*, p.149.

30.   *ibid.*, p.5.

31.   *ibid.*, p.26.

32.   Thomas A. Harris M.D. *I'm OK – You're Ok.* London: Arrow Books, 1995. p. 9.

33.   Upamanyu Chatterjee. *English August: An Indian Story.* op. cit., p.177.

34.   *ibid.*, p.153.

35.   *ibid.*, pp. 4-5.

36.   *ibid.*, p. 31.

37.   *ibid.*, p. 249.

38.   *ibid.*, p.10.

39.   *ibid.*, p.251.

40.   *ibid.*, p. 251.

41.   *ibid.*, p. 10.

42.   *ibid.*, pp.187 – 188.

43.   *ibid.*, p.188.

44.   *ibid.*, p.127.

45.   *ibid.*, p. 128.

46.   *ibid.*, p.128.

47.   *ibid.*, p.129.

48.   *ibid.*, p.129.

49.   *ibid.*, p.196.

50.   *ibid.*, p.31.

51. R. P. Singh. *The Concept of Anti-Hero in the Novels of Upamanyu Chatterjee.* Bareilly: Prakash Book Depot, 2010., pp.61-62.
52. *ibid.*, p. 288.

Chapter - VIII

CONCLUSION

M.H. Abrams writes:

> *Cultural studies designate a recent and rapidly growing cross-disciplinary enterprise for analyzing the conditions that affect the production, reception and cultural significance of all types of institutions, practices and products; among these literatures is accounted as merely one of many forms of cultural "signifying practices". A chief concern is to specify the functioning of the social, economic, and political forces and power-structures that produce all forms of cultural phenomena and endow them with their social "meanings", their "truth", the modes of discourse in which they are discussed and their relative value and status.*[1]

In this research work too, I have tried to limit myself only in one form that is Indian English literature and have endeavored to specify mainly the social and then only the economic and political forces (especially in its historical background) that have produced a cultural phenomenon, known as "Indian". In a way, I have tried to endow this 'Indianness' with its social 'meanings', its 'truth', the modes (rather, mood) of discourse in which it has been discussed in five different novels, and their relative value and status, if any.

K.R. Srinivasa Iyengar begins his survey of the Indian novel in English with the assertion that, "the 'novel' as a literary phenomenon is new to India".[2]

Although there was a rich narrative tradition in Sanskrit and in other languages, the novel as a literary form had its origin in the "literary renaissance" that swept Bengal in the later half of the nineteenth century. Inspired by the social revolution against some of the deplorable practices in Hindu society, Bankim Chandra Chatterjee (1838 – 1894) dramatizes the plight of the characters caught in the rigour and rigidity of Hindu joint families. Tagore, in his novel *Binodini* (*Choker Bali*), dramatizes the psychological tension of a young widow who confronts a hostile society when she tries to assert herself as a woman. Sarat Chandra Chatterjee, in a series of novels, tries to acclimatize the Indian mind to the uses of realism.

The spread of the English language and education in India brought the Indian mind into a happy contact with the Victorian novel. To quote V.V.N. Rajendra Prasad:

> *In any literary discussion, the word "influence" is a misleading term, and tracing literary influence may turn into a vague and slippery enterprise.[3]*

To quote Iyengar:

> *Before 1947 (the year of the withdrawal of Britain's political connection) the English models were the*

*major outside influence on the Indian novel.
After Independence, however, novelists in India
have shown themselves susceptible to the influence
of American and European (especially Russian)
models, and also models from Oriental countries.*[4]

While discussing the thematic complex of the Indian
novel in English, Iyengar says:

*After the advent of independence, the more
serious novelist has shown how the joy of freedom
has been more than neutralized by the tragedy of
the 'partition'; how inspite of the freedom there
is continuing (or even galloping) corruption,
inefficiency, poverty and cumulative misery;
how, after all, the mere replacement of the
white sahib by the brown sahib (or say, 'burra
sahib' as in Heat and Dust) cannot effect a
radical cure for the besetting ills of India. When
Independence came, the serious novelist in a sense
found his corruption gone, for the traditional
villain of the piece – foreign rule - was no more
in the picture. Making a new start as it were, the
novelist shifted his lantern side by side and that,
made his probes, and found little to satisfy him.
The old narrow loyalties were seen to wax as
eloquent as ever. Communal, linguistic, castiest
passions were seen to come into the open with
accelerated frequeny.*[5]

The process of intellectual and cultural importation in
India has created an imbalance in cultural trade as well as a

rift between knowledge and reality. The blind acceptance of modes of knowledge shaped in a distant island has resulted in a wide variance between life as it is lived and the modes of perception used to study it.

Ashis Nandy[6] (1983) has used the metaphor of a man-woman relationship to explain the psychology of colonial confrontation. According to him, in a colonial situation, the colonized culture (represented as female) tries to imitate the colonizing culture (represented as male), and ends up by becoming neither (represented as androgynous).

For the same condition, I put forth the term 'cultural allotrope'. A modern Indian more or less bears no flag (having dual citizenship), he owns no territory. He may simply be called an 'allotrope'[7], that is, the existing of the same person in two or more forms, having different properties at the intellectual or emotional level.

The three novelists Kamala Markandaya, Arun Joshi and Ruth Prawer Jhabvala have had the advantage of "mixed sensibility". All these three have first hand knowledge of countries of their adoption, especially both the women writers. R.K. Narayan knows the West through his frequent visits and Upamanyu Chatterjee is a direct product of anglicized generation. Hence, the landscape of these novelists is of global importance and their characters are typical examples of cultural allotrope.

Coming to the word 'culture', we can elaborate it as 'the accumulated intellectual, emotional and spiritual wealth of a nation."[8] As a mode of thought and action it evolves itself during the community life extending over centuries and embracing experiences, struggles, conflicts, failures and triumphs. In a way, culture includes unconscious and sub-conscious mind of a nation that determines and governs the conscious efforts of the nation. On the basis of my research work focused on five novels and discussed elaborately in the previous chapters, I have also tried to dig out few characteristics of being an Indian, and reciprocation of the west (my definition of 'west' for the purpose goes beyond the geographical longitudes and time zones and encompass all those who pretend to be 'modern' and 'put everything in doubt') at unconscious or sub-conscious levels to different Indian aspects that acknowledge the cultural allotropy at the conscious level. Also I have found that being 'Eastern' or 'Western' does not depend upon our origin or birth or ethnicity. It is, rather, simply a matter of exposure and how one takes his or her life into account. It is rather a name of a particular attitude, though, this synthesis is a by-product of these cultural crossfires and conflicts or cultural interactions only.

If the term "cultural allotropy" is not self defined, we can have a better understanding through different canvasses depicted suitably in different novels. The Great dam's site in *The Coffer Dams* is one of them:

> *The country was full of foreigners – Americans, west Germans, the Russian fresh from their triumph at Aswan … The Dutch with their ancient knowledge of dam-building…* [9]

and,

> *All kinds of men, tribals and technicians, English and Indian labor and management, otherwise disparate, who might be drawn together under this tenuous bond, and perhaps were.* [10]

This Cosmo-cultural situation is also witnessed by Sindi in America in *The Foreigner*:

> *I (Sindi) stood up and passed into the crowd. It closed me like the sea around pharaoh's legions. As I moved, the language changed until each layer seemed to have its own tongue. It was like switching a radio from one alien wavelength to another.*[11]

Once we go through the 'psyche' of these characters either in the novels or in the real world it is like moving in different isoglosses where languages change like 'switching a radio from one alien wavelength to another', we can trace out the spirit of real India which is ever-changing.

As to draw out a synthesis, I have underlined certain distinctive Indian features from the aspect of the culture and the westerner's degree of adaptability or abomination-which ultimately draw out the intensity of cultural allotropy reflected by and through the different characters of the five novels as discussed in the previous chapters in detail. This would help to draw out a sort of synopsis of different dimensions of "Indianism" in a systemic way as well as to know the response or bites of different characters from different novels focusing on a particular trait at a time.

Picking up different cultural traits one by one, I would like to begin it with *Gandhiji or Gandhism*. When Gandhi entered the socio-political scene during the thirties, it was the unprivileged section of Indian society that had attracted his attention. Inspired by Gandhi, creative artists in various Indian languages brought to a central focus the sociological and psychological problems of the untouchables whom

Gandhi rechristened as *Harijans*. With the passage of time, Gandhi emerged as an ideology to discuss, transformed into an 'ism' and gradually he became not only a face value of Indian currency but an integral part of Indian culture. Today, from the Tana Bhagats of Jharkhand to the Mumbai 'dibbawalahas'- Gandhi 'toppee' has capped the outer as well as the inner mental framework of each Indian. No doubt, he became a matter to be brought in life – both for Indians and the westerners. Everybody got a reason to talk about him - be it love or hatred at the core. So the first allotropic bondage seems to reside with Gandhiji. If it is assumed that there are several keys to open the territory of cultural study in relation to the Westerner's response to India, Gandhiji or Gandhism is certainly the 'starter' of the whole menu.

The impact of the Gandhian thought is all pervasive in R.K. Narayan's *The Man-Eater of Malgudi* (1961). Gandhian thought entered the soil of Malgudi, too. Nataraj like many other Indian families, "had been brought up in a house where" he was "taught never to kill" and when he "swatted flies", he had "to do it without the knowledge of the elders." Further, he was given instruction never to 'scare away the crows and sparrows that came to share "their food". This touch of Gandhian non-violence touches the soul of the real Indian. It denotes the patient and compassionate living in a land of 'ahimsa'.

If Gandhiji has touched Indians, the westerners are not left untouched. Not only he, but also his ideologies have become a matter of discussion for the outer world. Karl, the German character of Arun Joshi's *The Foreigner* (1968), has the curiosity (though a sort of irritation and envy is puffed out in his statement):

You Indians would bow down to the first man who comes along anyway. I don't know who put the non-violence, non-cooperation, non-nothing stuff in your heads.[12]

Though, the image of Gandhiji has become a bit confusing for the young 'cola' generation, he still exists in the political 'fables' of India's struggle for freedom. Agastya, the protagonist of *English, August: An Indian Story* comments:

Of course, they had all heard of Gandhi, the Father of the nation (but to some, Agastya remembered with a laugh, he was the Uncle — it must be so confusing, that Nehru's progeny were also Gandhis.[13]

The second aspect is the value - oriented *Indian tradition.* The intellectual traditions are culture bound. They come into existence because of the specific needs of the society and period that give them birth. When these traditions are transplanted, they tend to lose their authenticity and even their utility. Sudhir Kakkar has argued, in his psychoanalytical study of childhood and society in India[14] that many Western paradigms of psychology believed to be universal in application need careful scrutiny and adaptation before they are used in a non – Western cultural context. He clearly shows how different the nature of childhood and upbringing in India is, when compared to the childhood and upbringing in the West. That 'upbringing' may be one reason that Sindi, the protagonist of Arun Joshi's *The Foreigner*, is unable to understand the meaning of chastity and virginity of a woman. At one place, he asks Sheila, an Indian girl:

> *So you think one of those Marwari girls is really*
> *superior merely because of a silly membrane*
> *between her legs?* [15]

Sindi, being unknown to Indian values, is ignorant about the fact that even in the twenty first century, single girls living in metros go for colpoperineoplasty[16] as to restore their lost virginity before marriage. Things like virginity are no more a 'silly' issue even in today's India.

Indian religiosity and western bewilderment can be seen going hand in hand. Through Mackendrick, the character of *The Coffer Dams*, we could come to know that Indian religiosity causes a cultural discomfort to the Westerners. At one place, he quotes:

> *But what weight if any ... could attach to the*
> *words of a people who worshipped birds and*
> *beasts and probably snakes, ducking the forest*
> *with scruffy hutches which they knocked up out*
> *of driftwood and flowers for their deities?*[17]

Here, we should not forget that he is the same Mackendrick whose total project is at stake. It depends on the shoulder of these people only 'who worship birds and beasts'.

The reaction of Mrs. Blyth of *The Foreigner* is not much different on the same issue:

> *One thing I don't like at all about Hinduism is*
> *their nonsense about idols. It just isn't human.*[18]

Basically, this bewilderment is not a matter of 'longitudinal differences' as it has already been discussed that the term 'west' or 'western', rather, stands for a particular set of attitude. As Vasu, an Indian man of 'scientific approach' and villain of R.K. Narayan's *The Man Eater of Malgudi* mocks at Kumbh-Mela and the faith associated with it:

> *At Kumbh Mela, thousands and thousands gather; less than the original number go back home – cholera, or small pox, or they just get trampled. How many temple chariots have run over the onlookers at every festival gathering?* [19]

In his opinion, these *melas* are arranged 'so that the population may be kept within manageable limits' [20]. Here, Vasu pretends to be dipped into the Western soup. If he is not pretending, he seems to be too influenced by the "western' exposure that his each action, knowingly or unknowingly, goes on the line of Macaulay's design.

The same is the case with Mohan and Agastya in *English, August*. Mohan states:

> *... some like Rohini, who thinks sex is dirty, will think all this is OK because it's a temple. Didn't Mrs. Srivastava tell you just now. You have an 'intellectual; attitude to temples ... have you ever seen how women behave in front of a shivling? It's like a blue film. So what if the cock is Shiv's, it's still a cock.* [21]

For anglicized August (an anglicized version of Agastya), 'Religion was ... a remote concern' and he 'was not conscious of any blasphemy.' [22]

These western satires and bewilderment stood just against the religiosity and faith of millions of Indians but are widely accepted as a by-product of cultural amalgamation.

The Indian God and rituals and the Western perception standing in contrast are also quite interesting aspects to ponder upon. In *The Coffer Dams*, the crane is compared with a 'Devi' (Goddess). Further, Ruth Prawer Jhabvala amuses us with the description of "the principal God – he was in his monkey aspect, as Hanuman was kept in glass case; there were two other gods with him – each in a separate glass case."[23]

Tikku Ram of *Heat and Dust* is nervous not because he is going to be hanged. His anxiousness or nervousness is a caste-based inhibition. He wished to make it sure that the hangman should not belong to any low caste otherwise he would not get an entry pass of the heaven. Listening to this, the narrator goes off his nerves. Being a man of high caste, at the very last moment of his life, he "was worried about the caste of the hangman (if he was not 'chamar') who was performing this last intimate function for him. It was apparently his only worry at that moment of departure."[24]

The religiosity of Nataraj, the central character of *The Man- Eater of Malgudi* is unquestionable.

> He *hung up a framed picture of Goddess Laxmi poised on her lotus, holding aloft the bounties of earth in her four hands, and through her grace ... did not do too badly.* [25]

In the same novel, we come to know that "Garuda,... is sacred .. the messenger of God Vishnu."[26]

The narrator of *Heat and Dust* is all puzzled with the ritual of accepting 'prasadas' at the end of a 'puja' or say prayer as she "… was given some bits of rock sugar and a few flower petals …still clutching them on the bus back … respectfully tipped them out the side of the bus, but they … left the palm of (her)… hand sticky and with a lingering smell of sweetness and decay that is still there…"[27]

Another feature about India though negative in shade, is the prevailing inequality since time immemorial which in the colonial era was widened. The colonial rule, in fact, widened the gulf between the rich and the poor. In *Heat and Dust* we witness that, there is a "washerman that could be seen through the arched doorway eating his food in his courtyard … pollution- infection – seemed everywhere."[28]

Whereas, at the same time we have an Indian family in London who "had a tape playing of sarod music … a red sofa which had once been a swing and was fixed to the ceiling by long golden chains …"[29]

The post -Independent India is also not changed as the Rowling's bungalow can easily be seen:

> *always well lit, was a blaze of light when they gave their parties … proud of … lighting effects.*[30]

It may be one reason that Sindi, before coming to India, 'had read much of inequality in India'.[31] For posh boys like Agastya and Sathe, it is just 'whisky'[32] that means everything and Mr. Khemka who pronounces that 'India is working towards a new age … an age in which each man will be equal to another,"[33] loves to decorate his drawing rooms all filled with 'imported liquors'.[34]

Another striking feature of India is her landscape and more interestingly, the most striking thing is the same prejudiced approach of the Westerners to clique more often its lop sided pictures with much relishing zeal:

> *In the slums across the street, bundles of soggy humanity shuffled out of their huts and spread their miserable rags to dry. Full – breasted women, their thighs naked under wet saris, scurried back and forth like animals quarrelling over small bits of tin. Naked children rolled in the filthy pools, squealing with delight…*[35]

The narrator of *Heat and Dust* could see only 'many, many beggars"[36]. The Indian beggars (and people as a whole) appear so filthy to the Westerners that it is awful to listen to them. But we have to bear with them. The narrator after serving to the beggar women says:

> *I went home and bathed rigorously, rinsing myself over and over again. I was afraid. Pollution – infection seemed everywhere.*[37]

Even anglicized Agastya could only see

> *Snatches of other lives – veined hands on bicycle handled bars, and behind them a man emptying a bucket into a drain, the tensed calves of a rickshaw – wala, sweat-wet shirts round a stall selling fruit juice.*[38]

If Sindi could see 'naked children rolled in the filthy pools', Agastya could also easily locate them on "shabby stations of small towns where the trains didn't stop, the towns that looked nice from a train window, incurious patient eyes and weather beaten bicycles at a level crossing, muddy children and buffalo at a waterhole."[39]

The Westerners also find the ugly Indian richness. The narrator in *Heat and Dust* reports:

> *The rich men all seemed to look the same: they were all fat, and wore spotless loose white muslin clothes, and shone with oil and jewellary.*[40]

Sindi also notices the same:

> *...Old men grown fat with success come with their plump wives. They drank and then they had gorgeous dinners. They talked of money and how to make more of it. They left the impression that they could buy up anybody they wanted.*[41]

Quite remarkably, all these keen observations have come from the non- Indian community as we ourselves have become pachyderm and insensitive to our follies.

As far as the two basic infrastructural sectors of India – Indian postal service and Hospitals (the former being the life line of Indian people and another is the last resort of Indian health) are concerned, the condition seems to be pathetic and horrible as they have been reported by two different foreigners in two different situations. Their two different reports bring out the same conclusion- the condition is disgusting and condemnable. The narrator is impelled to write about the Indian Postal services:

> *Those impersonal post office forms which seem to constitute, along with stained and 'illegible postcards, the bulk of the mail that crosses from one end of India to the other. They always look as if they have been traveling great distances and passed through many hands, absorbing many stains and smells along the way.*[42]

And she does not forget to make a contrast:

> *Olivia's letters – more than fifty years old – look as if they had been written yesterday. The scent still seems to linger. Chid's crumpled letters, on the other hand, appear soaked in all the characteristic odours of India, in spices, urine, and betel.*[43]

If we dare to look upon the condition of the hospitals as reported by the anonymous narrator, we are bound to put down our eyes. According to her, in Indian hospitals men were observed as 'dispensible.'[44] The pathetic condition of the Indian hospitals is not a hidden issue even for the outsiders:

> *The patients sit in rows holding out bowls into which are thrown lumps of cold rice and lentils and sometimes vegetables all mixed up together.*[45]

Water is another element which binds two or more different cultures. But here it is another case of allotrope which works as an agent building up a *repulsive* bond with another reason and we can feel the surface tension quite easily. The people from Western countries are skeptic about coming to India as it causes a lot of problem to those hygiene – conscious people. In *The Coffer Dams*, Clinton warns Hellen "not to drink polluted water, reminded her that they were in Tiger country."[46] This statement points to the one-sided socio-economic development of the West.

Even in *Heat and Dust*, the narrator's neighbour at the society of missionaries warned her to "be careful with ... food in the beginning; boiled water only ..."[47] In the Independent India, in *English, August*, naib tehsilder was asked to "tell the cook to boil Agastya's drinking water as there was endemic jaundice and epidemic cholera"[48] and we find that the tag of "a country with polluted water" is still hooked with Indian's identity although millions have been drained in the Clean Ganga project. Srivastava, the IAS officer, senior to Agastya is worried about Agastya's health and enquired, "Are you boiling your water?"[49]

Apart from the polluted water, India is also renowned for its mosquitoes. Even our oldest epics confirm their presence since time immemorial. Who does not know the Mosquito –avatar (incarnation) of Lord Hanuman in the Holy Ramayana. But, the people from the Western longitude cannot stand mosquitoes that irritate even the urban – educated Indians a lot:

> *He slept under a mosquito net, but the mosquito got him anyway. He surfaced, struggling, out of sleep thrice at night, only, to hear the mosquitoes droning in the glow from the veranda.*[50]

Some may argue how a small thing like a mosquito can be a part of discussion under the cultural aspect, though it should be a geographical or biological question. For some it may be ludicrous also. Truly a mosquito is not at all a cultural entity but 'living with it' may be a cultural issue in a country like India where patients die of it's bite more than they do after contracting AIDS. It causes the Westerners to move around with a safari folding net when they tour in this snake charmers' country. We know how to live with it but the level of irritation for them, at times, is so high that it may also be suicidal as it happened with the westernized Vasu in *The Man- Eater of Malgudi*. Rather, the mosquito has been used as a major device by R.K. Narayan to reach the climax.

Dysentery has also given us a special status. Foreigners come to find here peace, as the foreigner girl of *The Foreigner* reports, "but all" they find is "dysentery"[51]. Whereas Avery, the tourist in *English, August* is seen traveling in India with 'Anti-dysentery pills'[52] along with the 'anti-sun burn lotion'.

Indian Bus Service has also carved out a special niche' and the recorders from the West or even developed Indians have not let it go unnoticed. This Bus service of India reveals the typical bus culture of India "much talked - about - much - mocked about". If we have sharp contrasting eyes to locate it, it is good; or else we can have a glimpse of it in *The Foreigner*:

> *Bright red buses of the Delhi Transport undertaking sloshed through the mud splattering pedestrians with grime. In spite of the rain they were full; in India things are always full whatever the circumstances.*[53]

In *Heat and Dust*, the narrator has "not yet traveled on a bus in India that has not been packed to bursting – point, with people inside and luggage on top; and they are always so old that they shake up every bone in human body and every screw in their own. If the buses are always the same, so is the landscape through which they travel."[54]

At the same time, Nataraj of *The Man-Eater of Malgudi* also records it objectively:

> *The bus arrived … although the bus itself was an old one picked off a war surplus dump, rigged up with canvas and painted yellow and red. It was impossible to guess how many were seated in the bus until it stopped at the tea-shop and the passengers wriggled and jumped out as if for an invasion. They swarmed around the tea-shop, outnumbering the flies.*[55]

Further, the cultural cross-fires occur especially on ethical and moral values as it differs from region to region, country to country. Chastity is one of the major virtues of Indian culture. Sindi, though a cultural mongrel, is conscious of this monogamous India. Once he says to Babu,

> *In your part of the world you marry only once in a life time.*[56]

Chastity of a woman is a riddle for Sandy, a cultural allotrope. For us, his question to Sheila, "So you think one of those Marwari girls is really superior merely because of a silly membrane between her legs?"[57] appear disdainful and embarrassing but it was asked too innocently or ignorantly.

Here comes a great issue of cultural divide. Had Sindi met Nataraj of Malgudi, he would not have dared to ask such a question. Forget about girls -single or married- even men in India, that too in a male - dominated society, reveal the social commitment that a married man in India carries with him. When Nataraj saw Rangi in the silent hour of a calm night, like any other ordinary man his "blood tingled with an unholy thrill ... no longer a married man with a child and home ... completely sealed against and seductive invitation she might hold out for (him), but, but, (he) hoped he would not weaken .. to dissolve within the embrace of her mighty arms all the monogamous chastity (he) had practised a whole life time."[58]

If Indian men are morally so sound, dutiful Indian wives claim appreciation and worldwide approbation. As Sindi, a global man, is filled with 'a sense of sympathy for all Indian women who always had their back arched, stooping to someone's service"[59], we feel the same for the mahout's wife in *The Man- Eater of Malgudi* who is "such a wonderful woman, she won't eat food" unless her husband is "back home, even if it is midnight" and when he is out for days and days she simply "starves, that is all ... a dutiful wife."[60]

Indians are also globally known for their compassionate nature and emotionality. Bashiam in *The Coffer Dams* pronounces:

> *We are emotional people. The spirit has been bruised as much as stomachs.*[61]

Vasu, a man who wears the mask of a 'scientific outlook' in *The Man- Eater of Malgudi* seems to stamp the notions of Bashiam of *The Coffer Dams:*

> *You are sentimental: I feel sickened when I see a*
> *man talking sentimentally like an old widow.*[62]

Paying respect to elders and a strong filial bond is another chief trait that distinguishes Indian culture from the Westerners. Nataraj records:

> *All our four brothers of my father with their*
> *wives and children, numbering fifteen, had lived*
> *under the same roof for many years. It was my*
> *father's old mother who had kept them together,*
> *acting as cohesive element among members of*
> *the family.*[63]

Shankar echoes the same voice in *English, August:*

> *In India we treat our parents and other people*
> *so well, they always stay with us, and help out in*
> *the house and everything.*[64]

The faulty education system is also one of the socio-cultural aspects that India is known for. Illiteracy has given India a bad name and the World Bank funded "Sarv Sakasharata Mission" is a by-product of this ill-reputation. Clinton of the pre- Independent India rightly registers; "Half these Johnnies can't read"[65] and the condition is almost the same even after a span of fifty years as Dhrubo of *English, August* records:

> *But all over India… education is biding time, a*
> *meaningless accumulation of degrees. BA, MA,*
> *then an M. Phil …*[66]

Indian society which is based on 'Athithi Devo Bhava' (Guests are God) philosophy, is also known for its magnetic and cordial hospitality. This time Gopal Rao becomes the mouth-piece and brand ambassador of Indian hospitality:

> *You are guests in our country … we like you to be comfortable so we adopt ourselves to your ways. Would you not.. do the same for us in your country?*[67]

Indian submissiveness is also a much ridiculed and hated aspect, sometimes within the country itself, and very often, it is an indigestible stuff for the outsiders. Krishnan, the progressive labor leader, yelled upon his own fellowmen:

> *Cattle, Look at them! Lined up, like passive cows … No organization, no discipline, cowards!*[68]

Almost the same notion is conceived by Vasu, though he oozes it out with a sarcastic touch, it carries some bitter truth and vitality in it

> *They (Indians) must show better spirit; they are spineless; no wonder our country has been a prey to every invader who passed this way.*[69]

As far as the paramount question "what is it to be 'Indian'?" is concerned — a mixed response comes from different corners of the mixed society. For an unprejudiced answer and to draw out a conclusion, we have to listen to both the 'outsiders' and 'insiders' honestly. Helen, the pro-Indian in *The Coffer Dams*, (though, she hails from the land of "memsahibs") finds many holes in her own western world as she admits:

> *Our world (western) ... has forgotten what fresh*
> *air is like. Our animals... we deprive them for*
> *their rights ... they don't know about sunshine*
> *or rain either. We've cut ourselves off from our*
> *heritage. We've forgotten what we know.*[70]

But for Rawlings, "it's the weather that depresses him"[71]. He finds "something has gone bloody wrong with this country."[72] The neighbour at the society of Missionaries also feels that, one "can't live in India without Christ Jesus."[73] But on the other hand, we also have June Blyth of America, who keeps her vibes positively warm for the people of the East. She opines:

> *People from Asia ... are so much gentler – and*
> *deeper – than others.*[74]

But once again, the foreigner girl in *Heat and Dust*, reports that Indians are "dirty and dishonest."[75] She further believes that "nothing human means anything here. Not a thing."[76] Agastya verifies almost the same, "One of the unhealthiest places ... Hot, humid, disease, everything."[77] Millie calls it "a bloody country."[78] Rawlings finds the essence of irrationality among Indians: "... Indian were an excitable breed, a quality that diminished the rational behaviour"[79] and for that he blames the climate, "Tropical climates do have extremes."[80] Mackendrick warns his wife Millie, "Never trust the blacks"[81] and feels that "Changing

India" is a product of their efforts as she acclaims, "We're behind them here."[82]

It is true that in India, as Vasu reports, "India is a big country with many jungles"[83], it does not mean that we should be called "Jungli wallah"[84]. Kamala Markandaya notices it via her narrator:

> *Anyone ... who adopted the panoply and pomp*
> *of an English archbishop would find himself*
> *jeered in an Indian town.*[85]

This is ill-health and sickened ethos of the Indian town that forces many outsiders to leave the country, the sooner the better. Mrs. Saunders in *Heat and Dust* represents those whole lots of Europeans who are desperate to leave India on the very first invitation. "Millie, let's go"[86] is not only her cry but that of many westerners and it has got eternal resonance equivalent to that of Catherine's "I'm Heathcliff" – resonance in *Wuthering Heights*.

At the same time Clinton's "bloody ... wish" is not to be in India. Chid also plans to fly away from India accusing her "smell". He confesses, "I can't stand the smell."[87] And then the narrator comes to his support, "Well of course, I know what he means — the smell of people who live and eat differently from oneself; I used to notice it even in London when I was near Indians in crowded buses or tubes."[88] It reveals that the Westerners find Indians obnoxious also.

This research has also found out that most of the westerners come to India either 'for a spiritual purpose'[89] or 'in the hope of finding a simpler and more natural way of life'[90] but all they "find here is dysentery".[91]

After passing through a subjugation of more than a couple of centuries, India today has got a whole lot of hexa - and septuagenarians who are transfixed in the twilight zone of new changes. As a result, their condition has almost become that of an 'allotropic' (that is full of paradoxes). They 'eat beef too ... corned beef sandwiches and wears dhoti and reads the Upanishads in Sanskrit."[92]

As a whole, we can say that "there are many ways of loving India, many things to love her - for the scenery, the history, the poetry, the music, and indeed the physical beauty of men and women"[93] but owing to cultural differences, the westerners put forth their allegation on us to 'find out (their) weak spot' and pressing on it.[94] The skepticism of the Westerners would probably never end:

> *It is very well to love and admire India – intellectually, aesthetically, ... sexually ... – but always with virile, measured, European feeling.*[95]

The above novelists have brought out all the specified cases and patches of cultural allotropy with the assertion that 'India always changes people' without 'exception'[96].

And with pronouncement that 'India is working towards a new age'[97] and 'nowhere else (except India) could languages be mixed and spoken with such ease ... American and Urdu...'[98] Indians are ready to hug anything western, beginning from the names itself (denying the Shakespearean cry 'what's in a name' and supporting the Oscar Wilde's bunburryism) that is why, we love to be called "August" in stead of "Agastya"[99], 'Sandy' for Zahira,[100] 'Sindi' for Surrender Oberoi,[101] and 'Chid'[102] for Chidananda.[102]

Discussing these aspects of the Indian novel in English, Rajan observes:

> *India today is facing radical challenges not merely in its sociological landscape but perhaps even in that immemorial landscape of the heart. The clash is not simply, between the East and the West (a conventional but deceptive stylization) but between the 'mores' of a pre-urban civilization and one committed to drastic industrial growth. The question to be answered is whether the Indian tradition with its capacity for assimilation and its unique power of synthesis can come to terms with the new (and the new is inevitable) without deep erosions in its fundamental character. In creating an image of this challenge there is perhaps a part to be played by the man of mixed sensibility, caught between crossfires, whose own mind is a microcosm of what he seeks to convey.*[103]

And, after deep analysis of our characters, be it Nataraj or Vasu of *The Man - Eater of Malgudi,* Sindi or Babu of *The Foreigner,* Helen or Bashiam of *The Coffer Dams,* Inder Lal or Olivia of *Heat and Dust* or Agastya or his 'cola generation' of *English, August,* it can be acclaimed that the rich Indian culture has shown its capacity of assimilation. It defiantly "changes people" by assimilating them all in her soil, and that too, without having deep erosions in its fundamental character. We, as readers, can very easily establish oneness with these characters. Like these characters, today we all are caught between the crossfires and have become microcosms of our own conscious minds, guided by the sub-conscious mind of the nation. We – the allotropes!

References:

1. M.H. Abrams. *A Glossary of Literary Terms.* N. Delhi: Harcourt Indian Pvt. Ltd., Seventh Edition,1999. p. 53.
2. K.S. Srinivas Iyengar. *Indian Writing in English.* N. Delhi: Sterling. Rev. Edition. 1984. p. 314.
3. V.V.N. Rajendra Prasad. *The Self, The Family and Society in Five Indian Novelists.* New Delhi: Prestige Books, 1990. p. 11.
4. *ibid.,* p.319.
5. *ibid.,* p. 319 – 20 (bracket and italics mine).
6. As quoted in G.N. Devy's *After Amnesia,* op.cit. p. 26.
7. Dr. G.D. Mishra. *Physical Chemistry.* Delhi: Motilal Banarasides, Rpt. 1987.
    This definition of "allotrope" bears reference to Ostwald's definition of allotropy. According to him, allotropy is "the existence of a substance – element or compound – in two or more forms, having different properties, physical or chemical.
8. Dr. Ravi Chopra. *Advanced Essay.* Delhi: Bookhive, 1988.p. 149.
9. Kamala Markandaya. *The Coffer Dams.* G.B.: Hamish Hamilton, 1969. p.10.
    All the references to the text are from this edition.
10. *ibid.,* p. 129.
11. Arun Joshi. *The Foreigner.* New Delhi: Orient Paperbacks, 1993. p.26.
    All the references to the text are from this edition.
12. *The Foreigner*
13. Upamanyu Chatterjee. *English, August: An Indian Story.* London: Faber and Faber, 1988. p. 197.
    All the references to the text are from this edition.
14. As quoted in G.N. Devy's *After Amnesia.* op.cit., p. 22.
15. *The Foreigner,* p. 52.

16. A tissue grafting operation for repairing tears in the vagina and the area surrounding its opening. The term is taken from L.M. Harrison's *The Pocket Medical Dictionary.* New Delhi: CBS Publishers & Distributors, Reprint, 2000. p. 89.

17. *The Coffer Dams.* p. 76.

18. *The Foreigner.* p. 62.

19. R.K. Narayan. *The Man-Eater of Malgudi.* Madras: Indian thought Publications, 17th Reprint,2003.p.149.
   All the references to the text are from this edition.

20. *ibid.,* p. 149.

21. *English August.* pp. 127 – 28.

22. *ibid.,* p. 128.

23. Ruth Prawer Jhabvala. *Heat and Dust.* G.B.: John Murray, 2003. p. 13.
   All the references to the text are from this edition.

24. *ibid.,* p. 178.

25. *The Man-Eater of Malgudi.* p. 7.

26. *ibid.,* p. 53.

27. *Heat and Dust.* pp. 13 – 14.

28. *ibid.,* p. 31.

29. *ibid.,* p. 97.

30. *The Coffer Dams,* p. 61.

31. *The Foreigner,* p. 16.

32. *English, August,* p. 47.

33. *The Foreigner,* p. 38.

34. *ibid.,* p. 14.

35. *ibid.,* p. 40.

36. *Heat and Dust,* p. 11.

37. *ibid.,* p. 110.

38. *English, August,* p. 21.

39. *ibid.,* pp. 4 – 5.

40. *Heat and Dust,* p. 37.

41. *The Foreigner,* p. 16.

42. *Heat and Dust,* p. 95.

43. *ibid.*, p. 95 (bracket mine)
44. *ibid.*, p. 112.
45. *ibid.*, pp. 156 – 57.
46. *The Coffer Dams*, p. 25.
47. *Heat and Dust*, p. 3.
48. *English August*, p. 6.
49. *ibid.*, p. 15.
50. *ibid.*, p. 7.
51. *Heat and Dust*, p. 21.
52. *English August*, p. 212.
53. *The Foreigner*, p. 40.
54. *Heat and Dust*, p. 11.
55. *The Man-Eater of Malgudi*, p. 41.
56. *The Foreigner*, p. 100.
57. *ibid.*, p. 52.
58. *The Man-Eater of Malgudi*, p. 121.
59. *The Foreigner*, p. 183.
60. *The Man-Eater of Malgudi*, p. 99.
61. *The Coffer Dams*, p. 70.
62. *The Man-Eater of Malgudi*, p. 134.
63. *ibid.*, pp. 11 – 12.
64. *English August*, p. 31.
65. *The Coffer Dams*, p. 73.
66. *English, August*, p. 3.
67. *The Coffer Dams*, p.71.
68. *ibid.*, p. 69.
69. *The Man-Eater of Malgudi*, p. 102.
70. *The Coffer Dams*, p.138.
71. *ibid.*, p. 167.
72. *ibid.*, p. 192.
73. *Heat and Dust*, p. 5.
74. *The Foreigner*, p. 29.
75. *Heat and Dust*, p. 21.
76. *ibid.*, p. 6.
77. *English August*, p. 15.

78.   *The Coffer Dams*, p.56.
79.   *ibid.*, p. 18.
80.   *ibid.*, p. 20.
81.   *ibid.*, p. 37.
82.   *ibid.*, p. 38.
83.   *The Man-Eater of Malgudi*, p. 80.
84.   *ibid.*, p. 80.
85.   *The Coffer Dams*, p. 48.
86.   *ibid.*, p. 62.
87.   *ibid.*, p. 139.
88.   *ibid.*, p. 139.
89.   *Heat and Dust*, p. 22.
90.   *ibid.*, p. 95.
91.   *ibid.*, p. 21.
92.   *English, August*, p. 281.
93.   *Heat and D*ust, p. 170.
94.   *ibid.*, p. 170.
95.   *ibid.*, p. 171.
96.   *ibid.*, p. 2.
97.   *The Foreigner*, p. 38.
98.   *English, August*, p. 1.
99.   *English, August.* the very title
100.   *Heat and Dust*, p. 32.
101.   *The Foreigner*, p. 191.
102.   *Heat and Dust*, p. 24.
103.   Balchandra Rajan. *"Identity and Nationality Commonwealth Literature: Unity and Diversity in a common Culture"*. *Considerations*.ed. Meenakshi Mukherjee. London: John Press, Heinemann Educational Books, 1965. p. 3.

BIBLIOGRAPHY

Primary Sources:

1. Narayan, R.K. (Reprint, 2003). *The Man Eater of Malgudi.* Madras: Indian Thought Publications. 1961.
2. Joshi, Arun. *The Foreigner.* New Delhi: Orient Paperbacks. 1993.
3. Jhabvala, Ruth Prawer (rpt.2003). *Heat and Dust.* G.B.: John Murray.1975.
4. Markandaya, Kamala. *The Coffer Dams.* Great Britain: Hamish Hamilton. 1969.
5. Chatterjee, Upamanyu. *English, August: An Indian Story.* London: Penguin in association with Faber and Faber.1989.

Secondary Sources:
(a) Books and Dissertations

6. Abrams, M.H.. *A Glossary of Literary Terms* (Seventh Edition). N. Delhi: Harcourt India Pvt. Ltd.1997.
7. Agarwal, R.C. *Ruth Prawer Jhabvala: A Study of Her Fiction*, N. Delhi: Sterling.1990.
8. Agnihotri, G.M.. *Indian Life and Problems in the Novels of Mulk Raj Anad, Raja Rao and R.K. Narayan.* Meerut: Shalabh Prakashan.1993.
9. Aschcroft, B. Griffiths. G. & Tiffin, Helen. *The Empire Writes Back: Theory and Practice in Post- Colonial Literatures.* London: Rout ledge.1989.

10. Bakhtiyar, Iqbal, ed. *The Novel in Modern India*, Bombay.1964.

11. Bhatnagar, Anil Kumar. *Kamala Markandaya: A Thematic Study*.N. Delhi: Sarup & Sons.1995.

12. Bhatnagar, O.P. *The Art and Vision of Arun Joshi*. Bareily, PBD.1983.

13. Biswal, J.K. *A Critical Study of the Novels of R.K. Narayan*. New Delhi: Nirmal.1987.

14. Bois, Cora Du. *The Cultural Interplay between East and West* in *The East and West Must Meet: A Symposium*. Michigan: East Lansing.1959.

15. Chadha, Romesh. *Cross – cultural Interaction in Indian English Fiction: An Analysis of the Novels of Ruth Prawer Jhabvala and Kamala Markandaya*. N. Delhi: National Book Organization.

16. Chopra, Ravi. *Advanced Essays*. Delhi: Bookhive.1988.

17. Cooper, David (ed.),. *The Dialectics of Liberation*. G.B.: Penguin Books.1968.

18. Cronin, Richard. *Imagining India*. N. Delhi: Macmillan Press.1983.

19. Dale, James. *Kamala Markandaya and the Outsider in Individual and community in Commonwealth Literature*. Edited by Daniel Massa Malta. Old University Press.1979.

20. Dass, Veena Noble and Dhawan, R.K. (eds.). *Fiction of the Nineties*. New Delhi: Prestige Books.1984.

21. Dhawan, R.K., *The Fictional World of Arun Joshi*. New Delhi: Classical.1986.

22. .... *The Novels of Arun Joshi*. New Delhi: Prestige.1992.

23. .... *The Fictional World of Arun Joshi*. New Delhi: Classical Publishing Co.1986.

24. Divivedi, A.N., ed. *The Novels of Arun Joshi: A Critical Study*. Allahabad: Kitab Mahal.1987.

25. .... *India Writing in English*. N. Delhi: Amar Prakashan.1991.

26. Driesen, Cynthia Vander. *The Novels of R.K. Narayan*, Nedlands: University of Western Australia Centre for South and Southeast Asian Studies.1986.

27. Ganguli, B.N. (ed.). *Readings in Indian Economic History.* N. Delhi: Asia publishing House.

28. Ganguli, S.N. *Tradition, Modernity and Development: A Study in Contemporary Indian Society.* N. Delhi: Macmillan.1977.

29. Gaur, K.K.. *R.K. Narayan: A Study of His Female Characters.* Delhi: S.S. Publishers.2000.

30. Girla, Shiv, K. *R.K. Narayan: His World and His Art.* Meerut: Saru.1984.

31. Gokak, Vinayak Krishna. *English In India: Its Present and Future.* N. Delhi: Asia Publishing House.1964.

32. Goyal, Bhagwat S. (ed.) *R.K. Narayan: A Critical Spectrum.* Meerut: Shalabh Book House.1983.

33. ... *R.K. Narayan's Indian: Myth and Reality*, N. Delhi: Sarup.1993.

34. Gultman, Ann. *The National of India in Contemporary Indian Literature.* New York: Palgrave, Macmillan.2007.

35. Gupta, R.S. and Kapil Kapoor, (eds). *English in India: Issues and Problems.* N. Delhi: Academic Foundation.1991.

36. Holmstrom, Laxshmi. *The Novels of R.K. Narayan.* Calcultta: Writers Workshop.1973.

37. Iyenger, K.R. Srivastava. *Indian Writing in English* (New Edition) N. Delhi: Sterling publishers Pvt. Ltd. 1984.

38. Jha, Rekha. *The Novels of Kamala Markandaya and Ruth Prawer Jhabvala: A Study in East West Encounter.* N. Delhi: Prestige Books. 1990.

39. Kachru, Braj B.. *The Indianization of English: The English Language in India.* New Delhi: OUP. 1983.

40. Kain, Geoffrey (ed.). *R.K. Narayan: Contemporary Critical Perspectives.* East Lansing: Michigan State University Press.1993.

41. Kripal, Viney. *The Post Modern English Novel: Interrogating the 1980s and 1990s.* Bombay: Allied Publishers Ltd. 1996.

42. Kumar, A.V. Suresh. *Six Indian Novelists: Mulk Raj Anand, Raja Rao, R.K. Narayan, Balchandra Rajan, Kamala Martmandaya, Anita Desai.* New Delhi: Creative Books. 1996.

43. Lang, P. *R.K. Narayan: A painter of Modern India.* New York. Micheal Pousse.1995.

44. Lannoy, Richard. *The Speaking Tree: A Study of Indian Culture and Society.* London: OUP.1971.

45. Mathur, O.P. *From Existentialism to Karmayoga: A study of Arun Joshi's* The Foreigner. *Perspective on Commonwealth Literature.* Eds., Srivastava, Avadesh K. *Alien Voice.* Lucknow: Print House.1981.

46. Mohan, Devindar. *Arun Joshi: The Foreigner. Major Indian Novels.* Ed. N.S. Pradhan. N. Delhi: Arnold – Heinemann.1985.

47. Mukherjee, Meenakshi. *Journey's End for Jhabvala* in *Dhawan. Explorations in Modern Indo-English Fiction.* N. Delhi: Bahri Publshers.1982.

48. Mogaral, Namratha. *Confronting Modernity and Post-coloniality:* The Last Burden *and* English, August: An Indian Story. *Indian Writing in English: Perspectives.* New Delhi: Atlantic Publishers. 2003.

49. Mund, Subhendu Kumar. *The Indian Novel in English, Its Birth and Development.* N. Delhi: Prachi Prakashan.1997.

50. Mujeebuddin, Syed. *R.K. Narayan's* The Man-Eater of Malgudi: *Problematising the Nation. Indian Fiction in English.* N. Delhi, Atlantic Publishers and Distributors.1992.

51. Mehta, P.P. *Indo-Anglian Fiction: An Assessment* (2nd Revised Edition). Bareilly: Prakash Book Depot.1979.

52. Mishra, G.D. *Physical Chemistry.* Delhi: Motilal Banarasidas.1987.

53. Nasimi, Reza Ahmad. *The Language of Mulk Raj Anand, Raja Rao and R.K. Narayan.* New Delhi: Capital.1989.

54. Naik, M.K. *The Ironic Vision: A Study of the Fiction of R.K. Narayan.* New Delhi: Sterling.1983.

55. Nair, K.N. Padmanabuan. *Irony in the Novels of R.K. Narayan and V.S. Naipaul.* Trivandrum: CBH.1993.

56. Nandy, Ashish. *At the Edge of the Psychology.* Delhi: OUP.1980.

57. Narayan, R.K. *Toasted English in Reluctant Guru.* N. Delhi: Orient Paperbacks.1974.

58. .... *Next Sunday.* N. Delhi: Orient Paperbacks.1965.

59. Naik, M.K. *A History of Indian English Literature.* N. Delhi: Sahitya Akademy.1982.

60. ... *Twentieth Century Indian English Fiction.* Delhi: Pencraft International.2004.

61. Nicholson, Kai. A *Presentation of Social problems in the Indo-Anglian and the Anglo-Indian Novel*: Bombay. Jaico Publishing House.1972.

62. Naravane, S. Viswanath. *Modern Indian Thought.* N. Delhi: Orient Longman.1978.

63. Pallan, Rajesh K. *Myths and Symbols in Raja Rao and R.K. Narayan: A Selected Study.* Jalandhar: Indian ABS Publication.1994.

64. Parleshwaram, Uma. *Kamala Markandaya.* Jaipur: Rawat Publications.2000.

65. ... *Native Aliens and Expatriates – Kamala Markandaya and Balchandra Rajan. A Study of Representative Indo- English Novelists.* New Delhi: Vikash.1976.

66. Prasad, Madhusudan, ed.. *Perspectives in Kamala Markandaya.* Ghaziabad: Vimal Prakashan.1984.

67. ... An Anthology of CRitical Essays. N. Delhi: Sterling.1982.

68. Prasad, Hari Mohan. *Response: Recent Revelations of Indian Fiction in English.* Bareilly: PBD.1994.

69. Pathania, Usha. *Having and Being: A Study of the Foreigner. The Novels of Arun Joshi.* ed., R.K. Dhawan. New Delhi: Prestige.1992.

70. Parsons, L & Shils, E. ed.. *The Theory of Action Towards A General Theory of Action*. Mass.: Cambridge.1951.

71. Pandey, Mukteshwar. *Arun Joshi: The Existentialist Element in His novels*. Delhi: B.R. Publishing.1998.

72. Radha, K. *From Detachment to Involvement: The Case of Sindi Oberoi. The Novels of Arun Joshi*. ed. R.K. Dhawan. N. Delhi: Prestige.1992.

73. Rajan, Rajeshwari Sundar. *The Lie of the land: English Literary Studies in India*. Delhi: Oxford University Press. 1992.

74. Rajan, Balchandran, ed.: *Identity and Nationality*. Commonwealth Litearature. London: John Press.1965.

75. Ram, Susan and Ram N. (1996). *R.K. Narayan*. N. Delhi: Viking.1996.

76. Ram, Tulsi. *Trading in Language: The story of English in India*. N. Delhi: GDK.1983.

77. Rao, A.V. Krishna. *Continuity and Change in the Novels of Kamala Markandaya. Perspective in Kamala Markandaya*. Ed. Madhusudan Prasad. Ghaziabad: Vimal Prakashan. 1984.

78. Ramane, R.S. *Message in Design: A study of R.K. Narayan's Fiction*. New Delhi: Harman.1993.

79. Rahman, Mustafizur. *The Elusive Searchlight: The World of R.K. Narayan*. Dhaka: Popular Publishers.1998.

80. Ramamurti, K.S. *Rise of the Indian Novel in English*. Bangalore: Sterling Publishers Pvt. Ltd.1987.

81. Ramjan, P.K. (ed.). *The Growth of the Novel in India: 1950 - - 80*. N. Delhi: Abhinav Publications.1980.

82. Rao, G. Subba. *Indian Words in English: A study in Indo-British Cultural and Linguistic Relations*. N. Delhi: Oxford University Press.1954.

83. Rao, A.V. Krishna. *Continuity and Change in the Novels of Kamala Markandaya. Perspective in Kamala Markandya*. ed., Madhusudan Prasad. Ghaziabad: Vimal Prakashan. 1984.

84. Radhakrishnan N. ed. *Arun Joshi: A Study of His Fiction.* Gandhigram (TN): Gandhigram Rural Institute.1984.

85. Rao, Raja, cf. *Foreword* to *Kanthapura.* Madras: Oxford University Press. 1938.

86. Ravi, P.S. *Modern Indian Fiction: History, Politics and Individual in the Novels of Rushdie, Ghose and Chatterjee.* Delhi: Prestige Books.2003.

87. Rose, Beulah. *Arun Joshi and Upamanyu Chatterjee: A Study.* Madurai: Kamraj University.2001.

88. Saguna, Krupabhai Satthianaadan. *The Story of Native Christian Life.* Madras: Christian College Magazine.

89. Sinha, U.P. *Patterns of Myth and Reality: A Study in R.K. Narayan's Novels.* New Delhi: Sandarbh.1988.

90. Sidhu, Nazar S. *Human Struggle in the Novels of R.K. Narayan.* N. Delhi: Bahri.1992.

91. Srivastava, Ramesh K. *The Novels of Kamala Markandaya: A Critical Study.* Amritsar (India): Guru Nanak Dev University.1998.

92. Sharan, Nagendranath. *A Critical Study of the Novels of R.K. Narayan.* N. Delhi: Classical.1993.

93. Sahane, Vasant. *Ruth Prawer Jhabvala.* N. Delhi: Arnold Heinemann.1976.

94. Saxena, O.P. & Solanki, Rajini. *Geography of Jhabvala's Novels.* New Delhi: Jainsons Publications.1985.

95. .... *Glimpses of Indo-English Fiction.* N. Delhi: Jainsons Publications.1985.

96. Saxena, O.P. *The Spiritual Porn in Jhabvala's Novels, Glimpses of Indo-English Fiction.* Vol. II. New Delhi: Jainsons Publications.1985.

97. Singh, P.K. *The Novels of R.K. Narayan: A Critical Evaluation.* N. Delhi: Atlantic Publishers and Distributors.1999.

98. Singh, R.S.. *Indian Novel in English: A Critical Study.* N. Delhi: Arnold - Heinemann.1977.

99. Sengupta, C.. *Upamanyu Chatterjee's* English August*: Metaphor of Contemporary Youth's Quest for Self-Realization.*

Indian Literature Today: Vol. I. Drama and Fiction. ed., R.K. Dhawan N. Delhi: Prestige Books.1994.

100. Singh, R.P. *The Concept of Anti- Hero in the Novels of Upamanyu Chatterjee.* Bareilly: Prakash Book Depot.2010.

101. Srivastava, K.R.. *Indian Writing in English.* N. Delhi: Sterling Publishers Pvt. Ltd.1994.

102. Sundaram, P.S.. *R.K. Narayan.* New Delhi: Arnold – Heinemann.1973.

103. ... (1988). *R.K. Narayan as a Novelist.* New Delhi, B.R.1988.

104. Thieme, John. *R.K. Narayan.* Manchester: Manchester University Press.2007.

105. Varma, R.M. *Major Themes in the Novels of R.K. Narayan.* N. Delhi: Jainsons.1993.

106. Vatsayan, S.H. *Contemporary India Literature.* N. Delhi.1959.

107. Verghese, C. Paul. *Indian Writing in English* in his *Essay on Indian Writing in English.* N. Delhi: N.V. Publications.1975.

108. .... *Problems of the Indian Creative Writers in English.* Bombay: Somaiya Publications.1971.

109. Walsh, William. *A Manifold Voice.* London: Chattor Windus.1964.

110. ... *R.K. Narayan.* London: Longman.1971.

111. .... *R.K. Narayan: A Critical Appreciation.* London: Heinemann.& Chicago:University of Chicago Press.1982.

112. ... *Sweet Mangoes and Malt Vinegar: The Novels of R.K. Narayan* ed, K.K. Sharma. *Indo-English Literature: A Collection of Critical Essays.* Ghaziabad: Vimal Prakashan.1977.

113. ... *R.K. Narayan: A Critical Appreciation* London: Heinemann and Chicago, University of Chicago Press.1982.

114. Williams, H.M.. *Indo-Anglian Literature 1800 - 1970.* New Delhi: Orient Longman.1976.

115. Williams, Hayder Moore. *The Fiction of Ruth Prawer Jhabvala.* Calcutta: Writers' Workshop. 1973.

(b) Journals/Newspapers

116. Aithal, S.K..*Indo - British Encounter in Kamala Markandaya's Novel*. Journal of South Asian Literature. 22, No. 2, 49 - 59.1987.

117. Bhatnagar, O.P. *Arun Joshi's the Foreigner*. The Journal of Indian Writing in English, I, No. 2.July, 1973.

118. Chadha, Ramesh. *Heat and Dust and the Coffer Dams: A Comparative Study*. Journal of Indian Writing in English. 10. 1 & 2.1982.

119. Chandan, P.S. *Kamala Markandaya's* Sense and Sensibility. Literary Criterion. 12. 2 - 3.1976.

120. Chatterjee, Upamanuy, in conversation with Nambisan, Vijay. *The Hindu (On line)*. April 1, 2001.

121. Desai, Anita. The Indian Writers Problems Language Forum.

122. Dhawan, R.K. Journal of Indian Writing in English. Vol. II. P. 62

123. Ezekiel, Missim.ed. *Bombay Indian Writers in Conference*. The Sixth P.E.N. All Indian Writers Conference - Mysore, 1962. The P.E.N. All Indian Centre.1964.

124. Geetha, P. *Kamala Markandaya: An Interpretation*. Commonwealth Quarterly 3, 9.1978.

125. Gondal, Yogesh Cnadra. *Indian and the West in the Indian Novel: A Note*. Viswabharati, Quarterly 38.1972.

126. Goyal, Bhagwat S. *The World of Women Novelists*. The Hindustan Times, 13 August, 1978.

127. Gupta, Balram (ed.). *Journal of Indian Writing in English*. Gulberga.

128. Gooneratne, Yasmine. *Contemporary India in the Writing of Ruth Prawer Jhabvala*. Westerly 28. 4. Dec. 1983.

129. Iyengar, K.R. Srinivasa. *The Fiction of Arun Joshi*. The Humanities Review. 3.2: 39 - 40.1981.

130. Jalloun, Tahen Ben. In an interview with Naravane, V. in *The Sunday Times of India* (Delhi Edition) Jan. 28, 1996.

131. Jhabvala, Ruth Prawer. *Autobiographical Essay, Living in India*. London Magazine. Sept. 1970.

132. Mukherjee, Kenakshi: *The Anxiety of Indianness in our Novels in English*. Economic and Political Weekly. 27th Nov., 1993.

133. Nagarajan, S. *A Study of English Literature in India*. Commonwealth Literature.1965.

134. Narayan, R.K. *English in India: The Process of Transmutation*. The Times of India. Bombay Dec. 2, 1964.

135. Nayak, P.M. *Cultural Change and Quest for Identity: A Study in Indian English Fiction*. Quest (Ranchi) 7,1.1999.

136. Prasad, Madhusudan. *Arun Joshi: The Novelist*. Indian Literature 24, No. 4, 103 – 114.1982.

137. Rao, Vimala. *Indian Expatriates*. Journal of Commonwealth Literature. Vol. X, No. 3.1976.

138. Rao, C. Malathi. *The Foreigner: Arun Joshi*, Literary Criterion. 8 (4).1969.

139. Robello, Snehal. *Kindly Adjust, this is India*. Hindustan Times (Delhi Edition) April 14, 2008.

140. Ram, N. *Malgudi's Creator*, Cover Story of *Frontline* Vol. 18, Issue II.2001.

141. Saxena, Sunil. An Interview with R.K. Narayan, *Probe*. Sept., 1987.

142. Sharma, D.R. *Arun Joshi and His Reflective Insiders*. Literature East and West No. 21 100 - 109.1977.

143. Sharma, D.R. *The Fictional World of Arun Joshi*. The Indian P.E.N. 43. 9 & 10: 1 - 5.1977.

144. The Indian Journal of English Studies. The Indian Association for English Studies. N. Delhi - 60 (Yearly)

(c) **Webliography**

145. www.google.com.http://www.google.com.
146. www.worldlibrary.com http://www.worldlibrary.com.
147. www.languageindia.com.
148. www.gzyn.com.
149. www.indianetzone.com/41/history-indian englishnoter.
150. www.indianetzone.com/2/english-literature.htm.